If this is a book about the deeper aspects of acting, it is well to start it with a simple question that requires a compound response.

What does the below paragraph describe? Can you fill in the blanks and solve this small mystery?

'**At the simplest level this is because this photograph, in composition and content, is a very great photograph. It is both the first and last word in ___ting, insofar as ___ting consists of making instinctive what begins as a set of quite unnatural motions. In this image ___ seems to achieve the complete reconciliation of the orthodox and the spontaneous, the rehearsed and the original, the conscious and the unconscious. His shirt seems both loose and taut; his arms appear both gloriously free and tensed for action; the movement is both instantly recognisable and uniquely his.'**
With thanks to Gideon Haigh who in 2009 wrote this about a certain Victor Trumper.

If you thought the above describes a wonderful acting performance, you'd be right, but only in theme - not in fact! In reality this highly poetic evocation of a 1905 photograph celebrates of the most lyric batsman in cricket history, whose charisma bewitched and enchanted even his opposite players. Of course the reader of a book about acting would know that such a panegyric **should** apply to theatre performance, and that is the WHY of this book, and the poesy on one side can be doubled over, to redouble the other (but HOW?), and the training zone is the When and Where it's owned

The thumper's Trumper....If you want the pic, Google Vic!

This book is dedicated to

Jacqui Carroll
meus socius totus

a devil pokes the actor
Frankly Acting 2

by
John Nobbs

illustrations by Peter Berkahn

Frank Theatre Press Brisbane

John Nobbs and Peter Berkahn

Copyright © 2010 John Nobbs

All rights reserved under International and Pan-American copyright conventions and no part of this book can be stored, reproduced or transmitted in any form or by any means without express written permission of the author [or publisher].

First published 2010-08-09

ISBN 978-0-9775071-1-5

Frank Theatre Press
PO Box 7023
East Brisbane
Queensland
4169
Australia
ABN: 52 274 080 202
www.ozfrank.com
Email: <info@ozfrank.com>

Front cover design features the author as MC Black Angel in Up Jumped the Devil: photography by Michael Andrew Dare

Back cover features the author as Death in The Reckoning of Badengood: photography by Florence Forrest

Table of Contents

Introduction
Prologue

The Way of Muscles

MP1	How Hamlet was stooged…	13
MP2	Machina Didactica	52
MP3	"No Dummy…it's training for football"	60
MP4	St Kilda's running midfield rules OK	68
MP5	Eskimo Inclinations	76

The Way of Meta Muscle

MMP1	Peter Sellers through the Looking Glass	85
MMP2	About a boy-o called Blake	96
MMP3	Peter Berkahn's Coldplay moment	106
MMP4	David Attenborough's Arm	114
MMP5	The Day Artaud stopped the clock	126
MMP6	Words get in the Way	134

The Way of the Migraine

WM1	Two Tad Jerzy Club	143
WM2	Controvski over Grotowski	164
WM3	True and False and partly True	184
WM4	A Soft Scrutiny of 'An Acrobat of the Heart'	214
WM5	Agar Gel is not a microscope	252

The Way of the Molecule

WMo1	Butoh and Charles Laughton's attitude	258
WMo2	Iggy's 'suctional' Charisma	266
WMo3	Teddy Bear: concierge of the unconscious	276
WMo4	Jung's heuristic moment	288
WMo5	Brighton Rock	300
WMo6	Audio Plasma	310
WMo7	Spirit Speed: the 5th Dimension	322
WMo8	Quantum Thespians leaping from Newton to Einstein	329

Ozfrank History Gallery

Acknowledgements

Inspiration:
Tadashi Suzuki

Editorial:
Jacqui Carroll

Sponsorship:
Margaret Nobbs

Contributors:
Jacqui Carroll, Peter Berkahn, Stephen Wangh, David Mamet, Glenn Taylor, Caroline Dunphy, James Anderson, Ira Seidenstein, Benjamin Williams, Fran Barbe, Kathleen Doyle, Andrew Lazarow, Kate Lee, Ross Hobson, Tracy Shoemaker, Glenn Johnson.

Performance Photographs:
Michael Andrew Dare, Phil Hargreaves, Carl and Kelly Berggren, Florence Forrest, Werner Rolli.

Front cover and illustration photography: Michael Andrew Dare.
Back cover photo and design: Florence Forrest.
Without the provocation, harassment and counsel of the following persons, this book wouldn't be half of what it is:
Jacqui Carroll, Peter Berkahn, Florence Forrest, Christopher Mueller, Hilary Regan.

Introduction

It is said that it is easy to write your first book, as it is a portrait of all your life up until then. I penned **Frankly Acting** during the last half of 2005 so I could pack in a lot of 53 years ruminating into it. So, after a few more years this book is not about discovering wider horizons so much as burrowing deeper into the existing ones.

This second book has been written for a number of reasons.

1. Since book one I have thought a good deal deeper and longer on all the various aspects of what we do. The **Frank Suzuki Performance Aesthetics** and the **Suzuki Actor Training Method** have continued to give me a more profound comprehension of the actor's potential and craft.

As well, I have spent a lot of time debating the connection between thought and action with my three best dramaturgicals Jacqui Carroll, Peter Berkahn and Florence Forrest all of whom give me considerable fertile space in which to concoct these provocative probes.

2. Another reason is that the next book reveals the first one as it leaves the previous book behind, unveiled and extant. When one moves on, relinquishing what went on before is the act that furthers self individuation.

I was inspired to this position after watching a wicked Suzuki Pantomime called **Kachi Kachi Yama**. It is a dark classic Japanese revenge folk tale of Bunny Rabbits and Tanukis (sort of a Japanese badger). Those of Suzuki's versions that I have seen have always been pretty raucous and very funny as he has introduced a mad 'Yakuza' gangster element into the animalia.

Jacqui and I have seen 4 versions in all and were especially impressed with version No. 2 a number of years ago. More recently we saw version No 3, and we expected pretty much a re-run of version No 2. We found, however, that Suzuki had jettisoned huge chunks of V2 and, following a rehearsal of this new version, while standing on the road in the moonlight afterwards, I marveled at Suzuki's ability to move forwards. I remember saying: "Suzuki's rejecting that to which other directors are aspiring!"

We, as audience, have in our mind's eye what he used to be, so when we watch the new version, he is moving away from us. But, paradoxically, we are also not left behind - he is taking us with him.

When I think on't, **Robin Williams** did something quite similar when he played **Mork** in the television series **Mork and Mindy**. Williams would be doing some dazzling improvisation, and as he got into it, he would get deeper and better, moving away from you, but paradoxically taking you with him. Breathtaking stuff!

In both cases, I feel that they represent the moral imperative of performative self individuation.

This book is Round Two of going further...

3. In 2009, Jacqui directed a musical theatre production called *Up Jumped the Devil*, in which I played a character called **MC Black Angel**. Everybody thought I was the Devil, which I suppose is not surprising as the cover photo of this book, showing me in this role, might indicate. To compound this inference, earlier that year Jacqui had prepared a performance for Suzuki's festival in Japan. It was a version of a mediaeval morality play 'Everyman', which we primped up to make it not so Olde Worlde and re-badged as **The Reckoning of Badengood**. I played **Death** which many people misheard or mistook for the devil......

On top of all that, even though Jacqui and I have been together since 1975 in a surprisingly robust partnership, many friends and not so friends, might consider that many elements of our creative relationship resemble a 'dance with a devil'.

But most of all, this book is a dialogue between doubt and desire, those twin horns of a dilemma that dog a bod who hopes he's doing something interesting.

Prior to writing my first book, my life was an unconnected panorama of clusters of extreme and idiosyncratic interests. **Frankly Acting** was the mechanism whereby those disparate constellations came together. In the writing of that book, one could say that my life became unified - I found myself. Unexpectedly, the book's gestation and completion was most gratifying, and I found it stabilizing for my somewhat excitable nature.

Subsequently, writing has become an even more prominent part of my life. I spend a good deal of time in gentle, and not so gentle, wrestling with scripts and articles, and they all represent an articulation of an evolving cosmological attitude, and the portrayal of that attitude is a reconciliation between the personal and the universal.

Each chapter is a provocation, a deeper question arising from the Frank and Suzuki exercises and these provocations are grouped under four headings. They start being purely practical The Way of Muscles, and accelerate thematically through Meta/Muscles and Migraines to the realm of Quantum Psychics, The Way of the Molecule.

1. The Way of Muscles.......
2. The Way of Meta Muscle.......
3. The Way of the Migraine.......
4. The Way of the Molecule......

NOW YOU KNOW WHY I WROTE THIS BOOK.......WHO OR WHAT POKED ME INTO WRITING IT.......?

Frankly Acting was provoked by Jacqui Carroll, my partner in everything. She, while we were teaching in London, was incensed by a twee account by a bubbly actress of her precious time spent doing jejune acting games. "Hey John! Our aesthetic runs rings around that...Why don't you write a book about what we do and how we got it from Suzuki?"

So I did!

Antonin Artaud once wrote of his drawings: "None of them, to speak exactly, is a work. They are all attempts, that is to say blows - probings or thrustings in all the directions of hazard of possibility, of chance, or of destiny"

The chief provocateur for **this** book, however, was even closer to home.......
Since all of us are somewhere between the devil and the deep blue sea, what better place to start a dialogue...... than with a devil of your own.......

PROLOGUE

These provocations are a series of fevered conversations, all bedded, tamped down lightly……..do not disturb....in the black magic hours between the deep midnight and the leavening of the dusky dawn.......because.....metaphorically......

Up came a devil that loomed large behind: at my desk just past twelve on a saturated Brisbane summer night, coming out of my past, cool and slow and smiling mean, with one express purpose to drag me back, back into a prior uncertainty - to a time when.........when......I was so unbolder then...

For a long time he stayed still, not speaking, gradually insinuating his way in: that chill, sly think that starts just on the outskirts of the brain, and increasingly asserts itself, sliding into the central cortex, thrumming until all other thoughts are struck out. Suddenly he spoke with a style that was slightly old and slightly new:

"And who, precisely, do you think you're kidding, Mister, Mister?
"And……………………….
"Where are all these 'I'm goingta's'.... going to stop?
"And…………………….…
"For all your blaspheming time's gone by, you still don't have a blessed clue as to who you are, and what you've got?"

To answer this triple inquisition, I tracked through the backlog of my mind, to hunt for the thoughts that hold and stem the swoon of this derision.

"Not quite true! I know who I am, but not quite sure where I stand!"

"I can smell your doubt and taste your desire, but doubt and

A Devil Pokes the Actor

desire are just double-ended see-saws of the deceptive kind. I plant these wanton seeds and watch them grow to be weeds in your febrile mind. But notions aren't motions - they're just bubbles in the brain, synaptic sparks that briefly scintillate before they evaporate. The road to hell, and Buddy Boy! I know it well...... is paved with good intentions.... but in your case? What's the proof? Where's the portrait?
Have you nailed your message to the mast?"

"But I've already written one book! You know that!"

"Well then, after one book, and a few more years, you look a mite between. Caught betwixt two elusive worlds, both assembled from your own deceptive dreams"...
Digs me in the ribcage with one knuckly digit:
"One is what you are"...
Pokes again...
"and the other is what you want to be...Well?...... What's going to fuse them together?"

"Right! I've got twenty five deep thinks to throw at you. I thought them up for a slew of reasons and through a series of seasons. One reason is that since that first Frankly Acting book, I have ruminated a great deal as I gazed over the variegated inlays of our theatre company, Ozfrank Theatre. The first book was an autobio of the Frank Suzuki Performance Aesthetics and its evolution as a filial variant of its parent, the Suzuki Actor Training Method. We have been riding it hard and soft for 18+ years, and its swingeing curve has carved out the glory of the actor's sublime potential, and the craft needed to crack it".

"Hellzapoppin! How did you go about gaining this oh! so special 'sublime' potential?"

"I have also spent a lot of time debating the connection between thought and action with my three best dramaturgical mates Jacqui Carroll, Peter Berkahn and

Florence Forrest, all of whom give me considerable oxygen with which to fan a few flames".

First off: Jacqui Carroll, short, bright-eyed and bushy tailed, by turns ferocious at work and placid at play, my wife and art-partner since 1975. Here's a provocative sketch of her that I recently wrote for our website:

Artistic Director Ozfrank Theatre

Jacqui Carroll

Jacqui Carroll is uniquely placed within the Australian performance spectrum as one of the very few international practitioners who has had a significant career as both Choreographer and Theatre Director. As choreographer her works cover the entire range from Post Modern (the John Cage songbooks) through modern dance *The Lotos Eaters, Stabat Mater* to Strippers and Opera, to full length classical ballets such as *The Tempest, Scherherazade* and *Carmina Burana* (with 80 voice choir, 3 soloists and 100 piece orchestra accompanying the Queensland Ballet dancers).

Her dance style can be described as a combination of the organic strength derived from Martha Graham and the clear lines of Classical Ballet. In similar fashion to her mentor, Glen Tetley, this amalgamation of the extreme technical strands has led to works of great sinuous, trenchant and archetypical impact.

As well she is the only dance teacher in Australia capable of teaching master classes in the big Five: Classical, Graham, Horton, Limon/Humphrey and Cunningham techniques.

In 1991 she first witnessed the training and aesthetic of Tadashi Suzuki and was inspired to break away from pure dance to develop theatre works combining Text, Movement and Music.

Since 1993 she has created 14 works for Ozfrank:

- ***The Romance of Orpheus:* A Whirling Tale of Underground Love and Death**

- *The Tale of Macbeth*: Super Distilled and Simple (Suisse, Croatia, Turkey, Czech Republic, Mongolia, Nepal)
- *Oedipus Rex*: 2 versions: 1st Spinning Reduction; 2nd Grand Oratorio (Croatia)
- *Salome*: Oscar's Fear and Greed x Three (Japan)
- *Heavy Metal Hamlet*: Disaffected Black Sabbath Boy (Japan)
- *Rashomon*: 'This is not a Love Song' of Relative Truth
- *Doll Seventeen*: Epigrammatic Fantasy of Classic Ocker Text
- *Midsummer Night's Romeos*: 1st Non Linear Carroll 'essay' (bi-lingual Japan)
- *Manga Ulysses*: Popster, Funhouse Odyssey co-prod with a Qld uni
- *Hamlet Stooged!* Wayne's World Dudesworth (London, Wales and Chicago)
- *VooMac*: Somnambulistic Voodoo Witchcraft for Macbeth
- *To Have Done with the Judgement of God*: A Short Waltz around Artaud's Proto-Butoh Radio Play
- *The Reckoning of Badengood:* Everyman's Morality Hipped and Primped, (Japan)
- *Up Jumped the Devil*: Grotowski Guignol for Nick's Cave

In the process she has transposed her unique choreographic voice to create a series of highly individual stage portraits with thick light, dense movement and sonorous vox.

Carroll's Theatre of the three C's:
Caravaggio: Hyper Real and Hyper Now!
Chiaroscuro: Light and Dark, Both for Good Measure

and Cornucopia: There's Plenty More Where That Came From.....

A scary mini monster indeed!

Then there's Peter Berkahn: Tall, soft, paternal - Uncle Arthur with Eisenstein glasses, lugubriously charming, but for all that....quietly intense. A peripatetic painter and writer, though he thinks of himself deprecatingly as merely a scenarist. He's also an extremely successful freelance Psychiatric Nurse. His proximity to those lost souls whose unconscious has overwhelmed their conscious, has gifted him highly perceptive insights into La Conditione Humaine. Also extremely adept at reading the back of the brain, he's AKA the Kirlian Geometer. We go back quite a few years to 1998, when we met standing in a back paddock in Limpinwood, bucolic Northern New South Wales.

He had just seen our outdoor performance of Jacqui's directorial take on Oscar Wilde's **Salome**, and he said it was the first time in a long while that he had been excited by theatre.

I, of course, found this pleasantly flattering but I was bowled over by what followed.

He went on to say that in daily life one has to be very logical, and that time and space were very circumscribed and linear. He murmured.....daylight, everything 'seen' and 'obvious'. But, he said, Art should deal with other realms, where time and space are elastic and polymorphic. This was the landscape of the night. How long was a dream or a nightmare? He said that most theatre was like daily life - everything was known and it was just ticking boxes as they came and went, and it all left him cold and wondering: "Is there something wrong with me because there's something I'm not getting?"

He was very gratified to have seen **Salome** because finally he had found a show that talked to mystery in the dark. He felt it was a testament to our acting and Jacqui's direction, that we had achieved this rarely seen phenomenon. To paraphrase Bogie and Rains in **Casablanca**, this was the beginning of a beautiful friendship. He's also the only man, woman or child I know who can give you the back of the story.

Last of the Quartet is Florence Forrest. Tall, dark, very pretty - the sort of girl that's both old and new fashioned. Florence is an internationally exhibited soft toy maker, who first appeared faintly on our screen after congratulating Jacqui on the production of **Doll Seventeen** in the Powerhouse foyer in 2002. Over the years she has loomed larger and larger in **Ozfrank** life, doing hands-on costumes and props as well as acting as an acute sounding board for myself as designer and especially Jacqui as director. Exceptionally well read esp. on Jung, Blake and other arty stuff....very strong on the spiritual/fey side of the ledger, with a deeply holistic but feminine approach.

"Hells b,b,b,bells, that's two male and two female... a quartzite, smells of Carl Gustav Jung ...... Uh-Oh! That Jung was hacking at my heels alright, on and off all of the night; he sat in his tower and divined the power......"

"Glad you brought that up, you're going to hear a lot about him later when I talk the teddys - Jung's so very, very key, that he's almost got his own section..... actually the word you want is quaternary...... nimbly summed up by Florence thus:
The Ozfrank Quaternary
Jacqui: Feeling (the passion and drive to create the work on stage)
John: Intellect (processing all incoming info to conflate into Ozfrank aesthetic)
Peter: Sensation (input of information coming from the physical and mental world)
Florence: Intuition (input of information from the invisible and liminal world)

"OK! OK! Enough of the wafty words!"
A dismissive wave of his flinty wrist.
"Get weaving!"

"But wait, just like a bad television ad..... there's more.... There are also other collaborators, Ozfrank actors, quite a few of which, like Glenn T and Caroline, have been with us for a long, long time. All of those listed below have said or done something that revealed an important aspect to me and will be poking their noses into these probes:

*Ira Seidenstein, Benjamin Williams, James Anderson
Caroline Dunphy, Glenn Taylor, Kathleen Doyle
Fran Barbe, Andrew Lazarow, Glenn Johnson
Kate Lee, Tracy Shoemaker, Ross Hobson.

"Now we have the team checked and set, where to now, bright eyes."

Provocation 1 is the 'Six journeys of a performance....

The Devil winces, frowns, licks a scab or two with his lathery tongue, the eyes flick up and he says: *"Why?...in nine lines or less........pul-eeze"*

"My life as a performer has been a very convoluted journey, starting as a beginner dancer at 19 and proceeding in fits and starts in an inexorable but variegated fashion since. Until recently, every few weeks, I'd collapse into a slough of despond….. and say to myself: "Why am I doing this....I'm going nowheres-ville!" The black cloud would evaporate just as quickly and meaninglessly and I'd be left with "what was that all about? Why?" But, oddly enough, I never pulled up stumps and loped off in quest of more distractive leisure, but stayed on this idiosyncratic course to find myself anew. Maybe the search through these performative journeys will give me a clue."

"Roll on Provocation 1......."

Muscle Provocation 1
How Hamlet was stooged....
The Six Journeys of a Performance
using the evolution of
'Hamlet Stooged!' directed by Jacqui Carroll
for Ozfrank Theatre as an example.

This is an outline of the six inter-dependent journeys that occur inside a live theatre performance:

1. The journey of the playwright
2. The journey of the play
3. The journey of the character
4. The journey of the actor playing the character
5. The journey of the director
6. The journey of the audience

> I've left out designers, composers, et al, because they are the same ilk as director.

As an aid to explaining these six journeys, I use as a sample Ozfrank's production of director Jacqui Carroll's **Hamlet Stooged!**, which was developed over a period of two years and premiered in its final form in Wales in 2006.

In terms of each of the six journeys, the samples are:

1. **Writing**: A combination of Shakespeare, Jacqui Carroll and John Nobbs
2. **The Play**: Jacqui Carroll's thematic reduction of Shakespeare's tragedy Hamlet
3. **The Character**: The part of Yorick as developed and played by Ira Seidenstein
4. **The Actor**: Yorick as performed by Ira Seidenstein
5. **The Director**: Jacqui Carroll
6. **The Audience**: I have asked an audience member, Benjamin Williams, who saw the show before he started

working with Ozfrank.

All the journeys under discussion can be viewed as having two separate but related parts.

Overt: the obvious, visible manifestation which includes the unfolding of the story and what happens to the people involved in terms of real time and space.

Covert: The inner journey, the passage of the 'soul' or 'psyche'. What happens to the 'spiritual essence' of the various elements as they proceed/unfold?

Each outer journey can, more often than not, be easily tracked as they are linear 'maps' in real time and relatively quantifiable. The inner journeys are much more complex to 'read' and analyse because of their more amorphous nature, but precisely for that reason, they are finally much more important as their subliminal components are the real content of art and are what truly communicate with audience and history.

1a. The journey of the playwright.

In outer terms:

From the playwright's perspective, what is the trajectory of the writing of the play, from initial thoughts to final presentation? These initial stimulae range from the operational (it may or may not stem from a commission depending on the writer's public profile) to the thematic (what event may have compelled them to write the play?). Well known writers have a track record in dealing with certain genres for a certain clientele. They are therefore commissioned by theatre organisations, wishing to service their own particular political and aesthetic requirements, because they are perceived as having a successful 'politico-aesthetic' view. This is generally a commercial and ideological combination (ie an ideology that has a market!).

Beginning playwrights do not have that reputation, so they have to hawk their emergent wares around the traps, eventually prevailing upon the shrinking theatre strand that deals with new plays by untried playwrights. This requires considerable serendipity/luck as there's not a lot of opportunity and a heck of a lot of competition and, in an age of retro and recapitulation, it's difficult for a neophyte to establish that he/she has a new voice.

Once our playwright, fledgling or no, has lit upon a 'story' he wants to tell, it's nose to the grindstone time. Text, plot devices or story may come first, second or third depending on personal methods.

In inner terms:

Playwrights are driven by a deep emotional/psychological need to have their innermost thoughts/feelings displayed as words and actions by people on a 'public' stage. As with most other artists, it is the 'public' demonstration **and** acceptance of their highly personal view that is the ultimate affirmation. Without that external validation, the value of that inner feeling remains unresolved.

The writing of the script is the playwright's revealing of his thoughts, expressed as poetic literary hard copy. After some sort of first draft, the play begins to 'talk back' to our playwright, stimulating all types of revisions (before any rehearsals). As the writer responds to his thoughts and feelings as a reaction to the efficacy of his 'story', he may make changes accordingly. As the play 'talks', he would sense that there may be better mechanisms, devices, text, subplots, etc., in both logistical and psychological ways, to convey his 'message'.

Before rehearsals the play exists only as a literary document, much the same as a book. Once rehearsals start the chemistry between the actors and the director can influence the script, and may stimulate further revisions as the play begins its existence as performance. In the early performances (known as previews) more revisions are generally made as the further 'chemistry' of the audience is encountered, and if the director and writer are particularly assiduous, the revisions are ongoing for the life of the work.

When a play is first being written, it is essentially an expression of a single mind. As it matures it becomes a collaborative effort between the words, the actors, director and audience. As such, the journey of the playwright proceeds as his singular idea develops into a schematic combination, determined by all the personae at the performance.

The Devil twitches his tail, cracks a knuckle and leans in, looming invasively with his ghostly gimlet pupils………..looking for the first faint hint of boredom in the crosshairs of his eyes, I falter but press on:

1b. The journey of the playwright of Hamlet Stooged!

As I said earlier, the 'writing' of **Hamlet Stooged!** involved three people:
1. Shakespeare, who wrote the original words and scenario
2. Jacqui Carroll who chose which sections of the script and story interested her
3. and myself. Jacqui asked me to rewrite the original language she had selected into modern vernacular speech.

Shakespeare the writer:
In terms of Shakespeare and the aspects of his writing of Hamlet, we are faced with a huge sea of often contradictive conjecture. He wrote almost no letters about himself or his plays, so we have no real idea of the mechanisms, either logistic or psychological, that could give insights into his creativity - it is a truth that we know much more about many of the people he was writing about than the man himself! Because so little is known about the man there are a myriad of theories and conspiracies surrounding his story. Whatever! Can't backtrack in truth, but some commonsense applied to what is known leads me to make a few observations.

a. His company must have had some pretty compelling performers as the plays were all performed in daylight to a

varied audience demographic - high born down to yokels. These actors must have been convincing because they had to play witches' scenes such as *'double, double, toil and trouble.....etc'* in broad daylight in front of an audience half of which could be 'rustics' ready with the rotten fruit. There is evidence of the actor's considerable skills as improvisers and, given the large chunk of time between the writing of Hamlet (around 1600) and its first printing 1632, it is inconceivable that, in an era of Commedia-like improvisation, there were not many permutations, additions and interpolations, eg.......... "Hey, Will, why don't I add the "…. "and drop the……." etc.
(Apparently the actors were only provided with their own lines which meant that they could never know what their co-actors' actions or reactions would be, this must surely have encouraged greater spontaneity).

b. The plays as we know them were first printed well after Will retired and some years after he had shuffled off his mortal coil. This probably means that for the first few years after he retired the rest of the gang figured: "Well, Will was a pretty good scribe, but another one will come along soon enough...." As time rolls by it becomes increasingly obvious that nobody else quite comes up with the goods and that Will's work is a bit of a stand out. One day they all aver "Er.r.r, maybe we underestimated the situation somewhat and we should jot all this down before we forget..... Er.r.r...Which bits did you do?"

c. He never seems to have made a big deal out of writing. He seems to have regarded himself as a tradesman, reeling off the stuff more in the manner of a plumber than an artiste.

For myself these three aspects substantiate that there was no over-riding psychological driver to what became a communal writing event and that the only knowable truths are in Shakespeare's supreme gifts of story-telling, poesy and psyche insights.
Any confusion aside, Hamlet is the most popular and revered play in the world, reckoned to be so because it is the

first play where man is in dialogue with his soul, making it a high watermark of Humanism - and this from a country boy who didn't finish high school!.......at the end of the day nobody knows why he wrote it.......

Jacqui Carroll as adaptor/scenarist:
Why:
Jacqui Carroll, the adaptor/director, has as one of her main interests the reinterpretation of classics, as she believes that an artist should engage with the panorama of great myths and issues that exist throughout time, but in such a way that truly reflects the artist and the 'Now'. She also believes that the 'Hamlet' myth contains many levels and manifestations, making it ripe for many stylistic interpretations. As such this was not a commission but an extension of her personal artistic curiosity.

How:
This is Jacqui's third adaptation of Hamlet. The first was **Heavy Metal Hamlet**, an hour and a quarter linear distillation of the original using as leitmotifs the apposite music of Led Zeppelin, Black Sabbath and Deep Purple. The second, called **Ratzhamlet!,** was a more chromatic dissertation featuring 5 Hamlets and 5 Ophelias/Gertrudes. Whilst **HHH** dispensed with the side plots and subtexts, **Ratz**, was even more narrowly focussed on the relationships between Hamlet and the two main women in his life, his mother, Gertrude, and his fiancée, Ophelia. **Ratz** was created, rehearsed but never performed (although it may one day.......) eventually morphing into **Hamlet Stooged! HS** started life using the same text adaptation as Ratz but this text was further added to and expanded as **HS** developed during the gestation/rehearsal period. **HS** has 5 main characters, Hamlet, Ophelia, Gertrude, Yorick and Horatio (in this version Horatio is Hamlet's dog) plus the minor roles of the three psychiatrists.

The writer John Nobbs:
Why: The major thrusts that influenced the final re-writing of the text came from two different but connected ideas that Jacqui and I had discussed. One idea came out of watching a worthy, conventional production of a lesser Shakespearean play. We

were in the audience watching the actors rattle through the entire play at the regulated fast clip when I realised, with a jolt, that I was barely keeping up with the language; now, if I, having a very good ear (and ken the lingo, so to speak) was barely keeping up, what about the unwitting punters either side of me?

With the dumbing down of the English language and with most people being unfamiliar with Shakespearean idiom, almost all modern audiences would have great difficulty understanding the ancient and alien sounding words. This effectively becomes a language barrier preventing them from participating or being 'inside' the play. Because they can't identify with the words, they attend the play as though they were dutifully watching stuffed exhibits in a museum. Not so much art as an anthropology lecture!

In discussing this situation Jacqui and I decided to update the words to a more familiar vernacular, while maintaining the cadences, meanings and rhymes of the original text. We also decided that since Hamlet was a youngish man, we could pick through the stylisms of **Wayne's World**, **The Simpsons** and even **Clockwork Orange** for the lingo. An interesting corollary to this is that not only do audiences relate more to this vernacular, but the actors, as well, also find it easier to speak and understand.

The other idea that triggered this writing style was my desire as a writer to talk to the stand up comedy demographic. This is one of the fastest growing areas in the theatre and has, as its centre, a self-satisfied smart-arse-sity. For a long time I pondered how to re-orient the Ozfrank aesthetic to engage with this expanding audience, and reconfiguring distracted Hamlet into a disaffected Dude seemed just the ticket.

How:
The 'rewriting' of the dialogue occurred mainly over three nights in a B & B high in the Japanese Alps while we were guests

attending Mr Suzuki's Toga International Festival in 2006. I found it surprisingly easy to translate verbatim using the Shakespearean text as an exact template. As an example: 'To be or not to be ' became 'to exist or to exit'. The challenge was to find words that were modern but appropriate whilst keeping the poetic cadences. As much as possible I kept the rhymes and it was exhilarating to find modern vulgar words such as 'wanker' that could be introduced as rhymes for the original ones such as 'canker'.

At a mental level I found it rewarding not so much to see myself as re-inventing Shakespeare but to 'translate' his great poetry and psychological insights into a modern idiom. I would also suggest that this 'trans-copying' is a very instructive learning process, being the literary equivalent to apprenticing oneself to a master painter in Renaissance Italy.

The Journey of myself as writer:
As a writer, I found it quite gratifying to hear my versions of Shakespeare's words spoken, first in rehearsal then later in performance. Because the words had moved from my cortex onto the page, then into the voice of the actors, it felt as though they were coming from a different space. It seems to become a form of multi dimensional witnessing; a type of multiple affirmation.

In my case it became further refracted, acquiring another layer as I am also one of the 5 actors, playing different parts at different times. I played Hamlet in London and Wales and Gertrude in Brisbane and Chicago.

I might add here that previously I had harboured no thoughts of being a writer, whether for the stage or just on the page and I was quite bemused at the enjoyment I derived from it, both in the short and long term.

The devil coughs and splutters to interrupt, before ticking me off in a cavernous basso profundo:
"Funny hunny! The heavenly spunk of the writer sprung upon

you like that. They cun hardly say you're in it for the munny."

2a. The journey of the Play.

Outer:
This is the story or tracking of the play as it evolves, and in most cases it is framed by a linear narrative which, at its simplest, can be: Boy meets Girl, They argue, Boy loses Girl, they reconcile, Boy keeps Girl.

In Hamlet the play, the 'real time' storyline concerns Hamlet's discovery of his father's murder and the gradual process of convoluted revenge, in tandem with other subplots (some involving Hamlet and some not) that converge to a bloody denouement with the deaths of some 11 characters by the end of Shakespeare's play.

Inner:
There is also an inner 'journey of the soul' of a play that is often masked by the external aspects. The playwright (an experienced one even more so) is often driven by deep psychological urges, not necessarily apparent to the audience. These hidden subliminal drivers are contained and presented inside more comprehensible conventions (such as a good juicy story) to render the message more accessible and digestible.

While there are always plays being written, most rely on topical resonances for their validation, and contemporary politics to propel them forward. These range from sexual politics, social justice issues to broader clashes between the left and right politic. These plays that 'explore contemporary themes', which is another way of saying 'exploitational' enjoy considerable short term success contingent upon the relevance of the themes they are married to, but generally fade as fashions shift. Their very contemporary relevance fixes them in time because that relevance is their most important attribute. In the fullness of time, most plays turn into 'museum exhibits' because they only reflect their era and its mores.

Very few theatre works transcend their time as it requires the paradoxical combination of universality plus the unique personal 'voice' of the writer. Most plays suffer from the reverse: on one hand too simplistic or one dimensional with their topic, and on the other hand, the play's 'voice' is too often generalised, indistinct and lacking Poetic Individualisation. By lacking PI, I mean that the language, tone and rhythm reflect a competent, generic ability that is acceptable but lacks a personal attitude and vision.

The plays that last, that continue to fascinate and involve people of all cultures and eras, are those most concerned with soul, for as the bad Lord Byron said: "The soul outwears the shield" and such a one is the play **Hamlet.**

When dissecting the 'outer' journey, there are many theories about 'good' story playwriting, but most can be simplified into: introduction, conflict and resolution.
Concerning the much more interesting 'inner' journey, it is instructive to note that there would be no quantitative way of analysing, rationalizing or dissecting the requirements for a 'good' soul's journey.

In truth, the success of a great play is in the alchemical relationship between the inner and outer stories, the outer passage being an amplification of the inner.

2b. The Journey of the play: Hamlet Stooged! (HS)

First of all, a precis of the play as written by William Shakespeare:
Hamlet is the local prince of Denmark, noble of bearing, and the very picture of a polymathic prince. As the play starts Hamlet is inconsolable over the untimely death of his father. That night Hamlet hears from the ghost of his father, the former king, that he had been assassinated by his brother **Claudius**. Claudius, now king, has, in what appears to be great haste, married

Hamlet's mother, **Gertrude**. All these happenings have severely affected Hamlet.

One of the complexes inside the play is the degree to which Hamlet is affected - is it real or feigned? Over the intervening centuries there have been reams written about whether William put that in, or we, as the witnesses, imagine it. This is what makes the guy such good copy.

Once Hamlet believes the ghost of his dead father, the cat and mouse game of retribution gradually unfolds. To avenge the regicide Hamlet pretends to go mad. Nobody in the court, except his one best friend **Horatio**, really understands his cruel behaviour, most believing it results from his breaking off the engagement with his fiancee, **Ophelia**, daughter of the court chamberlain, **Polonius**, who becomes Hamlet's first victim after an episode of unnecessary advice,

Hamlet decides he needs more proof of his stepfather's guilt. He writes a play about the regicide, and commissions a bunch of strolling players to put it on for the court. Claudius freaks out at the climactic moment and this action appears to confirm the ghost's accusation. Claudius decides that Hamlet is getting to be a handful and ships him off to be surreptitiously taken out in England. There's a bit of offstage malarkey when Hamlet outwits his minders **Rosenkrantz** and **Guildenstern** and escapes from a mob of improbable philanthropic pirates.

Meanwhile Ophelia has topped herself by drowning. Why? Probably because Hamlet has been very mean to her, as he has been to many people. As the play progresses it becomes apparent that Hamlet can use his intelligence very misanthropically. Hamlet arrives back into Elsinore, the family castle, incognito and, unknowingly, appears at Ophelia's funeral and strikes up a conversation with the gravedigger and Yorick, the skull of his dad's former jester. Meanwhile Claudius talks **Laertes** (Ophelia's brother) into a sword duel with Hamlet. This sets in chain a trail of death by sword and poison, at the end of which Hamlet, Gertrude, Claudius and Laertes are killed.

Over the length of the play there are 11 dead bodies as a result of Hamlet thinking too much and not acting enough. His prevarication is what the play is all about - human indecision amplified in all its confused glory. Is he so reasonable (ie full of reasons), that he can't act instinctively? Maybe Shakespeare is having a dig at the Age of Reason's assumption that mankind can solve all problems by reason alone. Whatever that may be, Hamlet is said to be the first hero for the modern era, wearing the badge of humanism with its abolition of moral certainty. This is why it is THE GREAT PLAY as it ushers in the modern world of philosophical relativism, prefiguring the big three: Darwin, Marx and Freud.

With these implications the play is as au courant as it ever was....
Now back to the main game:

The journey of the play: Hamlet Stooged!
adaptor/director Jacqui Carroll

HS started as a choric essay, called Ratzhamlet, featuring 5 men as Hamlet and 5 women as both Gertrude and Ophelia. Gertrude (G) and Ophelia (O) are the only two significant female characters in the original, and the director, Jacqui Carroll, was deeply interested in the dynamic between both women (singly and together) and Hamlet (H). This was not a linear/realtime version of the play, but an essay on the disaffecting machinations wrought on H by G and O through their commissions, omissions and their very existence.

It became apparent, as we would be touring it internationally, that a cast of 10 was impractical and that a reduction to 4 performers was necessary. In fact HS eventually expanded to five. The name change to HS came about as a result of the 'Wayne's World rewriting' and it was felt that the word 'stooged', when added to the title, reflected the new style. The word 'stooged' came from an Australian sitcom about a dysfunctional

A Devil Pokes the Actor   25

Pizza bar. The mostly Lebanese actors referred to making a fool of someone as 'stooging' them. It seemed a suitably irreverent and puerile word.

The Stage Setting:
The setting is primarily a bare stage, with a white floor about 7 m by 7m square. At the back are 4 free standing white painted flats, spaced out equally so that there is a 750mm gaps between. The gaps are lit 'corridors' where the actors can be framed, as well as entering and exiting at different times. In this production the space behind the flats becomes a 'twilight zone' which alludes to the subconscious of H and the play itself. It works as a twilight zone because the audience knows the actors are back there doing something but it can't see them. As an example, the actor playing Yorick, offstage, whistles to the dog who is onstage, the dog looks up wondering where the whistle is coming from, deduces it must be coming from behind the flats and lopes off. The audience, matching the dog, also hears the whistle, knows it must be coming from the actor, knows the actor is upstage, but can't see him. The audience is aware of the actor's presence but is not exactly aware of what he is doing. They are conscious of the actor, but it is incomplete - he is really in their unconscious, so the audience completes the image with their own imagination.

This is a wonderful example of the types of psyche zones that can only be experienced in live theatre and which cannot happen in film. This is due to the fact that in theatre, the audience accepts that it is sharing a space with a group of actors, who may come and go on and off stage, but who are still in the 'room'. So even when they are not onstage, they are still in the consciousness of the crowd. There are no such possibilities in film because it is displayed on a two dimensional screen, and, if you're not on the screen, you've been effectively edited out of the mind of the watcher.
The props:
In order of appearance: a single mattress, a red and black sheet, a seat that looks like a very large red high heeled stiletto,

a small black box, a squeaky toy steak, a 600mm high Yorick/Stan Laurel-type doll, 3 hand mirrors, a suitcase and a toy plastic guitar.

The play HS:
The play starts when a man, who turns out to be the 'The Spirit of Yorick' (Y) the long dead jester to Hamlet's father, enters dressed as a life size version of the Yorick doll. The Yorick doll, which will appear much later at the denouement, is modelled on Stan Laurel (of the Laurel and Hardy comedy movie duo) and is the major emblem of HS.
Y is the Master of Ceremonies and his first step is to announce the characters. He whistles and a man dressed as a dog (D) appears. He is Hamlet's dog/mate Horatio and, as in the play proper, he is H's one true confidante. At another whistle the dog growls and pulls on the other three characters:

    1. Gertrude, played by a man in a tarty dress wearing fishnets, a raucous red curly wig, earrings and red high heels,
    2. Ophelia, an elegant, intense young woman in a punky miniskirt with a black 20s style wig and red stilettos,
    3. Hamlet, a young man dressed in punky tights and shirt to match Ophelia.

Y describes them mimetically by using vulgar and oblique gestures and noises, while they each perform a short spastic solo dance to music by the Tokyo Shock Boys.
(I describe it as spastic because each solo reveals the aspect of the character that is disturbing Hamlet).

Tokyo Shock Boys' music is the primary music source for HS because it has a unique, forceful, disjunctive style that mirrors the confused thoughts and feelings rattling around inside Hamlet's head

Once introduced, G and O disappear and H is put to sleep on the mattress by Y, who then interrupts the sleep with nightmarish vocalising and weird text which consists of fake Russian, the undecypherability of which denotes that Y is an unconscious

A Devil Pokes the Actor

force acting upon Hamlet. Y's speech wakes Hamlet with a start who then commences a dialogue with his dog as Y sits back and watches. This dialogue ranges from pejorative descriptions of his surroundings *"...this burping 'burb"* to acidic descriptions of his existential confusion *"...what sort of dude am I?"* The speeches end with a playful dogfight over a plastic steak, which is terminated by Y who whistles, orders the dog offstage and summons Ophelia on from the back.

Ophelia staggers on, outlining how she was scared witless by H's strange appearance and behaviour *"I have been so flashed and trashed.......His slacks all poo-ed on.... scans my dial as if to fax it, etc"*. During this speech H writhes up to the back miming O's account of the meeting. The speech segues into a full freak out dance for the Dog, O and H (all standing in the upstage entry points between the free-standing white flats). The movements are constructed to make it look as though they are finding and stamping on cockroaches. This movement alludes to the disconnected brain patterns of all three.

Exit Dog and O... Enter Gertrude in drag, carrying a red platform shoe chair, dressed in red platform shoes, fishnet tights, a black puffy knee-length skirt, a red wig, earrings and red lipstick. She is a manly woman on a mission and she upbraids H for his boorishness in front of his step-father *"....wipe that stupid black look off and let thine eyes look like pals upon your uncle's little plot...."*. H responds in kind *".....no way... I feel... I do not fake...."* During this testy exchange, H looks up G's dress in mock horror, reinforcing the Freudian sexual complexes in the writing.

The Devil........ deeply, softly scorning: *"Hairy fairy Priscilla, drag Queen of Denmark..... "*

Having an actor in drag is a very useful distancing tool when portraying sexual relationships on stage - especially those of a decidedly vulgar and graphic nature. A man groping a real woman on stage is fraught with sexual political challenges, but a man dressed as a woman subverts such problems. It inverts the reaction to the scene, refracting and diffusing the emotional relationships between the audience and the actors. This refraction is made even more potent if there is no effeminacy in the playing style. In this situation it is not a man pretending to be a woman, but a man playing an essence of woman.

G finishes by trying to sweet talk H into accepting his step-father ".... *remember you have a newer dad, one dad dead, a new dad in my bed..."* This speech, with its Freudian provocations, puts H to sleep in baby dreamland. To a slightly astringent lullaby, H starts to suck his thumb in his asleep, whereupon, with Y in attendance, G tucks him up and caresses him, with surreptitious attention to his privates. Y then escorts G off, showing the audience her scarlet g-string as an emblem of her sexuality, and revealing Hamlet's sexualised view of her. It is said that one of the worst things to befall a young man is to have a MILF, Mother I'd Like to ....

Horatio, the dog, comes on and Y commands the dog to windup H. The dog licks H awake. H delivers the great soliloquy of teenage angst with suicidal tendencies which, in the original is...."*That this too, too solid flesh.....*" In HS it has become "*.....so soggy, stale stinking and slack seems to me all the burgers at big Macs....*" Dog exits as Y and G re-enter, H turns the speech on her uttering the cruel insult.....*" Life's like some dumpster, full of junk, or a whore's old beaver, caked with dirty spunk..."* He slumps onto his mattress and Horatio the dog re-enters, commenting that Hamlet's mind is addled and we should watch the unravelling.

G advances in a placatory mood, H, goaded by Y, attacks her, pulls her wig off to reveal a bald pate and gropes about her crotch saying uncomplimentary things such as, *"methinks I groped her growler".......*"*not as bad, good mother as forget a dad and shack up with his brother...".* In the middle of this contretemps, O re-enters and accosts H with his misdeeds towards her *"... you promised before you tumbled me, you promised me to wed............ instead you wrecked my head."*

H responds even more viciously, uttering the famous rejoinder: *".....get thee to a nunnery"*. In the original it has a double meaning in that it is both an insult and also a warning because he knows the proverbial is about to hit the fan, and there will be carnage aplenty. In HS this becomes: *"....get thee to a rub'n'tug"* (massage parlour).

O runs up the back and, standing on the large red shoe-shaped chair, trades insults with H while Y and G look on. H finishes his tirade by pointedly insulting what could be both G and O *".....corrupted lust, deep in your veins, creates a canker, do not spread your compost on the weeds, you stupid wanker."* As H goes to exit, ridding himself of both these maddening women Y thrusts a mirror in his face, making him really look at himself for the first time.

The others gather around while H sits on a chair and Y replaces the mirror with a toy plastic guitar. H accompanies the 'divinity' speech with onomatopoeic air guitar by saying: *"... There is definite divinity in the death of my little doggie....."* G grabs the guitar and, echoing his last line, introduces the 60s pop song: **'Locomotion'**. While the others enthusiastically jive around him, H becomes a spastic with Tourette's syndrome. Once again, his inability to function, to engage with those around him, to be part of life, is pointed up by showing him alienated inside the landscape of a popular song about having fun.
The Devil's lewd voice lugubriously loops out and rumbles in my left ear: *"If you're playing Locomotion, can you procure for me Kylie's private number?"*

Using very accessible popular songs to corroborate discrepancies is one of Jacqui Carroll's directorial hallmarks, and they work because the audience hears songs that trigger enjoyable memories and that is contrasted or confirmed by what they see on stage. Because music bypasses the rational brain and connects directly with the soul, such songs create psyche spaces where audiences can make their own connections with the unfolding stories.

During **Locomotion** Horatio the Dog places mirrors in G, H and O's hands and all 3 main characters end up in the gaps between upstage flats. H places his mirror in Y's hand, toys with Y's face (the first time in the play he has acted upon Y- ie coming to terms with his own unconscious) and dismisses all 3 (G, O, and Y) with the speech: *".... since my mind got on the job and could pick the dudes with 'tude, my stupid fury has made me a stooge!....".* With this realisation (in effect the act of becoming mature), H and Horatio lie on the bed and Horatio comments on how life treats everybody with equal disdain, regardless of fame or achievement. He uses the *"noble dust of Alexander the Great becoming a beer barrel plug"* speech, but transposes it with more vulgar and puerile references to *"Acky-Wack's pubic hairs"* making a *"fortune cookie."*

Suddenly there is the afore-mentioned off stage whistle and the dog/Horatio trots off. At which point the three other actors re-appear dressed in black coats, black trousers and with black-framed spectacles on. One of them carries an old suitcase. They have morphed into psychologists bent on studying Hamlet's brain, and make pseudo- scientific comments while H lies under his sheet. H springs up *"baby plastic axe"* in hand and accuses them, *"..... you toy with me.....you push my pegs to set me off......"* referring musically to his toy guitar, before once again covering himself with the sheet.

One psychologist (formerly Y) arouses H by opening the suitcase and bringing out the 600mm high 'Yorick doll'. H immediately recognises it as his father's former jester *".....a witty sod, as slick as spit......made my father's mates all piss their pants...."* H places the doll gently on the ground and begins the 'to be' speech by saying: *"to exist or to exit, that is the question facing moi....."* The psychologists take up various strands of the speech as they move upstage and each stand in front of a flat. When H finishes *"....when we have scuttled off this skating rink........might even make a yobbo think"* the dog returns, licks H and they speak an edited version of the original 'to be' speech, falling asleep at the end.

As a coda, the Bee Gees song **'I Started a Joke'** plays and, while H and the dog lie crunched up in a ball on the mattress, the others silently walk forward and gaze dispassionately over them, and exit as the song plays out. The song is a wonderfully plangent paean of existential disconnectedness, couched in novelty pop melodies. It mirrors so many aspects of H's mindset with its anguish, self importance, sacrifice and melodramatic irony.

'I started a joke' is a gentle epitaph for H himself and for **Hamlet Stooged!** as a theatre piece. As the actors quietly withdraw away from the audience upstage into the shadows, the song lingers in the air, leaving an emotional vapour hanging over both the stage and the audience.

3a. The Journey of the Character:

This journey is what happens to any individual character as they traverse the landscape of the story. A character's journey in any play is primarily, either instinctively or by design, the acquisition of knowledge and the steps and sacrifices that enable that knowledge. In parallel with the play, this also has the two major manifestations of external and internal. In this context by external I mean the life and physical circumstances of the character evolving as a response to the people and situations he meets. This external aspect might also be called 'real time', which, even though it is compressed for logistical reasons, is the dramatist's temporal and spatial landscape.

By internal I mean how his emotional and psychological states transform as the story unfolds. This might be also called psyche time as it is non-linear in terms of time and space.

External:
In the case of a classic such as Shakespeare's Hamlet, what happens to him as the script progresses? In external terms there is his gradual realization that his uncle is his father's killer, the

ambiguity of his mother's complicity, and the various steps he takes to avenge the murder. A play such as this has a trajectory, an overall arching through-line as it were. On the one hand, it does have a straightforward beginning, middle and an end. As well, there are various fits and starts, and a few sidetracks such as Polonius' mis-adventurous slaying. There are also various sub-plots involving the secondary characters that flesh out the story, so that rather than being just a portrait of a life's singular revenge, it also a mosaic outlining several person's stories, their interactions and complications becoming a complex and unstable panorama through which Hamlet moves.

Internal:
As a mirror of his external journey, there is also the journey of Hamlet's psyche, his emotional and psychological shifts as he engages the other characters. These are both positive and negative shifts depending on his relationships. These have a trajectory too, but this time it is less linear - the mapping of a human mind is much more complicated and convoluted.

In this play Shakespeare has provided soliloquies as emotional and psychological way-points on this complicated quest for knowledge. They are Hamlet's thoughts made manifest as visceral and literary expressions of his 'state of mind' at the various conjunctions with the other personae and situations. Many other characters have solo speeches as well, mapping their journeys inside the interior life of the play. There is, also, another deeper level in the internal journey of the character. It has been said that Hamlet is the first, and possibly the best, portrait of a man's dialogue with his own soul. If it is the best, it would be because Shakespeare has no equal in his ability to render thoughts into poetry - all the soliloquies are the individual actor's conscious and subconscious thoughts offered up as poetic insights. (In this Shakespeare appears to be unique).

Once we see Hamlet's soul as undergoing a journey, then reductively, we can recognise that his emotional and psychological relationships with others are really also amplified portraits of an inner dialogue between the emotional sections of his own personality.

3b. The Character: The part of Yorick, An Outline of the experience of playing Yorick in Hamlet Stooged! by the actor <u>Ira Seidenstein</u>.

Ira S., is a very accomplished clown and actor, who was with Ozfrank from 2003 to 2008. He has performed and taught all over the world, and he is an expert in mime, circus and commedia dell'arte. He left us to join Cirque de Soleil because the lure of big bucks to recompense his great skills was too attractive to an impecunious gypsy. **(see Ira's pic in back of book)**.

I played **Yorick** over a period of two years in three evolutions of the production and performed it on very different stage settings in four different countries.

The journey of the character of Yorick began in a surprising way. Originally **Yorick** was actually called "Igor - a Russian Jokester". I was assisting as a sound operator for Ozfrank Theatre's production of **Macbeth - Crown of Blood.** The venue technician didn't quite catch my name and rather than Ira, he called me Igor. Our director, Jacqui Carroll found that quite amusing and said "Yes! That's what we need in the company, an Igor ". Thus, I suddenly had a nickname: Igor!

At another time, in a large theatre in Brisbane we were bumping out the **Rashomon** set. When the bumpout was nearly finished I started to invoke my own fantasy as a Russian actor from the Moscow Art Theatre. When I do such a character, surprisingly, my voice changes drastically and sounds to me as though I could have walked right out of the magnificent heritage of the Moscow Art Theatre.

Ozfrank Theatre had done a version of Hamlet many years before called **Heavy Metal Hamlet** that toured nationally and to the Shizuoka festival in Japan. In 2004 Jacqui began a convoluted process to create a new version of Hamlet. First, there were to be two small-cast adaptations one female-cast and the same adaptation with a male-cast. At some point it seemed more viable to go for an all-male adaptation. This too went through a permutation until finally Jacqui decided to contemporize the language.

Thus was *Hamlet Stooged* born. The 'stooge' was not a reference to my heroes the Three Stooges, but to Iggy Pop's band who John held in high esteem. At an early stage, with John as Hamlet, Jacqui asked me to improvise in a scene using my Russian accent.

After major roles in **Rashomon** and **Manga Ulysses,** I felt that I knew that, as demanding as Jacqui was, she was equally patient in waiting and allowing an actor to stretch their creative freedom. During rehearsals of **Rashomon,** in which I played the role of **The Woodcutter**, I thought I would test my theory that the actor had to be willing to improvise and that also meant be willing to accept Jacqui's wrath if things went awry. So, accepting the risk, I came in one day and tried to push my vocal work ie improvise using one or two lines of my role as the Woodcutter (**Rashomon**). I thought Jacqui would either respond positively, as I had observed, or she was going to chop off my head. I went for it and, within one minute, Jacqui intuitively responded and began to coach me in the more advanced way. I then tested my theory and nerve in a monologue when the Woodcutter was a 'witness'. Again Jacqui responded very positively. I believe this was somewhat of a breakthrough in the way the company rehearsed, whereby less experienced actors also started to receive the best-case-scenario coaching from Jacqui.

After that the stakes were raised, and I began to wake up about 2 or 3 am, suddenly doing my lines and doing Suzuki movements in bed. After a while, I would get out of bed and rehearse and about an hour later I would go back to sleep. Working in the 'best case scenario' level with Jacqui put a touch of the fear-of-God in an actor as there clearly was a psyche

connection between her and the actors at certain times during the rehearsal.
Then it was time for **Igor** aka **Yorick** to emerge. The first version I spoke some gibberish with a Russian accent. For the next version, Jacqui came in excited, saying that she realised that Igor was actually Yorick. Something that I and the others had thought about but hadn't broached with Jacqui.

As well, there was a time when Jacqui had found a porcelain doll of **Stan Laurel** complete with tails, bowler hat and red bow tie. So I was made a matching costume creating a Chaplinesque affect. During this second version Leah Shelton, who was also playing Ophelia, took on the costume design of *Hamlet Stooged*.

That is the process, as I recall it, of how the character of Yorick came about. First, there was a period of training with the company for a few years, and then playing a variety of cameo roles. The shifts that deepened the creative relationship with director Jacqui Carroll gradually became more daring as the **Woodcutter** in **Rashomon** and then as **Hermes** in **Manga Ulysses**. It was further amplified with the playfulness with Igor, who evolved into **Yorick**.
Ira Seidenstein 2009

4a. The journey of the person playing the character.

Outer:
What happens externally to each actor as they play a character?

Parts of this journey are notional because, for instance, whilst a character may die on stage, the person playing that character has to feign death. Other forms of physical conflict such as fisticuffs are likewise problematic - watching 2 guys fight on stage is really to watch two men trying **not** to hurt each other! Because of the problematic nature of real violence, all forms of Capital and Corporeal contact are better alluded to rather than actually enacted.

However, other aspects of the outer rites of passage transcend the notion that an actor should 'go out and give it everything they've got' to paraphrase Warner Baxter's famous words to Ruby Keeler in the film, 42nd Street. This exhortation describes the total commitment required of any actor in any and all types of theatre, regardless of their style, content or accessibility. It implies the devotion of one's entire psychic and physical energy and, if so, then the actor should have expended his physical and mental powers at the end of the performance. It's as if he has run a marathon. Each performance is then a microcosm of a life's journey, where the actor experiences the symbolic ups and downs that the character undergoes.

Inner:
What happens to the psyche of the actor as he/she follows the path of the character?

The actor cannot convincingly re-enact Hamlet as 'Hamlet' never existed – he is a myth created in the mind of the writer! And.....in the case of a real life historical figure, how can you convincingly impersonate someone that existed centuries ago? When attempted in most conventional theatre we inevitably see a display of inverted atavism - contemporary Aussie suburban dude aping a fantasy Danish nobility that never existed. Therefore an actor can only play an aspect of Hamlet.

First, he must be highly self-defined. The audience cannot witness an idea on stage - they need something or someone concrete to identify with - someone with highly idiosyncratic, but charismatic behaviour. For example, John Wayne, who was not so much an actor as a monument to a certain attitude or mode of behaviour, was a very good filmic example of this concrete charisma - he not so much acted as behaved. He wasn't impersonating any one so much as he was just being John Wayne.

Second, however, the actor's performance must unveil much more than just a static display of self; he must also be on a journey of self-discovery. This means that, while having definable and emblematic character traits, he must also be psychologically mobile - he has to be able to be affected by the emotional and psychological vicissitudes that the environment may impose on him, undergo these experiences and to be seen to be transformed by them.

"*vicissitudes!*"
The devil caresses my temple with a scaly burnt black fingernail:
"Precious! I do my best to make those vicissitudes as vicious as can be!"

Any successful performance has inside it an intertwining of these paradoxically separated essences. Without a strong sense of self, the audience is left trying to connect with a set of airy, quasi-universal notions. If the actor is not also psychically and physically mobile, he is stuck in time and space with nowhere to go; as it were a metaphysical insect in amber. His persona has to undergo some form of transformation. The audience witnesses this transformation and can identify with it vicariously. That transformation is the heart of the actor's journey.

4b. The Journey of the Actor
playing the character
Yorick played by Ira Seidenstein

At some point in the first production of Hamlet Stooged! I started to view Yorick as a Shaman. Via Jacqui's mise en scene and dramaturgy, and John's script, as well as improvisations in rehearsal, Yorick became the first to enter the stage and he became the master of ceremonies, with the assistance of the second character to enter, Hamlet's dog. I called him Scotty-Dog after the actor in the role, Michael Scott. He was later called **Horatio** - because he was Hamlet's only friend. Scotty-Dog then was commanded to fetch each of the other characters in the following order – Gertrude, Ophelia, Hamlet. Yorick then encapsulated each character via use of mime and vocalising, then shooed them off stage, until only Yorick and Hamlet were left; Yorick puts Hamlet to bed under a large black and red shroud.

When Hamlet is shrouded, Yorick then uses his full hara (the Japanese word for anger and for centre) to cast a spell on Hamlet, and there I utilized both my Frank/Suzuki voice and my own fantasy of a Russian basso-profundo from the Moscow Art Theatre.

At one point in rehearsal we had a guest actor and director from Mongolia. One day, Lisa O'Neill and I were to take the guests for a day out at the beaches north of Brisbane. Along the way, I asked for the Mongolian words for star and moon. If I remember correctly they were sut and ut. Jacqui told me that tree was mut. So when Hamlet fell (literally, as Yorick pushes him) to sleep I began to invoke the nature spirits of ut, sut and mut into the sleeping Hamlet. From the earliest of these rehearsals I considered that Yorick was not just a clown, a story teller, but also a shaman.

I do have some experience with various aspects of traditional shamanism. Certainly, as one Gershon Winkler has researched and proven, the Jewish religious culture is in fact shamanic. The first time I saw an official shaman was in Sweden when I saw a performance by a Korean shaman who, like most Korean shamans, was a woman. Certainly that performance gave me some information that influenced FrankenKlown's show Chaplin's Eye. Rarely have I seen performers whom I would consider shamanic. Two that come to mind are Archie Roach and Yasmina Levi. The roots of Japanese Noh theatre are directly shamanic and since Suzuki Tadashi draws at least some elements and exercises from Noh, then there is a lineage from the indigenous Japanese shaman to Noh, to Suzuki, to OzFrank and the various company members. OzFrank pursue a shamanic path drawing from Suzuki, rock music and Gurdjieff and perhaps other influences.

As a company member I draw my shamanic interpretation from those sources, but also from my own cultural practices as well

as the Korean shaman that I had witnessed. For vocalising I used a gibberish that some feel is Russian but that Russians would feel is Polish. Additionally I used Mongolian, Welsh, Hebrew, Yiddish words or phrases. I was also using a Stanislavskian approach as I created an inner monologue or inner truth to my character. Throughout the duration of the rehearsals and performances I had to constantly reinvigorate my journey as a Frank/Suzuki actor ever-watchful to engage as fully as possible and then move in a wholly intuitive fashion, appropriate in our preferred performance aesthetic.
To get to that stage, I had to engage with regular training led by Jacqui and John and during their times away senior colleagues such as Lisa, Caroline, Leah or Ramsay. Then, during rehearsal, one needs the constant prodding, encouragement and challenge from Jacqui.

Additionally John would always offer either advice or encouragement when he felt it was appropriate. As well, I had to engage as fully as possible with the other actors in various incarnations of Hamlet Stooged including John, Leah, Michael Coughlan, Michael Scott, Emma Pursey and Conan Dunning. Like actors in any company, each is different and engagement with one is not the same as engagement with the other.

The challenges of acting the role of Yorick kept evolving. I enjoyed the inversion of the traditional Hamlet story when Hamlet finds the skull of Yorick. In our production, Yorick invoked a nightmare into the sleeping Hamlet's skull. The remainder of the show then was the nightmare that I at one point referred to as the 'toothed vagina' of the Native American Indian's cultural myths. Another aspect of Yorick was that he was both guardian angel and tempting devil at any one moment, with a slight leaning towards the devil on Hamlet's shoulder.

In my career of about 35 years, I can recall my three hardest days as a labourer hired to put up a huge three-ring circus in the USA with my selected labour partner being a black-American built like Mike Tyson. It was an absurd pair. The second hardest day(s) was my audition for Cirque du Soleil under the excellent coaching of Michel Laprise.

The third hardest day was our first performance day of **Hamlet Stooged** at the Hoxton Hall in London. Since the spacing adjustments were huge for that tiny historic vaudeville venue, we had to do 3 full runs of the show and then the performance, all in one day. Due to the blocking changes that I had to learn, the only way I could find what I needed and could give Jacqui a real view of her adjustments, was to do each run-through full-steam. In the actual performance, in sweltering heat, there was one point where I had to stand still for a few minutes in a classic Suzuki-style statue, fully engaged like an animal ready to pounce. I was soon standing in a pool of my own sweat - a memory and a challenge I shall never forget!

In summary, just as the development of the character went through many phases, so too did my experience of actually engaging in the role. Certainly the challenge, to fully involve with the training exercises, rehearsal, and finally the performance, is one of the most satisfying in my career. The point is that the engagement is the ultimate aim. In our Frank/Suzuki and in my other work, the fuller the engagement the more profound possibilities arise inside the experience.
Ira Seidenstein 2009

5a. The Journey of the Director.

The director coordinates all the forces that constitute a performance. These include selecting and matching -
1. the actors,
2. the text,
3. the accompanying music or sound-scape,
4. the designer and or/the design style,
5. the movement style and/or the choreographer,
6. the lighting style and/or lighting designer

Directors often have assistants and researchers, people who buttress the production by filling in gaps in the director's knowledge, but the director is the point of last resort - the buck stops there. She may be a gatherer of minds and visions; she being the glue bonding them all together to create a unified aural and visual sculpture. Most of the great directors own several of the 6 functions above but only a few have truly singular visions wherein they encompass every attribute themselves. Those few have the most original, irreplaceable aesthetics because there is no other figure mediating between them and their conceptions.

They assemble the 6 basic materials above and gradually amalgamate the elements, either in fits and starts or slowly and deliberately, by a process of accretion or by ablation. Their journey is the process by which the final product is arrived at, and would include at least three synchronous and circular steps:

1. Aggregation - putting all the elements on the same page,
2. Re-arrangement- placing the elements in relationship to each other,
3. Scrutiny – reading the developing work, witnessing its evolution from the viewpoint of a third person to gain objectivity.

These 3 steps can run both separately and/or simultaneously, often in an instinctive and convoluted fashion that really only makes sense to the director herself. Whereas the actor is primarily a searcher for a new self, the director may be a searcher, but is primarily a displayer. By that I mean that she must have a world view, an attitude to the cosmos that she intensely desires to display in some concrete form. A director needs to see her 'world' displayed. In her own way, she's also a searcher for ways in which to reveal and articulate her vision, to make it more apparent and appreciable.

During the development phases she's effectively her own audience, but in the final phase, the performances, she uses the audience as a landscape against which she can read and perceive the work. The aesthetic of a production is very much a map or display of the cosmology of the director and the journey of the director occurs as she observes the unfolding of the story using the audience as a witnessing landscape.

5b. The journey of Jacqui Carroll as director of HS:

Outer:
JC writes........It is part of my aesthetic while pursuing my versions of the classics to:

1. Excise all subplots and material not germain to the thrust of the central theme eg there would be no references to Rosencrantz and Guilderstern or trips to England and outlandish escapades with unwicked pirates.
2. Eschew all attempts at 'realistic' sword fighting and fisticuffs (as it **always** looks like two guys trying **not** to hurt each other!)
3. Reduce the amount of dialogue by about 90% so as not to baffle the audience with too many words. My philosophy is that the audience comes to experience/feel the show, not just listen to it as if it were a talking book.

Inner: Jacqui Carroll:
- My reasons for tackling and re-arranging Shakespeare's Hamlet was a powerful sense that here was a play with many doorways in it to other worlds and that mining and re-mining it would lead me into some fascinating labyrinths.
- The stage setting which contained the 3 corridor-style openings at the rear of the stage represent the corridors and doorways of the mind, the conscious world in front and the unconscious world behind.
- RatzHamlet revealed to me the keys to open the door on Hamlet Stooged!
- Hamlet is an incomplete man who, though moderately bright, vacillates and finds the only people he can truly dominate are the women in his life, Ophelia, his fiancée, and Gertrude, his mother. I used these two women as the doorways through

- which the audience could witness his deep problems.
- In the final casting mix I cast John (Nobbs) as Gertrude. This choice of drag for the portrayal of Gertrude allowed me to realise a more crude, boldly physical Freudian relationship between Hamlet and his mother
- At first the character, Yorick, was called the Russian Joker because he spoke a quasi-Russian lingo, it was only when the whole play had been created did I realise that what I'd made was Yorick, the old King's Jester, reincarnated. The clue was Hamlet saying, 'I knew him well.'
- Yorick is an aspect of Hamlet's troubled mind. Only Hamlet and Horatio, Hamlet's dog/friend, could see and hear Yorick, a powerful device which kept the metaphysical aspects of the work fully alive.
- All these things, the dog's name, Horatio, the Russian Jester's name, Yorick, only came after the work had been fully made and these characters spoke back from out of the play revealing their 'true' nature within the story that I had made.
- I was very pleased with my invention of the three 3 'psychologists' who make an appearance at the very end of the work to comment on Hamlet's state-of-mind and to mock him.
- I made the decision to ask John (Nobbs) to re-work the dialogue into a more witty and 'hip' lingo because I felt that the weakness in RatzHamlet had been the retention of the original Shakespearean text, which, though adapted and edited, was still in the original language and was, I felt, a barrier to realizing the core intent of my adaptation.
- I chose the Tokyo Shock Boys and the Bee Gees as the principal source of the music to accompany HS!. The TSB's discordant and wacky soundscapes ideally suited the madness that pervaded the work and the Bee Gees '*I started a joke"* seemed a fitting epitaph for Hamlet's mangled life.

6a. The journey of the audience:

The audience is both the ultimate witness to and the ultimate judge of a performance.

They are required to be the witness of final resort for all the other journeys, all of which only come to completion in front of a group of lay people; that is a group of disparate individuals who do not have a pre-existing knowledge of all the intricacies of the gestation and evolution of the work. Their reactions are instinctive rather than analytical due to their brief and transient relationship with the actors and the story.

For a performance to be successful from an audience's point of view, they must be able to experience one or more of the following:

1. Distraction (Sensual): Many people come to be entertained as a way of temporarily forgetting their cares and anxieties, a release from their daily concerns.

WoWoWoah! I sense the rancid beery smoky sniff of last night's bar-room carpet, as I get thumped face first, flat on the desk. Groaning, I look sideways to see Disco Dev gurgling his way through a lurid Macarena, licked off with a wolf tongue slobber. Is this the delinquent devil's idea of sensual? #?@*%+!!! Bruised but unfazed, I return to the lofty realms of philosophy and metaphysics.........

2. Affirmation (Philosophical): Audiences also come to have their essential beliefs affirmed. Most performances contain struggles between notional good and evil elements that are introduced, played out and finally resolved to the satisfaction of the moral underpinnings of a community.
3. Revelation (Metaphysical): At this highest level, they come to be shown new ways of thinking and feeling that may have been latent and previously unrevealed.

All audiences seek one or more of these experiences at a performance and these levels can be seen as analogous to Ezra Maslow's hierarchy of needs, ranking in order of sophistication from Distraction up to Revelation. The great and enduring works of theatre have elements of all three, the great moral driver being the last, but carrying with it the first two. Distraction and Affirmation are often the presented or outer face of an aesthetic.

In Hamlet, entertainment and distraction is provided by:
- Shakespeare's words, especially the keynote speeches,
- attractive costumes and set,
- attractive competent actors.

The affirmation is provided by Good overcoming Evil, as well as the keynote speeches (the hearing of 'to be or not to be' offers a real sense of re-capitulation).

The revelation is provided especially by the witnessing of Hamlet's soliloquies, which are poetic manifestations of his soul's inner dialogue, as he wrestles with the moral dilemmas associated with revenge.

The audience comes to a performance for many reasons; entertainment, snobbery, desire for revelation, and those reasons are bundled together in some form of secular communion with the other audience members. This communion is a journey that starts and continues as long as the audience feels connected to the presentation.

From the start the audience must feel that they are part of the play and that they are comfortable with the situation because their self beliefs are not essentially under threat:

To be successful, nothing throughout the duration of the performance should fracture that zone. The audience's relationship is instinctive - it is based on 'feelings' - going behind the mind's analytical processes to speak directly to the soul. If they start to think in rational terms (if they become critical) it is because they have dropped out of an instinctual relationship with the play - they are no longer IN the play. They have become excluded from the magical aura surrounding the production by a breakdown in any number of the elements; from technical problems such as lighting mistakes to the style and focus of the actors or weakness in the director's conception.

At the highest level, they come for a new experience - to have revealed to them some part of themselves of which they were not heretofore aware. This is why performances must have charm as well as challenge. The audiences' psyche experiences must be revealed and expanded without their psyches being threatened. In many ways it is not so different from a sporting event, where people go for an uplifting experience by witnessing positive human energy in controlled conflict.

Where performances differ from sporting events is that sporting events are purely affirmational. The crowds come to have their beliefs verified in their witnessing of the 'success' of their team. If there are any revelations it is the crowd's witnessing of special physical virtuosity. **Benjamin Williams**, (see pic at back of book) as audience, comments below:

6b. Journey of Benjamin Williams as he watched HS.

Among the unique and undeniable features of theatre is the art form's transience or impermanence. For both the performer and for their witness the particular sensual, sensory and visceral experience of the best theatre is powerfully immediate yet sadly passing – it remains the memory, both mental and physical that we each savour. That Jacqui Carroll's unique production of Hamlet Stooged that I have witnessed and will hereafter reflect upon has had such an enduring bodily effect on me as a witness speaks much then of this production; its performance, its direction, and its design; but also of Ozfrank; and of the work of Master Shakespeare.

Ozfrank's production Hamlet Stooged, as played on the Roundhouse Stage in Brisbane fits squarely within both the performance traditions of the Brisbane based Suzuki- inspired ensemble's work, but also, and as significantly, within the world of Shakespeare – theatrically, performatively, socially and culturally.

The particular balance effected by the dangerous marriage between these two traditions is communicated through a production which though respecting the theatrical and literary tradition of the bard, and a greater tradition of English theatre in which he is a central player, nevertheless ruthlessly subverts the play's language and themes in a way unquestionable Australian – convict, burlesque, anti authoritarian, puerile, rude, larrikin, and deviant. It is this effect that, though placing it within the ever-evolving world of Shakespeare as a world language, also claims both he and his imaginary, especially his socially disaffected teenage Hamlet, as fair-dinkum Aussies. It is this aspect of the production, I believe, that makes it an OzFrank production – built upon the training methodologies developed both in-house and from those learnt with Tadashi Suzuki – for both these houses train actors in performance for inter-cultural exchange.

In Hamlet Stooged John Nobbs plants much of the seed for this exchange in his extensive rewriting of the script. Working from the colourful (read fabulously crude) Australian vernacular many of the original play's famous speeches and soliloquies are poetically transformed to realise a distinctly Australia feeling to the language and arousing within a willing audience participant both a sense of distaste for the vulgarity of the scene but also of darkly affirmative familiarity.

Though the immediate literary sense the words and dialogue may be considered, superficially, to be as popularly unintelligible and indigestible to a typically uninformed and disinterested 21st century audience as those of the original work. However, for those theatregoers, such as myself, who seek both affirmation but also revelation in their experience as witness, the language of Nobbs' new script and its embodied play takes you, and the darkest corners of your imagination, on a journey, most immediately with Aussie-teen Hamlet, but also with a Danish prince hundreds of years past and the famed writer of his tragic demise apparently separated from us but 400 years of history and cultural evolution.

In just one short hour, our intimate dialogue with Hamlet (stooged), engaged between he and his audience from his bedroom, cramped, confined and made chaotic by the often unwelcome and always discomforting visitation by those 'significant others' in his life, be they real or imagined (or really imagined), reveals that though our anxieties and foibles remain distinctly and distressingly, but also joyously our own (whether we like it or not), little separates the anxieties and foibles of we 21st century Australians from those of seventeenth century Poms, or indeed, from those of an imagined and esteemed Danish prince. Considering the production as a whole, this I find a most significant accomplishment for, with this work OzFrank shares with its audience a deeply personal yet profoundly shared appreciation and knowing both of our own distinct Australian culture and psyche – one which exists beyond, but not to the exclusion or denial of the traditionally ocker notion of the bushie or the digger – and also, of our seemingly distant and forgotten forebears.

I have, here, spoken a great deal about what may be considered the 'bigger picture' or the 'take home message' from Hamlet Stooged – of my intellectual engagement with the work – and little of the immediate effect of the production upon my self, my body: sensually, sensationally, emotionally or viscerally. This may seem a significant, even negligent, omission for throughout the show my body, my self, was wholly and honestly engaged – engaged with character, with bodies, with story and attitudes, with noise and colour and music, with conflict, with darkness, with those things for which there are relievedly no words. It felt good. It felt awful. It felt delightful and shameful. It was enlivening. It is past. And yet it remains.

The best theatre is transformative, for both its craftsmen and most necessarily, for their witnesses. Of Hamlet Stooged, this is true absolutely of the production in its wonderfully, bodily and soulfully absorbing yet sadly transient immediacy – that which one experiences as witness to its play, but also, most significantly, in its passing. Hamlet Stooged is a culturally significant work of art. Yet, as a work of theatre, its endurance is not material, as it may be visual art or architecture but rather, it is visceral, of the body, of the indefinable undeniable self. Hamlet Stooged, its dark playful vulgar poetic memory now informs something of who I am as a man; as an Australian; as a citizen of the world in all its chaotic glory, and colours how I choose to live – with my self and with others.

Benjamin Williams 2009.

I turn to face the Devil, who's slumped on the stairs, sniffing and scoffing. Pulls out a finely Sobranie cocktail and lights it with a flick of a finger...A cool smoky chill settles on my skin like frost upon the sand.....he hisses subtly with a threatful softness:

"Burn that! Striking you should map and plan and plot and plat what most scribes would simply call a play. Why all those kilobytes elucidating......what?"

"All the probes I'm posting are enquiries into the arcane nature of acting, a pastime historically riddled with dodgy escapades and shifty evasions. However.....suitably tooled up, heroic types can wend their way through the emotional mud and muck, and emerge unscathed. The SATM and the FSPA are all about providing the tools, and the six journeys provoc was a tool, a demotic mudmap that shows the course with all its traps."

"And....Provocation Number 2 ?????"

"The second tool can be a shift in strategic thinking. The next provoc pushes the thought that chunks of life and art can be viewed anew as teaching machines………..''

"Hidey, Ho...Let's go!"

Muscle Provocation #2
Machina Didactica
The Machine that teaches the teacher

A few years ago whilst watching our company train, I realized how much I had learnt from the training. For the first few years of our existence the training had primarily been directed towards skill acquisition - exercises designed to strengthen the actor's voice and body giving them the ability to generate the most power and flexibility.

I was satisfied with this approach for the first 4 or 5 years because, working on myself, I was pushing my body's finite possibilities. As I reached my fullest physical and vocal potential, I found that I had hit a type of wall - I had reached a point where neither my voice nor my body were getting stronger. After weathering a period of frustration, I began looking at the more creative prospects that lay inside the body's enlarged capability. This led me to expand the training range by developing exercises that encouraged more imaginative shifts and levels - first of all in movement patterns and textures, and by extension into vocalising. The first such exploration was *'I Put a Spell on you'* by Screamin' Jay Hawkins in 1995.

By this stage many of the other **Ozfrank** performers had achieved similar levels of proficiency in accessing their latent power, so a shift in creative priorities was pertinent to their growth as well. This shift could not have occurred until after the actors had achieved their fullest physical potential (their figurative 'top speed'). A comparison can be made with the training of a sports team, where all the players, through a series of simple, demanding and repetitive exercises achieve a level of expertise which they can instinctively draw upon during the heat of play. More of this, however, in another chapter....

Some of the exercises then evolved to such a level that, whilst the actors were doing certain vocal and/or physical activities, I would be able to throw in a command with a generational shift.

A Devil Pokes the Actor

For example, if they were doing a 'spastic' dance sequence to the saxophone solo in *'I put a spell on you'* I could say: 'Dance with one hand stuck to the floor!' This shift in demand would create an extra frisson of energy in the entire room for a couple of reasons:
1. The actors would somehow maintain whatever they were doing, whilst adding the extra elliptical element.
2. They would often not fully understand what I had said (because I was in a new 'space' myself and very much thinking on my feet) and this provided an even greater frisson of energy amongst the actors as they went about their improvisation whilst asking themselves, "What did he say? What did he mean? What did he want?' This frisson is caused by the question that now hovers in the space, and we'll return to that point later.

I had a precedent for moving in this direction for during my times performing with **Suzuki**, I had seen him on any number of occasions give complicated instructions half way through an exercise. I sensed that the actors had often not quite understood his request, but nevertheless had maintained deportment and mission while they endeavoured to implement what he had said. <u>The Japanese are also culturally very adept at not dropping the ball whilst entertaining notions of renewal.</u>

As I did this more and more with our own actors I became more elliptical and less prescriptive with the requests/demands. This was partially because they had developed the requisite 'talent' to be compelling no matter what they did, and my being more vague meant there was more plurality in the group atmosphere. This meant that the actors owned the experience more, because they had made their own. The trainer, myself, by not making explicit demands was imposing less of himself on the group. The group had to be more self-generative and invent their own 'instructions' because they couldn't fully understand or hear mine.

As I noticed the shift in the 'temperature' of the room, either when Suzuki was taking rehearsals/training or when I was training Ozfrank, I began to feel the effect of the frisson on myself. Because the actors were on such a level of sophistication, I felt that the combination of their talent and my suggestions had taken the 'organism' of the training to a higher pitch, a newer more exciting plane. I then understood that I had learnt something from the experience - that the experience had taught me something. This frisson was most often something intangible - a feeling if you like, which would take time to homologate into something more concrete. Because I had learnt from working with the actors I was rejuvenated - I was not only in the position of just giving out information, I had achieved a situation where the actors were 'teaching' me.

The word 'teaching' is a simplified code for what is a complicated transaction. The combination of the actor's skills and my suggestions creates an atmosphere that I can 'read'. One could describe that 'atmosphere' as a type of teaching organism or **learning machine**.

In any teaching/learning situation, the less one prescribes, imposes or proffers, the more one is likely to learn. Witness the old adage: 'To learn, shut up and **Listen**!' The more elliptical my demands, the more compelling the atmosphere became, which I presume meant that the more oblique I became the more I could learn from the experience.

In our long term observations of Suzuki's process, one of the things that intrigued Jacqui and myself was.... exactly how had Suzuki gained his exceptional choreographic and directorial skills? In our understanding of his history, he was studying political economics (or something equivalent) at his university and gradually became attached to the undergraduate drama society. At one stage he found himself caretaking the situation when the movers and shakers became highly politicized and left to man the revolutionary barricades. He must have seemed at that point to be an unlikely candidate for future theatrical greatness, having had no training in any aspects of a director's craft.

A Devil Pokes the Actor 55

As he progressed along his artistic path he had to have picked up the necessary skills, because, now, in any estimation, he has considerable facility as a lighting designer, director, choreographer, vocal coach, costumier, scenic designer and dramaturg. So……….where did he get it??

Once I'd trained actors to a level where they could, in their improvisations 'teach' me, I began to conjecture that Suzuki had to have done the same thing. As I recalled my experiences of working with him as well as observing, I remembered the 'atmosphere' of the room when he was making suggestions. In the training the situation was more apparent because I was aware of the structures and formats and I could more easily feel the shifts. This must also have happened in the rehearsals but it was harder to tell because I don't understand Japanese, so couldn't read the complexities

A good example of this occurred while Suzuki was conducting a training session for myself and a group of his actors. We were all performing in the Shizuoka Theatre Olympics in 1999. We were doing an exercise called **Agiteketen**, where we stand rooted to the spot, legs and bodies still whilst our arms, as straight as rods, wave around chaotically as fast as possible.

This exercise is demanding and compelling as it stands, but one day Suzuki said: "HOLD IT! I want you to do it again, but this time just move as fast as you can, jumping, hopping what ever – just don't stop and make every movement as crazy as possible" I don't understand Japanese, but it must have been words to that effect as they all began hopping and jumping around like Colonel Parker's chickens at an early Elvis concert. The look on their faces was something to behold, as their expressions said: "I've got no idea what I'm doing or why I'm doing it, but I'd better keep going and try and work out what it is while I'm doing it!" Pretty impressive! Luckily I was in the next group so I had a bit of warning, but I'll bet I looked as confused as the others.

On reflecting upon such experiences and transposing them to

my training of the Ozfrankies it gradually dawned on me that this was the process Suzuki employed, however instinctively, to gain the immense and varied skills he has today. This means that he is using the training to train himself as much as the actors under his charge - much more than just telling the actors what to do, he was using the training in reverse as a **teaching machine**!

The more I applied this approach to our own work the more I began to see the deeper implications. I began to realise that one's actual cultural aesthetic - the whole shebang, could originate from this machine, and by extension the political and philosophical actions could likewise be given shape and focus from the 'organism'. Of course as they ripple out further, they become more conceptual and elastic.

I also don't see why this 'teaching machine conceit' should not be applied to any other field of endeavour. I'm sure that creative thinkers as diverse as Bill Gates, Edison and Einstein all somehow invented equivalent machines that propelled their innovative schemes, of course, the more 'creative' the field the more obviously applicable.

In 2004 Ozfrank was asked to take part in the Financing Innovative Growth (FIG) program. This was a Queensland Government sponsored series of seminars for young 'Turk' industries, predominantly in the IT sector, to gain the necessary smarts to go from the garage to the factory floor.

We were invited because we were seen as the hippest theatre company in the state. We were surrounded by very motivated, forward thinking people on the cusp of success and it was highly instructive to be in this milieu, even though their core businesses were quite different from ours. In the course of the seminars I could see that though there were many things separating our' businesses', there were also things we held in common. At the end of the day all businesses are essentially about coordinating and training people.

As I chatted and observed these people who were enterprisingly searching for ways to configure their aspirations, I could see that my 'learning machine' principle could apply to any other culture. I then cast back through all the biographies I had read over the years and found that all of the so-called 'successful' people had devised or discovered some device, organism, mechanism, zone, diagram, mental attitude, image, sound, that they could 'read' from a remove.

With all of these people the ability to 'read' was a crucial requirement. This 'reading' ability was the ability to think out of the square so to speak, to not think head-on, linearly, but from an angle, in an oblique fashion, to think laterally (in the words of Edward de Bono). Another way of putting it is to say they could think beyond rationality - they could think poetically. This put them in the position of being more receptive than projective. So, discoverers from Nicolai Tesla to Steve Jobs would invent something and see the invention not so much as their finite achievement but as a springboard for generating future creative shifts.

I think that when creative, successful people such as Bill Gates invent a device, they then don't have to initiate the next stage. If they turn their invention into a 'teaching machine' it will show them the next way to go.

A Devil Pokes the Actor					59

Yon devil's up too close and personal, skull to skull, steadily smoking, blowing smoke rings through my mind:

"How's a struggling punter going to connect the dots of Machina to Didactica?"

"This is not a new idea, it's a transposition. The idea of machine thinking has been around since 1923, when hyper-modern architect, Le Courbusier said: 'A House is a Machine for living in!' He was implying that, in a mechanised age, we need to crank up our brain rate by thinking creatively across the tracks and into the stacks."

"My next provoc details how Expertise is actually acquired, with a little kick from Beckham."

"Hell's bells, let's hop from Corb the Shaven Raven, to Bend it like Beckham!"

Muscle Provocation #3
Beckham says "No, Dummy! It's training for football"
The Acquisition of Expertise

Ozfrank often presents a demonstration of training to articulate our theatre practice. When watching our company members in the demonstration many people are expecting to see 'acting', ie actors doing scenes from plays. Instead, what they see are the exercises that we use to prepare an actor for rehearsal and performance.

Unfortunately most people are imbued with the attitude that an actor's entire world consists of pretending to be someone going through a range of emotional and psychological re-enactments. Most people, including many actors, would look upon our training as a non conventional 'style' of acting, whereas it is definitely **not** a 'style' but is, instead, a way of 'building' an actor with a methodology analogous with those of musicians, dancers and athletes.

In order to de-mystify our training we make comparisons with sports such as soccer, by positing that if one observes someone such as soccer great, David Beckham, practising, you will find him doing simple, repetitive, seemingly eccentric tasks, such as dribbling the ball between his legs while running backwards from the centre line to the goalposts. If one approached him and said, 'What's this weird stuff you're doing? Why don't you just play football.' he would probably reply, 'No, Dummy! It's training for football!'

Beckham would be indicating the pathway for the acquisition of expertise.

The vast majority of people probably believe that being an 'expert' is a lofty position occupied by people who can think and function in long convoluted patterns, generally due to some innate 'genius' not available to ordinary folk. They think gaining that expertness is a form of magic -

being naturally good at complicated routines, or systems, and that getting better at them is an automatic perquisite. It just follows, getting easier and easier etc.

<u>Not so!</u>

Many years ago I read an article deconstructing expertise. It articulated a much simpler pathway from that generally understood. It described expertise as deriving from the accumulation of a large number of discrete, simple experiences. The common perception of expertise is that it's a natural talent and you're either lucky to have it or you're not. Instead, the author went back to simple analogies to show that while innate talent is important, time and repetition are also two crucial factors.

He used as his example the act of driving a car, ranging from beginner to racing driver. He stated that in the process of learning to drive a car the learner was required to think and act in very simple and separated terms, ie in order to perform the simple act of changing gear he would have to:
(1) think and perform accelerator pedal off,
(2) think and perform clutch in,
(3) think and perform change gear,
(4) think and perform clutch out,
(5) think and perform accelerator on, etc.

In between each action would be a stop of up to a second during which the driver would mentally construct the next phase before moving on. Five discrete actions for one seemingly basic task and those of us who've done it will well remember the stumbling and intermittent progress we went through.

It is a series of discrete experiences with definite gaps between, and repeated until the function becomes semi-automatic. It never becomes fully automatic because it must always depend on decisions sent from the brain, not act of its own accord. The gaps in between the actions are also crucial in another way, because those gaps are where the action becomes logged into the body as a deeply ingrained process. While one may read many books about driving, this is the **only** way to learn how to **actually drive the car**. As the driver becomes more proficient the spaces between the thought and the action become shorter and shorter - the actions have been homologated into the body. The driver then ceases to perform them as separated experiences - and as he does this, his driving becomes more fluid, connected and instinctive.

Most of us don't remember any of the mechanical actions we perform when driving. In fact I can often recall driving in the country and suddenly realising that I'd absolutely no recollection of what had occurred over those past few minutes - I'd no idea what had happened and how I'd responded. Quite a shock, as my mind had been blank while I had been doing 110 kph. Now of course I realise that my mind, or parts of it, had organised all the necessary actions, without the rest of my brain being involved in any way.

In the original article which deconstructed the acquisition of expertise the writer expanded on this and stated that it would be impossible, even for someone as skilled as Formula One champion Michael Schumacher, to think fast enough in terms of discrete and separate neuro-muscular experiences at the high speeds he consistently drives at. He postulates, instead, that Schumacher has accumulated literally millions of neuro-muscular experiences such as ... clutch in ... brake ... turn steering wheel, etc. and they form something akin to a personal library stored somewhere inside the instinctive areas of Schumacher's brain. Therefore at any one moment in his driving, when a reflexive action is required, Schumacher intuitively and automatically draws on the history of the accumulation of those experiences. So, in this way, expertise in such fields is not about thinking faster, better or more creatively. Rather, expertise is the conscious accumulation of a series of experiences that the proponent can access subconsciously. Much more than being simplistically clever, it proves, like many things, that it is mainly hard, focussed, disciplined work!

A Devil Pokes the Actor

Another good pointer to this is the case of Don Bradman, the Australian cricketer whose scoring average was 50% better than his nearest rival, making him the greatest sportsman that has so far lived and statistically one in ten billion. His legendary facility was supposed to have been derived from his mythical ability to see the ball's flight in slow motion. When he was tested for reflexes he was found to have the same reflexes as any normal adult male. He did not possess special bodily talents. What he did possess was the ability to immediately and instinctively read the flight of the ball as it left the bowler's hand. This skill was something he'd acquired through countless hours as a boy, using a cricket stump to hit a golf ball against a corrugated iron tank. He didn't have special, God-given, facility - he had developed exceptional instinctive recall from his endless 'golf ball-and-stick tank practice' combined with the concentration and temperament to access it continuously.

Possibility one might ask what has such 'mechanical' training for sportsman got to do with art? In point of fact, great musicians and dancers, must, like the sportsmen above, employ great concentration and temperament to realise the full potential of their innate talent. Unlike singing and dancing however, the actor's skills of spoken voice and gesture are much less easy to quantify. The question becomes; how to construct systems that are functional but not mechanical, neither restrictive nor robotic - but elastic and creative?

Even though acting is much more art than sport, expertise for an actor can be achieved in a parallel fashion. Of course there are actors who seemingly have naturally beautiful sonorous voices, attractive, co-ordinated bodies and the ability to move an audience but on closer inspection these (apart from physiognomy) turn out to be hard won and mostly achieved under erratic and unstructured conditions.

I'm vividly reminded of the reductive, primitive way Richard Burton learnt to speak with his beautiful voice. It wasn't reciting 'peter piper picked...etc, etc' in elocution classes......it was by yelling under a train bridge (while a train passed overhead) until **it didn't hurt any more**! Hardly the gentle evolution one might expect.

If we look at the way training is applied to athletes such as a champion high jumper we can get closer to the idea of how an actor could be trained in the same purposeful, structured way as a sportsman.

The high jumper has accumulated 'jumping' experiences in terms of developing a technique that fosters efficiency, height, fluidity, etc. But, if you watch a training session, you will not find him endlessly and unsystematically just jumping over a cross bar. For the high jumper's preparation to have any developmental function, it would be an imperative for him to structure his training. He would, of course, spend some time doing the jumps themselves but he would also break the entire sequence into its constituent components, separate them and work on individual sections and aspects. On TV I have watched these long lankies applying themselves to a deep interrogation of the first three loping steps of their run-up! As I inferred, these 'antelopes' can look pretty extraordinary, even peculiar when they are preparing, but nobody's game to laugh when they grab that Gold.

The aims of car racing and high jumping are easily comprehended, that is, to win, and in the early days when the situation was more primitive and less crowded, there was no need (or possibility) of training. As competition has increased, natural God-given skills are no longer enough, and amateur notions with their cavalier attitudes have been superseded by a more rigorous and purposeful orientation.

The two structures that sports training shares with music training are their use of **time** and **space** formats. Meaning in music is the combination of time and the space between the notes, and the basic training routines are scales and arpeggios. In music, time is self evident and rhythm is half the story, but there is also the aural space between the notes and much of musical practice is addressing the space between the notes. Likewise the crucial focus in football training is borne of personal skill development, allied to space/ time structures between the players on the field…..where they are….and when…in terms of their interaction with the rest of the team.

Our skinny high jumper was once a slender stripling, and in his early days he would have spent his practice time doing endless jumps over a stick into a pile of leaves (I know I did when at the age of ten I had dreams of jumping immortality). But, as his expertise grew, our antelope would have found that his training would have to be more structured and forensic, identifying weaknesses and how to eradicate them.

And so with actors! At the amateur level, negligible training would be required as the stakes are very low, but for the more ambitious and enterprising the higher up the ladder of excellence the more assiduous and structured the training needs to be.

A Devil Pokes the Actor

As I trail off with the last few lines, I swivel in my chair. He's showing me a side-on pose, his muscled bum on what looks like a rock. He's Rodin's 'Thinker', with the big shift, that he's glaring at me with his blue grey eyeballs bulging. As I take in this bizarre contortion, I'm reminded that somebody once said that even though nobody thinks with his elbow on the wrong knee, everybody gets the picture.

Is the Devil trying to say the same thing: You have to show a lie to tell the truth!
Hmmmmm.... Have I got HIM thinking? He snarls sardonically through his loose lower lip.

"Athletes and antelopes you say.....showed you the way !"

Unwraps his fist, unwinds the bony bits and cracks his knuckles, crunch....crack..clunk ... Somewhat gnomically he drolled out some more:

"What's a devil got to do to get these champs to dance together?"

He wants more 'athlete-speak' so be it………..I opened up with both barrels:
"There's a suburb in Melbourne, Oz, home of a benighted Aussie Rules football club. They've only come top once, in the sixties, but their luck may change, and it may well be because of culture...of a different colour..."

Muscle provocation #4
St Kilda's running midfield rules OK
Teams turning expertise into culture

As a rule sports training for beginners is focussed on generating the basic skills to eventually develop a technique. Once a sports team has achieved the requisite technique as individuals, they are ready to play together. At that level the exercises build to a more expanded and elastic level, where the 'discrete steps' have turned into 'sequences or paragraphs', creating potential for more complex interaction between the players. If the exercise regimen remains locked into a player 'skill only' zone, it prevents the more complicated and subtle interaction between the players. This ability to negotiate with each other in complex and evolving environments is crucial because, in the game proper, the players have to contend with the continuous destabilising interdiction of the opposition. This means that in a match, the scenario is constantly shifting, and the team who wins is the one that adapts best to the circumstantial shifts that occur throughout.

Due to the opposition's 'interdiction', the success of sports teams is dependent on the ability of the coach to think at ever more sophisticated levels and to devise systems that bring those levels to fruition.

In sport the practice game is the bridging experience to the game proper by approximating the conditions of a match. These 'match conditions' actually represent the introduction of the 'opposing energy' of another team. This is the interdiction I refer to, because it involves having to face the combined energy of a group of individuals bent on the opposite purpose, and to adapt to and subvert those energies.

Likewise, as our training evolved, the actors in the room obtained higher degrees of skill and sensitivity, which brought about a greater awareness of each other and their space. This necessitates that we invent exercises with broader implications

A Devil Pokes the Actor

way beyond being purely concerned with craft, towards a more highly structured interactivity, which begins to take on the nature of a 'practice game'. This has different nuances from the 'performance' game because there was no effective audience apart from Jacqui, the trainer. Jacqui interdicts, providing conscious back up, whereas the audience provides tacit 'collective unconscious' input. As with many other aspects of our performance aesthetics, there is congruent analogy with sporting systems and attitudes.

As a nipper I was mad keen on sport, especially the ball sports: Cricket in summer and Aussie Rules football in winter. I still love sport and since one of my goals is to bring together widely separated interests into a unified field, I've tried to see my chosen art forms as incorporating sport and other interests.

In the 2009 season, my team St Kilda did remarkably well remaining undefeated for most of the season. During a break in one of their televised games there was a group interview with what is called the **Running Mid-field**. This was a group of St Kilda's smaller, faster players probably numbering 10 (out of the 24 in the squad). They have to work very closely together in groups of four to six, the others being rested off the field and interchanging every ten minutes or so to keep the group on the field, fresh.

This seems to be the 'engine' of the current game now because I felt, as I watched the interview that I was watching a strategic shift in the way the game was being addressed. The modern game now depends on speed of retrieval and quick handballing over very short distances to maintain possession so these players have to be highly adaptive and responsive to the game and especially to each other. Of the 10, maybe 4 to 6 would be on the field at any one time. Given the constantly shifting arrangement, they would have to have a highly developed awareness of each other with 360 degree sensitivity and response.

As I watched, I marvelled at the sophisticated attitude they displayed towards their playing. They had a tremendous sense of group cohesion and familiarity.

These young men were not the moronic monosyllabic sports-jock mentality of repute - no grunting in ill-fitting suits with fat ties. Their attitude was more than professional. Without really giving the game away, these men knew what they were aiming for, what they had to do to get it, and they had about them that undeniable but inexplicable frisson that what they were doing was special and new!

I was looking at **culture** - a concept not generally associated with sport!

Another particular aspect that struck me was the obvious respect the younger members held for the more experienced players - that hierarchy of respect (duly earned) for the holders of deeper knowledge. This further reinforced this idea of culture - more than belief in themselves was a belief in what they were doing. This was **Evolving Heritage** - culture as growth. I had earlier come across such an approach in an interview I had read with Leigh Mathews, who was a champion player and coach.

When asked where his main focus lay when coaching, instead of a predictable: "We work on skills and discuss tactics and strategy, etc, etc....." he replied: "We create a culture!"

This was a stunning declaration which indicates that:
1. he's not stupid
2. that the modern game with its complex, fluid variability is approaching an art form.

The culture he is talking about refers to the relationships between the players.

It is quite intriguing watching Australian Rules now, because over the past thirty years or so it has evolved from the 'kick-and-mark' with uber-macho admonitions to 'Go out there and kill 'em'. It is now a much more variegated and complicated spectacle. In gaining this new fluidity it hasn't lost much except a bit of 'biffo'.

It's now a game that has tremendous variation ranging from the elegance of the high mark, the speed and facility of the running 'possession' game all the way to the 'Irish' melee of a muddy scramble on a wet winter's day. As Neville Cardus once said of cricket 'it is symphonic in nature'; so too, though to a lesser extent, does that refer to Australian Rules Football. It can be majestic with the rare but spectacular aerial high mark or get bogged in a soggy stalemate in a sea of mud.

Previously (eg. in my school days), coaching consisted of really only two things – teaching kids how to kick a ball and, in the game itself, there was one coach whose main job was to incite players to be as aggressive and committed as possible. I am sure the adult game was a little more sophisticated, but probably not much, judging from the writing of the time. In the modern professional game the coach is surrounded by at least ten assistants, which indicates how far things have advanced.

This generational shift in the demands placed on contemporary coaching reflects the fact that skills development at a preparatory level has become so proficient that all teams in the top flight have access to any number of talented young players. Many years ago when sport was more regionally focused most footballers came from their own suburb. The coach's job then was simply to ensure that the best local players were in his team at any one time. In the current game the only local remnants are the fans. A player's loyalty to his club is no longer defined by where he lives and consequently he has become much more nomadic, looking for the team where his 'speciality' is needed and where he can fit in best.

Current coaching reflects this shift by moving from a purely skills and drills attitude, to one where the relationships between the players is 'managed'- focussing on the use of rhythm and space between the members of the team. To use an arts analogy, the football coach has become a choreographer. This contains inside it the basic requirements of technical proficiency (like the craft of dancing), but takes it to a new creative level by training the players in formats of space and time. In this the footballers have to not only know their abilities and liabilities but be very much aware of their fellow player's skills and proximities in a very fluid environment that is made even more complicated by the malign intentions of the opposite team.

It's all very well to talk of such lofty goals, but how do you bring such complex ideas to fruition?

In thinking of this, I remembered a report I had read concerning Manchester United beating Chelsea in a final held in Moscow in 2008. Apparently they won 2 to 1 in the last few minutes of the game, after it had begun to rain.

Sir Alec Ferguson, the ManU manager, was quoted as saying: "As soon as it started raining, I was trying to work out ways to bring Ryan Giggs on, he's so good in the wet... he has such balance." (Obviously Giggsy scored the match winner!). What struck me, apart from the sophisticated thinking, was the fact he must have made such judgements whilst observing his players in training.
It would be very hard to do it during the game, as factors such as luck, nerves, expectations and the interdiction of the opposition would preclude systematic study. However, at the training level, the manager oversees practice much as an army general, having assistants to take care of the nuts and bolts, while he constructs the big picture. His job is not to deal with the individual player's skill development, but on the broader level of integrating those skills with other team members.
That combination of skills and integration is the **team culture.** For team culture is born in the training, not the game. The game is the manifestation of the success of the culture - its footprint, so to speak.
Team culture builds the players (**actors**)
Team culture builds the coach (**director**) and as it does both of those....
Team culture builds the style of game (**aesthetic of the performance**).

A Devil Pokes the Actor

As I finish writing provoc 4 I hear a cataleptic wheezy groan.....I spin.....this devil had morphed into another variation of the thinker, Michaelangelo's Damned Man, fallen off the back wall of the Sistine Chapel.

He's covering his rheumy RH eye with his right claw....I recoil....Is he mocking me?......a sardonic allusion to the eternal abyss of the mis-appreciated artist who uses words too big for his boots? Applying 'culture' to footy! Culture to Coaches, Games and Players...He doesn't speak, just rasps away, a lazy vapour snaking up from his sneering lip.

Should I hang on to his every whim?

What will brother devil make of provoc 5 wherein I slam into reverse, hurling sporting hallmarks back at acting.......

Muscle Provocation #5
Eskimo inclinations
Actors attempt Absolutes

In the performative realms of dance, music and acrobatics it is accepted that training is focused primarily on attempting various types of absolutes. By absolutes I mean the use of extreme exercises to corral and coerce the body to go way beyond daily or domestic activities to achieve levels of skill beyond the ordinary, even though the body in question is in a sense ordinary as it has two arms, legs, etc - it is not a freak of nature.

In classical ballet - a 90 degree developee is an exercise where the leg muscles and bones are straightened so that the leg represents a perfect horizontal line. In music - a top C is the melodious result produced when the singer manages to control the shape of the vocal chords to convert noise into a breathtaking sound. It is highly artistic or poetic because of the effect it has on the listener and that artistic effect has a scientific dimension because this imaginative impulse is also a perfect mathematical formula - Art as Science. In acrobatics - a triple somersault is the action where an acrobat turns three consecutive forward or backward rolls in mid air before being caught or landing. It is regarded as the apogee of the craft because the body is spinning so fast that the acrobat temporarily blacks out during the second spin, and it is the ability of the body to wake up during the slowing down third spin that determines success.

Ballet, music and acrobatics require years of practice to take an ordinary body of unrealised potential and fashion an instrument capable of such extraordinary feats. Over time each of these disciplines have developed their own highly codified techniques in searching for the best and most practical systems for skill development, leading to superhuman achievements by what are, after all, humans not essentially different to you or I.

In dance and music I would call these endeavours

representational absolutes, as they attempt to conform the body into perfect shapes and sounds, highly pleasing and gratifying to the ear and eye.

Both classical ballet and music appeal to the Aristotelian sense of order (roughly translated as Art as a portrait of harmonised life in balance), precisely because the audience's witnessing of the performer's absolute affirms that their life is in balance. I remember that homework always seemed to be more pleasant when listening to a classical orchestra, especially if they were playing something attractive and balanced like Mozart.

In sports this sense of representative absolute does not exist in quite the same way. Whereas the performative arts are concerned with manifesting human psychology in space and sound, sport is more essentially concerned with triumphant human physical achievement. As an example: in the high jump, the goal is jumping higher than one's peers in the immediate competition and, by extension...... the final vision that nests in the minds of all high jumpers ....to be the World Record holder! Achieving the feat of universal pre-eminence, albeit temporary and transitory, is in itself a type of absolute, and all training is put to the service of astringently focusing to exploit every available avenue of human potential to take that further step towards immortality.

It is also compelling to realise that the reason sport is so popular is its straightforward concern with maximising and measuring human muscular potential, with no hidden meanings or ulterior motives. There are no caveats or subtexts - quite simply, who was the 'mostest' on the day? This gives sport a very clear moral dimension that is predicated on and measured in undeniable terms: highest, fastest, longest, etc. This absolute or 'perfect' measurement delineates unique achievement, and successful athletes are warranted high esteem as modern shamans, with magical powers and the super-successful are given god-like status precisely because they have achieved like gods - they have transcended their fellows by being the most triumphant over time and space.

This clear and easily defined sports absolutism crosses over to a certain extent into the performing arts, especially ballet and music. If we shift the emphasis away from overt competition to representing absolutes such as perfect sound and movement, we have replaced **absolute achievement** with **representational absolutism**, and we are now entering the area of metaphysics. The absolute achievement of sport can be described as relating to the 'material world' and the representational absolutism of art is more concerned with the world of 'spirit'.

Sport uses a number of structured overt absolutes to connect with the hearts and minds of the public and Art uses its own more oblique absolutes to connect with the soul of the audience. Thus the competitive nature of sport appeals to the linear, emotional, accretive side of man and the performative nature of art triggers a lateral imaginative psyche response. Sport appeals to the heart and Art appeals to the soul.

Somewhat paradoxically, Art had been around considerably longer than Sport - at least 4 thousand years! Millennia ago the cavemen of Lasceaux were making spiritual likenesses of animals - magic symbols that would give them the metaphysical leverage they needed in their hunt for survival. Ironically, sport has progressively gained more prominence as there has been a general lessening of conflict regarding survival. Facetiously……….has sport become the Health and Safety reconfiguration of war?

The enjoyment the crowd gains at a sporting event is paralleled by the delight that audiences achieve in the presence of the almost mystical feats achieved by dancers, musicians and acrobats. I say 'almost mystical' because the audience is witnessing real people in real time (no smoke and mirrors!) performing actions they can conceive but not imagine themselves doing. These 'actions' are thoroughly verifiable but only achieved by a very small number of people. A multiple pirouette and a top C are both undeniable, but extremely rare and done by very few. Unlike sport, where extreme physical experiences are used to gain success, performers concern themselves with **representing** experiences.

Historically western actor training has eschewed physical or vocal 'absolutism' as it has been primarily concerned with accessing emotionality and revealing psychology, especially in the misunderstood legacy of Stanislavsky. To a certain extent this is understandable as speaking and gesture are not easily measured in the same way as pirouettes or top C's. But modern western acting generally lacks moral impact because there is no sense of quantifiable achievement - of breaking new ground. It is very rare to witness actors discovering new 'space' in their acting. Most actors' performances consist of parading their 'history' in a comfortable static compact with the audience.

In our development of the FSPA, Jacqui and I, coming from a comprehensive dance and ballet history, were interested in providing **'attempting the absolute'** elements to the training of an actor. We call these *definities*. Whilst many other acting approaches mention absolutes, perfections or positives, none seem to offer exercises that realise them as concretely as the SATM/FSPA.

In the SATM the approach is instinctual because it exists inside the Japanese cultural process of un-prescribed ablation (water dripping on a stone). I believe that there are physical and psychological principles behind the visceral and moral power engendered by the SATM exercises. The FSPA is a Western translation that reveals those principles behind the moral impact of the original and much of the reason for this 'moral' power is that the exercises have such absolutist content.

A good example inside the FSPA is an exercise we often do called '**eskimoes**'.

It starts with two actors lying on their backs on the floor with the soles of their feet facing one another - about a metre apart. Saying a speech, they first make eye contact, then gradually rise to standing until they are touching noses - they then reverse the process, until they are once again lying on the floor eyes facing the ceiling. The aim of the exercise, once eye contact is established, is for the actors to 'ramp up' in a **continuous upward gradient** to the point where they are touching nose to nose (hence 'eskimo'). The speech, whether whisper, quiet or full, matches the action, adding both content (full commitment of body and voice), and timing (the span of the speech matches the gradient).

As in other FSPA exercises the linked voice and body actions are the primary concern, the actor having in their mind that the voice and body, being much more than simultaneous, are inextricably connected.

As one can imagine, this physical straight line is difficult to maintain as human bodies have bones, joints and muscles that do not work in a completely contiguous fashion and the actor has to work very conscientiously to achieve the sense of continuous gradient. Parallel with the 'gradient' movement of the body, the voice locks in to the same straight line of delivery. This develops in the actor the voice as a form of physical energy leaving the body as a 'tube of information' carried on the line the head makes as it goes from lying to standing and back.

This is in no way a replacement for emotional and psychological 'content', but it does give the actor the experience of perceiving his voice as having absolute properties alongside and augmenting the conventional aspects such as emotional colour and psychological depth.

Having actors face each other enhances the experience as each actor becomes the other's 'mirror' and they can, separately, and together, self-monitor their process and progress.

Another variant consists of doing it in a group in front of a full length mirror, which, by removing the other performer, amplifies the engagement of 'self' in another way, more of which later.

As in all the other SATM and FSPA exercises, there is

tremendous sense of focus, concentration and application. These are very much the easily understood outcomes for this type of training, but the really transformational function goes much deeper philosophically. That is: the transcendent effect on the actor by trying to achieve an absolute. It is the actors' intent to reconfigure their bodies and voices into absolutist terms that creates the potential for self-transformation - the highest and most profound goal of an actor as artist.

A Devil Pokes the Actor

As I talked the tales of eskimo exercises, I was scarcely aware of an intermittent soughing , like the sea or air, and I was sure I'd put him to sleep, but...no...once again the baleful glare drew me round, to find a devilish Peter Sellers polishing some chromey thing...... That pic! On a record cover my parents had when I was a kid. Sellers was breathing over the delicate, shimmering Rolls Royce statuette....how the devil did he know about the Sellers anecdote that kicked off the use of mirrors in the FSPA.

"What theme does this make you think?"

"Once upon a time I read a biog sometime about Sellers and at one stage it mentioned an occasion where Sellers was kissing a woman, and he suddenly glanced in a mirror and saw his reflection. As he looked, he felt that the image of him kissing was more material than the sensation of actually kissing! The copy was more real than the original! Maybe he only felt genuine when he was imitating someone else."

"In the words of Travis Bickle, vous dites moi? I know'st already, already ....let's get going with the program...."

"Yes! But wait a sec!   .....apparently during the filming of Dr Strangelove, where Sellers played 3 black comedic roles, he could only do one spectacularly funny take. Stanley Kubrik, the director, apparently had to have 5 or 6 cameras going at once so as to salvage a sequence where the rest of the cast in shot weren't cracking up."

"Let's get into gear, shall we?"

"But I tell you this, my Gog Magog ! ....Peter S. should have won an Oscar for listening to Sterling Hayden's 'precious bodily fluids' speil!"

"Move it, punk!"

"O.K. O.K. We're moving up a metaphysical notch onto the Way of Metamuscle!"

Meta-Muscle Provocation #1
Peter Sellers through the looking glass:
heuristic hand Mirrors

The use of a hand mirror enables the actor to see into his soul, and by extension, to see what the audience sees of his soul.

That's a big call, is it not?

Actually it is even more extensive than that, with a series of graduated aspects that lead in complexity and depth towards that spiritual endgame.

I developed the use of small hand mirrors in the FSPA. When a mirror is held immediately in front of the actor's face it becomes a most effective tool for building the actor's self awareness.

It is quite a different experience from that of a dancer, who grows up using a mirror from a distance of 3-5 metres as a monitoring device. A good two thirds of a dancer's life is spent in front of a mirror. Most studios have one wall of the room covered in floor to ceiling mirrors, and after the barre in classical or basic floor work in modern dance, the rest of the class is spent facing the mirror - likewise nearly all of rehearsal. Since dance is essentially a series of moving 'pictures', the mirror provides the dancer with an immediate reference point, both for the image that he presents to the audience, and in extension, to feel the position from the inside as to how it corresponds to the visual reality as seen in the mirror.

The dancer cannot really see the expression in his eyes from the space he is dancing in, keeping in mind that the focal distance is effectively double the distance to the mirror. Furthermore, dancers are generally obsessed with their body image rather than facial expression.

Ozfrank's use of mirrors is fundamentally different in that they are small hand mirrors which are held fairly close to the face, and used in such a way that the actor can observe himself very closely as he speaks and moves. The mirrors are not used to observe the movement per se, but to observe the effect the movement has on the actor's soul.

The idea of using such mirrors as a training device came to me as a direct result of using them in one of our productions, **Heavy Metal Hamlet** (HMH). We were performing in Melbourne and Jacqui and I were staying with Ian Carruthers, an academic with deep interest and knowledge of Tadashi Suzuki's work. I'm not sure how it came about, but during some discussions about the show, he suggested that we use some small mirrors as props for a certain section.

I went straight to Target and purchased some children's toy tennis racquets, then visited a plastics centre to buy some mirrored perspex. I went home and cut them into the small oval shapes that matched the insides of the racquets, and glued them in with silicone sealant and sprayed them metallic grey to match the rest of the props.

Later that day we had a rehearsal and it was a revelation!

From the first moment I looked in the mirror I felt a huge difference in what I was doing. I wasn't sure what it was or meant, but I did feel a profound shift.

An important aspect of our approach is the use of exercises taken from the training and used as a rehearsal sequence. We often rehearse speeches from a play whilst in standing or sitting statues, as this helps to implant the speech more firmly in the body. This not an aesthetic and may have very little to do with the 'look' or 'feel' of the final production, but we find that these experiences prove very instructive in giving the actor different insights and attitudes to his role.

It also works the other way, because we often use excerpts from the performance as temporary training routines. Often

these temporary excerpts turn long term when it becomes apparent that their effectiveness extends outside the show.

When we train just prior to a performance, we always use words or movements from the show as a preparation, and some of our most important training routines have evolved directly as a result of their incorporation in a pre-show training.

Other profound implications came for me on the day we first used the HMH mirrors in a **Tenteketen** exercise. The Tenteketen is highly formatted, in that there are very clear reference points in terms of where one has to be in the space at a certain moment.
Because of that, shifts in perceptions are very apparent, and it was during this exercise that I became very aware of the potential the mirror held as a bridging tool. As I looked at my reflection in the mirror from a distance of 300mm, my face became more composed and as a result, I became calmer inside. I could perceive facial tics and tensions, and by regarding them, could feel them ablate and fade from my face. I could feel myself becoming more centred, more balanced and more 'present'. When we used the mirrors while speaking, the benefits were even more powerful and profound.

We also use the mirrors in one of our more advanced exercises: **The Bacon Swipe**.
Its inspiration stems from Frances Bacon's 'deformed' portraits. It's done to a piece of Gothic Rock, and consists of a series of slow motion segments between which the actors use their hands to 'swipe' their faces into distorted grimaces, a la certain Bacon paintings.

This exercise is not about 'pulling' faces, but using the visceral energy of the song to impel the hands to physically mould the face into an extreme shape. This grotesque mask is held for the length of the each verse after which another swipe creates another grotesquerie. The actor observes these deformations in the mirror as they progress, and at the end of the song we say a speech three times, the first in the highly deformed position, the second in a half way position and the third in a neutral one.

The first speech is to be done with the grotesque intact, ie without moving a visible muscle, which means that the speech becomes a series of primitive noises. The actors are trying to speak the words properly but are unable to due to the fixed grimace. The second is 'half' articulate and the final speech is neutral, but with the primitive essence remaining inside, covert. This de-formation exercise, one of our most striking, is designed to 'de-civilise' the actor, to take him to a pre-cognitive state of primitive grace, and it uses the mirror so that the actor can witness himself in this 'primeval' experience. It is very good for making the actor less pretend and more real. I have no real idea of how I invent such exercises, but often their continued evolution is driven by the actors' instinctive responses. Sometimes an actor will make some elliptical comment which triggers another development. One such occurred when one of our actors, **James Anderson**, (see pic at back of book) said something very pertinent early on after a 'Bacon Swipe' routine. He said he couldn't recognize the image of himself in the mirror:

The use of the hand mirrors in training has been a revelation to me. My training as an actor up until I joined Ozfrank had been in various 'methods' or 'techniques', most notably Meissner Technique. I was taught that to use a mirror for acting was to somehow eliminate spontaneity and 'realness' from a performance. As such I was initially resistant to the use of mirrors, however I had come to Ozfrank for a challenge and so I went with it as best I could.

I had been training for a couple of years before I had an experience with the mirrors that was very profound. It was during one of the more intense exercises, Red Right Hand into Frenzy that I noticed something different about myself in the mirror and for a few moments I could not recognise the person in the mirror. It was me, and at the same time it wasn't me. I was watching this 'other' person talking to me and making the most extreme faces and after the exercise was over I realised that I had been completely unselfconscious and also very aware of my 'self' in time and space. The mirror had somehow defined me more.

The mirror, in its ability to define you more, makes you more acutely aware of yourself in time and space. As you observe or communicate with yourself, you are forced to feel the floor and your body with greater sensitivity.

Another interesting aspect that has occurred to me since we have been musing on Jung and Freud recently, is that the person in the mirror is my 'Id', the part of my psyche that is unable to make an appearance in the ordinary world but exists as a necessary part of who I am. If as actors, we are going to get to 'the next level' access to this dangerous part of the psyche is necessary and I feel without the mirror I may have only ever glimpsed that aspect of myself, but through the mirror I am able to see it in reality, but from the safety of the mirror. It exists within me, but can only be seen in the mirror. This makes it a safer way to experience a darker self, rather than 'method acting' where there is a danger of not being able to let go of the experience. Thus the looking in the mirror and looking away from the mirror within the confines of the exercise, which itself is controlled by Jacqui, the space and the music, one is able experience and develop this Id safely.

The mirror work continues to challenge me as the use of the mirror is expanded and deepened with new additions and challenges.
James Anderson.

As James suggests, we continue to use and develop this 'tool' since its inception in 2005. To summarize the reasons and benefits:

1. The actor can see himself very much as the audience sees him. At first actors find using mirrors very disconcerting as they associate mirrors with personal grooming such as shaving or putting on makeup. It is quite a different thing to carry them with you. Once the actors get over the: "Yoiks! That's what I look like!" factor, they acquire a greater sense of gravitas and clarity, and become much more compelling as performers.

2. The actor is talking to himself. It has been said that great public speakers are in reality not trying to convince an audience, but in fact are trying to convince themselves. We have found that the more an actor uses a mirror to 'talk' to himself as well as 'talking' to an audience, the more well-rounded and whole his performance appears to be.

3. The actor is also witnessing himself talking to himself. An important component in any performance is that, not only should the actor be involved in the action or speech (the first person), he should also be a witness to what he is doing (the third person). I am reminded of an anecdote concerning Laurence Olivier, who came off stage after a particularly fervid speech, only to say: "That overhead light in the prompt side top corner wasn't on!" This was remarkable, as, at no stage did he look up, and the speech was quite intense. This shows that even though he was very involved and appeared emotional, he was, AS WELL, highly aware of what he was going through.

4. There are two people there - the actor and his image. He is speaking to himself, this 'doubling' of the actor's persona compounds the effect as the actor is less alone - strength in numbers, so to speak.

5. What happens when the mirror is taken away? As I said previously, the mirror is a bridging 'tool', a stepping stone which opens a door on to further knowledge. It is not an aesthetic; one cannot wander around the stage looking in a mirror inside an actual play (unless it's Narcissus!). However, as a bridging tool, having provided a sample, it must be relinquished at some stage so that the actor creates his own image, without assistance. When the mirror is taken away half way through an exercise, the result is: what is left behind as a memory....... a resonance? What resides or remains in the body as a result of the experience?

So, very quickly, some way through an exercise I began saying, "Mirror away!"

This involves changing nothing but a slight shift of the angle of the mirror, so that the actor can no longer see his image. We

A Devil Pokes the Actor

stress that the objective is that the actor should remember the image or feeling of looking in the mirror. Then, in order to reinforce or re-capture the notion, I would say: "Mirror back!" These intermittent commands determine that the actor is in a more or less constant state of witnessing, whether the mirror be in gaze or not.

6. What happens when an actor witnesses another actor? We have extended the idea to invoke the same 'mirror as memory' tool in partner with other actors. Often we do the TKTN in couples with one watching the other as they traverse the space. The idea here is that the actor senses the other actor witnessing himself as he proceeds about his actions. The other actor becomes another 'audience', and, this, once again compounds the experience for the first actor. We have also done an exercise where we all watch some fixed point in the space as we all do a TKTN across stage. For example our mascot, **Francine the Gerbil** will be placed downstage centre and we all have to keep her in sight as we traverse. This involves continuously moving the mirror and our gaze as we move across - truly a compound action. This exercise led on to...

7. What happens when an actor witnesses his body in a different way - from a different angle? Once, when doing a TKTN with mirrors, I suddenly thought of using the mirror to view the body from a different angle.

This has a 'cubist' affect on the actor, because we are unaccustomed to seeing ourselves other than from the angle directly coming straight out of the eye line, I remember one of our students remarking when he held the mirror above and behind him: "I've never see myself from that angle!"

I remembered that comment for its innocent existentialism, as I realised he had gained a more three dimensional view of himself. He had **perceived himself as a sculpture, not a two dimensional cutout.**

Some time later, with this in mind, I thought of asking the actors, stick in one hand, to use the mirror in a wide position in the other, and view the end of the stick. When I did it myself, I found it quite dis-orienting to observe the end of the stick as I transitted the space.

Normally, when we observe the end of a stick as we cross a space, we are accustomed to the stick passing across the landscape in a certain way, because our perceptions are governed by the eye-line axis. Our eyes are effectively a fixed point, located as they are, in the one spot in the body, and we are used to seeing everything, body parts, the environment, etc, from that one fixed point.

When our gaze passes through a mirror, the angle of our view becomes refracted markedly away from the standard line and we find ourselves watching the stick traverse the landscape from a different viewpoint, in an entirely new way. Using the 'stick in the mirror' in such a way is another bridging moment.

The awareness of any part of the body from such a different angle gives the actor a much more three dimensional way of considering himself, a cubist view of himself - he is effectively doing what Picasso did when he first painted **'Les Demoiselles d'Avignon'** in 1905. With this, the first cubist painting, he created a three dimensional portrait on a two dimensional surface.

Using the hand held mirror does a similar function for an actor.

In 1905 Picasso's invention of cubist art in Paris was matched in Bern, Switzerland by Albert Einstein, when he articulated the special theory of relativity. To be put very simply, this was effectively a shift from linear thinking (Newton) to compound lateral thinking. Science was trying to solve whether light was a wave OR a particle. Einstein said, "Well guys, actually they are both explanations of the same thing from different perspectives". Instead of trying to resolve a problem from a single viewpoint, it involved thinking more holistically and saying that a single answer can be explained from different points of view.

As surprising as it may seem, the use of handheld mirrors creates in the actor a shift in self appreciation analogous to that of the shift from Newtonian to Einstein-ian physics.

"Let's move into the 21st century!" ……I hoped I'd convinced him…….but I hear a noise….a jangling clatter behind……I rotate to find this devil had cast down his perturbing black rimmed glasses, which have shattered against the steel stairs……WRRRONG……he wasn't captivated by Sellers and mirrors! His back to me, he'd adopted an angled stance/quel dramatique/slab shouldered and looking into a bowl of blood, all brawny back and scaly shanks.The original creature from the Black Lagoon……… Blake's 'Ghost of a Flea'! He wants a serve of William Blake.

"Now you're talking," I respond, deep in breath.

I've admired Blake's Flea painting a long, long time; heavy and delicate in one. Oleaginous in colour and luminous in its starry staging, for Blake, the painter, could never be truly nasty. If ever there was a man who personified my ideas of self definition and mythic self it is Past Master Blake.

Meta Muscle Provocation #2
About a boy-o born Blake:
Self definition becomes mythic self

Since my late teens I have been fascinated by the phenomenon that was William Blake.
For any halfhearted hippie in the 60s, he was a multiple exemplar:

- A Tolkien-like ability to invent a highly original spiritual cosmology
- An inspiration for the name of the psychotic and epigrammatic 60s rock band **The Doors** via Aldous Huxley's peyote driven **"The Doors of Perception"**
- A spiritual revolutionary that took on the prevailing cliches of religion
- Pacifistic and non-jingoistic with an incredible way with words
- A painter whose home-made unique vision was never over run by style and guile
- A softening spirit that was later picked up by the Romantics 70 years on
- An inventor of a highly personal engraving technique which both came out of and also stimulated an aesthetic that continuously evolved until the day he died
- A writer of some of the most special, elastic poetry ever written in the English language

Poems such as **"Tiger, tiger, burning bright"** have a child-like simplicity, but remain burnt in the brain for their fantastical allusions, prefiguring Rousseau and other hardcore naturals.

His poem: **'To see the world in a grain of sand ...'**
        heaven in a wild flower,
        To hold infinity in the palm of your hand,
            and eternity in an hour" has a haiku like simplicity, Zen-like credentials and is culturally transcendent in

the same way as John Lennon's song **'Imagine'**.
He was also capable of some very stretched and psychedelic thinking......he was once talking to a friend in his parlour when he left off and said: "Hold it! I've just seen the ghost of a flea!" He stopped everything else and proceeded to draw and then paint it. The result was one of the most extraordinary paintings of all time, a sort-of 'The Mummy's Tomb meets Creature of the Black Lagoon' - the sort of image that would have been pretty off-the-wall even in 1981 let alone in 1819. And he **wasn't** trying to be smart or scare people - he just said he painted what he imagined, what he saw in his mind. No wonder the locals would have been scared and despaired of same. Remember this was a good ninety years before horror started to become cute and vogue-ish. Good old England wasn't even Victorian yet so it didn't know how to be shocked even! It was so far ahead of its time that nothing seen was equivalent until guys such as Gustave Dore in the 1890s, and these guys **were** trying to be clever and scare people.

But he also had a soft sweet tempered faerie side. Witness this gentle little tale:
"Did you ever see a fairy's funeral madam?" he once said to a lady, who sat by him in company. "Never, Sir", was the answer. "I have," said Blake, "but not before last night. I was walking alone in my garden, there was great stillness among the branches and more than a common sweetness in the air; I heard a low and pleasant sound, and I knew not whence it came. At last I saw the broad leaf of a flower move, and underneath I saw a procession of creatures about the size and colour of green and grey grasshoppers, bearing a body laid out on a rose leaf, which they buried with songs, and then disappeared. It was a fairy funeral." Very well spoken or written, never mind which!

Not long ago I worked my way through an heroic biography of the man and the reason I say heroic is that he never flinched from going deeper and deeper into his own painterly and poetic myth. And most of it is as impenetrable as a horizontal forest in Tasmania! This bloke really did his thing and that meant coming up with huge rambling analogies on the hunt for godhead, complete with his own biblical nomenclature (Old Testament style) engraved and printed in phantasmagorical colours, groupings and levels. And, as I said, no backing off! - Blake just ploughed on through, industriously oblivious to whatever trends the punters may have been able to cope with. He was both uninterested in, and incapable of, being popular.

It is quite sad reading at times, going over how he never quite, so to speak, got given the keys to the car. Even though he could be wild eyed and explosive at times, this un-recognition never seemed to bother him too much, as later in life, he thought that if he'd lost his poverty, he may have lost his spirituality with it (which was a neat attitude to have, though not comforting to hear). There is much verbose and not particularly gripping poetry in some of these allegorical travails and the stories are not 'sexy'. But if that is what he had to grind through for us to get the gems, so be it. Something else I got from the book was that nearly everybody, even those that loved and sponsored him, thought he was bonkers. However those that were **really** close didn't think so, because everybody that actually dealt with him said he was as cute as a puppy, and was never overwhelmed by his 'visions'.

He always maintained that:
- he painted or wrote what was in his imagination, and
- anyone and everyone had the same capability if they were prepared to foster it.

Both of those answers are pretty lucid and logical, certainly linear enough to not be those of a madman. They are also introduce an inspirational example as they indicate possible pathways for any like-minded souls to develop a similar temperament.

The book also mentions many times how his ideas and visions were often more successful after they were somewhat diluted by more commercially savvy artists and entrepreneurs and, if it wasn't for the sterling efforts of a few hardcore fans, his body of work could well have languished unseen and unremembered.

Blake's more fashionable contemporaries have, however, been lost in the mists of time, while his panoramic personal visions have reverberated and expanded in the time since he died. He is now possibly the most imaginative figure in the aesthetic lineage of English history.

To digress for a second, I devise Ozfrank exercises that empower the actor in everything her body involves: muscles, voice, heart, mind and soul and this process involves bringing those various aspects together, to unify in one indivisible instrument.

We call this process **self-definition** - the act of being or making the most of what you can be, and, being aware of it. Accepting what you are and building on it. Once an actor joins those parts of her character together in a spirit of discovery, she acquires a great deal of presence or charisma. She seems to 'know' something special, and the audience comes to watch and hear her so they can access that 'knowledge'. I call this charisma **Mythic Self** because such people seem to be larger than life - their presence emanates to fill the space around them beyond the volume they actually occupy. People possess charisma if there is no apparent division between their 'self' and their environment - their spirit or essence seems to occupy the whole room.

Interviewer Michael Parkinson mentions that among the thousands of celebs he's met, Orson Welles, Muhammad Ali, Nelson Mandela and Richard Burton all had that special presence that seems to fill the room. They appeared to have a special inner 'knowledge', which attracts us to follow. Saying that is to suggest they are very self-defined. We all believe they have special attributes that ordinary people perceive themselves **not** to have. I believe these 'mythical' properties are manifestations of the individual's Mythic Self.

In considering Blake's life he doesn't appear to have been overtly charismatic, but, on the other hand, his legacy continues to be <u>very</u> charismatic. And I would hazard that his long term charisma is interdependent with his short term lack of charisma, and I don't think it is just coincidence. They appear to be inversely proportional and, in his case, extremely so. In considering his personal journey, one is struck by this relentless pursuit of a highly individual, esoteric vision.

His whole life's quest was to portray the search to create a document in poetry and painting that would be the outward illustration of his highly idiosyncratic inner path. His paintings and poetry are a road map and diary of, what Jung would call, his God Impulse - his spirit's search for an auto-gnostic godhead.

While he seems to have had no particular natural ability to promote his cause and sell his work, his lack of commercial success in anything he ever touched compounded his temperament and he was also forced in many instances to go deeper into his own artistic world. So, while to a certain extent this search was self induced, he was also never tempted to be sidetracked from it by fortune or fame.

There are many instances in the book where he was employed by contemporaries much more popular and successful than he. Much of the time he was treated as an eccentric lackey, spikily talented, but requiring strict control and dilution to make him more civilised, manageable and acceptable. There were instances where his designs, through chicanery, were copied and then engraved by other, more conventional artisans. These copyists cut down on the 'wild man of Soho' stuff making the engravings more palatable to the bourgeoise punters who wanted something 'noice' to match the aspidistras. It was a case of divide the extremity of the paintings by five, put a doily on them, and they run off the shelves and out the door!

Now of course, all those palookas with their kitsch kulture have fallen off the map and our man William B. has acquired true legendary status. While they may have been artists of their time, he has become an artist for **all** time. He wasn't regarded as an artist in his own life time, except by a very select few and those few were never particularly rich or connected. His death passed unnoticed, but gradually he became a cultural fixture with first, the Pre-Raphaelites and then the Bloomsbury Set who were taken by his poetic and painterly admixtures of mystic quest. The crowning irony is that in 1917 the words to his 'Jerusalem' poem were set to music, and it has become the unofficial English national anthem sung at the conclusion of the Proms, that most English of Classical concerts. This man regarded as an eccentric and subversive artist in his own time has, over time, become the definition of Englishness. That is paradox non pareil!

This original 'guy in the garage', plugging away industriously with vision and guts, (tout seul 'cept for his patient partner Catherine) has prevailed. The rest of Britain was oblivious to the cranky craftsman. He carks, unwanted and unmissed, too far ahead of his time. Succeeding hipsters, more savvy about the shock of the new and looking to reject the kitsch of their Ma and Pa cried; "Hey! Look at what those old fogies missed.......and right under their noses, too! This Dude Blake's our spiritual Dad!"

Every generation since has re-found him in its own image. He has become an artist for all times, even though he wasn't regarded as an artist in his time. And, if he had been, he probably wouldn't have transcended his time he would merely have been of it.

Just exactly how did that transition from private and unpopular to epic and emblematic happen?

Like many young artists who showed promise, he was accorded some support, watched and given preparatory sponsorship, with the proviso that he would act tame and play the game. Inevitably, he bridled at their lack of vision and chafed at the psychic bondage, became stroppy and was let go to do his own thing. This set a life pattern which became a circular self-perpetuating process and it's hard to tell if it's the chicken or the egg. Did he become more inwardly focussed because of outside rejection, or was the inner focus an instinctive truth that intuitively shut out the meddlesome shallow outer world. My guess is that it's probably **both** chicken and egg!

I am inclined to think that he was driven by a very strong moral inner compass and that created a white hot atmosphere of spiritual search around him. Under this he would neither suffer fashion fools gladly, nor work for them, and, sooner or later, he would drive them away, like money changers out of a temple. This lack of acquiescence to the social 'moment' meant that he gained neither flattery nor fortune. But it did accord him the time on his own in the Spartan surrounds of his workhouse, enabling him to work both on himself and his visions undisturbed by the deceptive distractions of celebrity.

There's another element too, that of the avatar snatched from us by the jaws of mortality. Those deemed to have a secret knowledge, evidenced by their private poetic art or prose, too personal in their time, are suddenly taken away. Unexpectedly, we want to now know what it is that they knew, to discover their secret which has been snatched from us forever.......

Blake was a great understand-er of paradox and his personal paradox was that the more he delved into his own soul, to explore and reveal a highly individual cosmos, the less fashionable he was in his life time, but the more valuable he was regarded after his death - when he became part of all time.

The more self defined he became, the more mythic he became.

The devil goes strangely solicitous, surprised by something I said……adopts a tone more in keeping with gentle man Blake…….

"I didn't think WB would mean so much to you. You seem so speedy and sensate - Neal Cassady and all that goes with beatific speed."

"Well, I chew the cud, too. And after being a long time fan of the Beat Generation's stellar avatar, I finally saw that he foolishly died trying to live up to his myth, so I re-jaggled my program with a nod towards the guys like Blake and Bacon who went inside and dug deep into the soul."

"Beastly beatitudes from Blake to Bacon, what about this bloke Berkahn ?"

"Berkahn? My Uncular dramaturg? Well, here's something linear and quiet brought about by PB's chance remark on a Tokyo tarmac."

Meta Muscle #3
Peter Berkahn's Coldplay moment:
Incompletion into Inclusion

A few months ago my philosopher/dramaturg mate Peter Berkahn was talking about the elegaic English popsters **Coldplay**. He suggested that apart from their rare ability to write a haunting melody he thought that the singer Chris Martin's melancholy vocal delivery left space for the audience to 'finish his up beat songs', because one could sense Martin's heroics to keep up with the song's mood. Even if the concept may be partially apocryphal, the idea is an extraordinary bellwether for judging communicability in art. What it implies is that an artist, in order to be successful, needs to create an atmosphere where the audience itself completes the story.

This reminded me of a description concerning Mick Jagger in the very early days of the Rolling Stones, when they were a support act for American R'n'B groups touring the UK. Mick apparently studied the mainly Afro-American singing styles from the sidelines every night and noticed that they never seemed to say the words 'properly' and often seemed to deliberately slur the words. Apparently he felt that it was a pretty cool thing to do and began to adopt this practice. This may be another way of 'not completing a performance' so that the audience could either finish or make their own 'sense' of it.

Yet another example of this 'incompletion' occurred recently in Switzerland when we were showing some DVD's of theatre productions, one of which showed an actor speaking Japanese, playing Macbeth in our version of the classic Shakespeare text. He was, admittedly, a very compelling performer, but I was struck by how riveting our Swiss audience found him, even though they manifestly couldn't understand what he was saying. I knew instinctively that if he had been speaking in English, which they could all understand fairly well, they may not have found him as compelling. It must be that, because they couldn't understand him in a pragmatic, logical sense, their lateral unconscious processes moved in to fill the gap. They were using him as a shamanic window, a gateway into their soul's own conversation with itself. The story ends up being more magical because it is not rationalized by language.

Similarly, Mick Jagger's not fully comprehensible lyrics affect the audience's minds in subliminal ways. Because the audience can't concentrate on the literal meaning of the words, they became far more immersed in the poetry and sounds they were receiving. This puts their psyches into a less analytical and more receptive zone where they are more moved by the experience than judging it. They are not standing outside the song and criticising it. Instead, by investing some of their imagination to complete the song they become integrated into the song.

This concept of completion is very much analogous to the idea of the audience 'filling the void'. The example of this that I've given many times has been the final scene of the early Talkie' film, **Queen Christina**. In this film Greta Garbo, as Christina, Queen of Sweden c. 1750, after meeting and falling in love with the Spanish Ambassador, abdicates her throne, travels to Spain to marry and hopefully, live happily ever after with her dashing beau. The final scene in the film has her standing on the bow of a ship leaving Stockholm Harbour with a fair wind in her hair. As far as the audience is concerned she is thinking the many hopeful/fearful thoughts that such a momentous decision would engender. A telling story concerning the filming of this scene has her asking the director: "How should I play this scene?" The director, an elegant and astute Armenian by the name of Rouben Mamoulian, answered her, "Think of nothing".

The tremendous success of this film, and that scene in particular, can be put down to the fact that by thinking of nothing in particular and remaining very still under the intense scrutiny of the camera, the audience, individually and also collectively could interpolate their own thoughts into the mind behind the image.

I found this a very inspirational instance and I managed in time

to re-apply it to the Frank/Suzuki Performance Aesthetics.
I have been using the Frank/Suzuki Performance Aesthetics /Suzuki Actor Training Method as training and preparation for performance since 1991 and, whilst I cannot precisely chart my changes in attitude towards it in the early days, there are certain aspects that have become much clearer and instructive in the last few years. I have noticed when doing an exercise over the long term that there occur profound shifts in my perceptions. As I became more experienced my awareness has become more holistic.

In the FSPA exercises there are many factors to focus on: leg and feet positions, upper body softness, relaxed, focused gaze, etc..... multiple possible individual components. It is easy to understand that these must be constantly monitored and addressed, but in order to achieve completion they must be connected to each other as well. Until they are collectively incorporated into the body of the actor, they remain separated and isolated, fragmenting and dissipating on each move.

The integration of all the separate elements indicates the beginning of completion for an actor, and, in my experience, consists of thinking of both everything and nothing at the same time. And, if I pose that question to any of our experienced actors they invariably give a similar response.
This is integrating a paradox which only the unconscious mind can countenance. More about Conscious and Unconscious in the upcoming Teddy Bear provoc.

In terms of thinking of everything and nothing, I also realized that using the word **void** can be misleading as it implies 'empty', whereas the opposite is true; it is, instead, a highly charged stasis, a form of **'empowered neutral,'** for which the explanation is that it is the agglomeration of many oppositional forces in equilibrium. Stillness is the physical manifestation of this. Stillness is a very powerful tool for making actors more mythic and this is achieved by encouraging the actors to perceive themselves as a portrait, an encapsulated 'moment' of a series of forces that arrive at a still point because they are balanced by their equal and opposites.

A simple example is for the actor, while standing still in a **Statue**, to imagine that he is being pushed by a force acting in a Northerly direction, and at the same time being pushed by an equal force acting in a Southerly direction. As a result there is equilibrium in the form of stillness. This stillness is a form of arrested 'conversation' between the forces, and the sculptural arrangement of the body is the three dimensional 'portrait' of that conversation. That portrait is what gives the actor a real 'presence', making him charismatic, compelling because of the inner energy produced by the balanced dialogue of opposites.

A short digressive anecdote that illustrates how mythically powerful stillness is.....when I was younger I avidly watched many classic films, especially those of the 30s, 40s and 50s. I read many books and biographies of the stars and these of course contained many still photos, some of which have become emblematic of that star's charisma. A very good example is the still of Marilyn Monroe in the film **The Seven Year Itch**, where she stands over a subway vent and her dress is blown above her knees by a passing underground train. A very erotic and emblematic 20th c. image indeed! Having seen the picture first, when I watched the film I felt that Monroe in movement didn't quite live up to the still image, that she was lesser in action than her photographic image would suggest. This 'disappointment' happened many times with 'stills' and 'actions' of famous film stars. It often took me quite a few viewings to reconcile the two - the still image with the person in action.

Only after I had done Suzuki Training and come to understand the mythic nature of the still body have I then been able to articulate the mythic nature of the still photograph. Such photos are mythic because they are 'perfect'. Everything is in balance, from smile to the swirl of the dress, and that perfect instant has been captured for all time. It is an eternal document that transcends daily time and daily activity. This effect of mythologising is enhanced when the person depicted dies, especially tragically or before their time, because the picture becomes a monument and a reminder that we can never see that action again - that experience has been taken away from us for ever.

Back to stillness as a sculpture......
The simple attitude of seeing the body as a portrait of forces in balance, gives the body an expressive muscular power - a physical charisma. This process can be expanded into a multiplicity of forces and directions, the more multiplicity, the more charismatic and 'present' the actor appears in the space. Furthermore, these 'physical' manifestations can be used as templates for invoking emotional, psychological and metaphysical ideas of opposites in the body and soul of the actor. This also shows that the physicality not only produces muscular definition, but it provides a blueprint for more profound creativity. It fosters this by evolving processes that emancipate the other more mysterious and elusive natures that lie deeper inside the mind/body matrix.

When Peter brought up this idea of Coldplay's incompleteness it seemed to me an extension of this 'filling the void.'

Just as I finish writing, I hear a cough at my shoulder, this devil persistently reads everything I write….. he comments in his best Blakean 'flea' voice:

"A singular discourse that one; euphonious to the ear and easy on the brain."

He perches over me, takes my nervy hands, pours some blood from his bowl through my fixed fingers and say:

"Taste it and taste deep………. 'tis the bones in blood of thy forebears……"

I crane forward, touch the warm red with my tongue…….not pleasant, but it certainly pressed a few atavistic buttons……..he's forcing me to dig deeper, to dive into blood memory. Time to talk of the tectonic shift that happened to me during Voodoo Macbeth………his kinda show….

Meta Muscle Provocation #4
David Attenborough's Arm:
The Four Stages of a Statue.

In the previous provoc I discussed the mythic stillness of the photograph. In many ways the idea came out of doing statues, a seminal exercise first devised by Suzuki. When you do statues umpteen times over a number of years you tend to do two things: you learn to remain very still AND you do a lot of thinking about what it means to be very still!

When I first saw and did the statues with Suzuki in 1991, I was struck by their simple yet profound power. Fascinated by this sometime later I realized why........by forcing the actor to be still, by interdicting an actor's movement, the Statue converted the actor's daily self into a type of mythic self. This is to do with the simultaneous condensing AND expanding of time! It is analogous with the still photograph which, by freezing an image into an instant, paradoxically transcends time by creating an image that lasts for ever!

Those still images taken from movies of stars such as Elvis or James Dean have become emblematic and etched in our memories and will remain part of a universal unconscious, even though their subjects have gone the way of all flesh.

The statue is a temporary way of making such an image, and it forges the same emblematic power because it suspends time inside the body.

When you make a statue, and hold it still for more than a few seconds, you are forced to think more profoundly, and eventually to engage with your true 'self'.

To explain this arcane statement I'd like to quote an excerpt from the film **Koyaannisqatsi**, a high speed and slow-mo doco made in 1983 by Godfrey Reggio. It is a quite remarkable document full of stunning and surprising footage. One scene shows a group of female croupiers from Las Vegas, standing still and looking straight at the camera. It was filmed in fast motion which means that it only lasts 20 or 30 seconds, but was maybe 4 or 5 minutes of real time. They were wearing short frilly skirts and started smiling artificially at the camera as they would be trained to do. But gradually, (imperceptibly in real life, but speeded up by the camera), the smiles evaporated to be replaced by a more natural, 'true to themselves', look. They started off looking like they 'should' look, but ended up looking like who they really were - they looked like themselves!

........this happened because they were still AND looking at the camera. They couldn't maintain a pretense, and their artificial pose ablated like a false skin. They were forced, by being as still as possible, to engage who they really were. If they had been allowed to move around and break eye contact with the camera, then they could have preserved their 'professional' smile.

In fact, when you observe similar situations where people are trying to look 'attractive', you'll find there will be subtle distractive movements, shifts and small diversions, so that the fake sincerity is not found out. By moving and shifting their gaze, they are trying to fool the viewer (and themselves) into thinking they are genuine, and mean what they are trying to promote. Many people in many occupations have to wear a social smile, a 'have a nice day' face, and that is properly an extension of the necessary pleasant etiquette that lubricates social intercourse.

But theatre is the place where daily social etiquette is more than unnecessary, it actually impedes true interaction between the actors and the audience. Women especially, who often spend their entire day being accommodatingly attractive, can take a long time to lose their 'nice' face.

In the case of the croupiers, the stillness actually forced them to show us their 'real self ' and by filming at high speed, then slowing down the playback, the filmmaker was making the transition more apparent.

Argued another way: at first we saw their Egos (their 'I want') predominant in their faces and, as time and stillness eroded away their ego's ascendancy, in its stead we saw a balance of ID (unconscious) and EGO (conscious).

The film portrayed much the same thing a little later with a fighter pilot standing in front of his jet. In this case, the officer's machismo evaporated, and he began to project who he really was. This was an even clearer case of the Ego dissipated by stillness and its accompanying deep thought. The same import can be applied to statues, and it is this process that creates the moral power that is so evident to the observer.

As well as thinking more profoundly about your self, another important function that occurs during a held statue is to receive and process information from the outside. How often do parents say to their kids: "Shut up, Be Still and Listen!"

In our training we do two main types of statues, standing and sitting.

Standing: This starts off in a neutral squat position with the legs wide apart and heels on the ground, the buttocks as close to the floor as possible (depending on personal facility). On command (stick hitting the floor) the actor rises to make a 'statue' in any position as long as the heels are OFF the floor and making sure the feet have not moved. On command, back to the squat.....repeat, etc.

Sitting: Starts with the buttocks on the floor, legs in parallel, knees bent and feet placed on floor as close to buttocks as possible, arms clasped together over the knees. On command the actor springs into a balanced position balancing on their bottom with arms and legs in the air. On command return to 'neutral' first position, repeat, etc.

The sub-tasks to be considered while making any statue are:

1. each statue should be a unique once off event. No repetitions,

2. the actor to spring into position immediately, as quickly as possible,
3. the statue should be finished before the sound of the command ends,
4. the statue, while an invention of the actor, should also be a portrait of the energy of the command

These subtasks are firstly challenged, but ultimately facilitated by the non-predictable timing and rhythm of the commands.

There are also advanced versions such as statue on one leg (supporting foot flat on the floor), but basically we have been doing the statue exercise, as described, since 1991.

What has evolved since is the level of functionality. By that I mean; more than what the statue is, what is it doing to the actor? Over time I have realised there are 4 distinct stages in the effect they are having on the actor, and by extension, the effect they have on the audience. They are:

1. **STILL** Can you be still?
2. **FEEL** Can you feel yourself in the statue?
3. **EXPRESS** Is the Statue a portrait of your imaginative impulse?
4. **RESPOND** Can the Statue trigger in you a poetic or imaginative process?

1. **Can you be still?**
For the neophyte, just to learn to be still is a major achievement. For most of us, stillness in daily life is extremely rare. It is only in moments of great intensity and drama that we are genuinely motionless, transfixed. So the actor first has to train himself to recognise when he is being still and when he is not (which is most of the time!). Although difficult, it is a very simple goal, and easily objectified as the actor can clearly know if he is/is not moving first, by observation, and later, by feel.
It also has a very clear moral determinant and that is DON'T MOVE A MOLECULE! No matter how:

a. Exhausted you are,
b. Nervous you are,
c. Experienced/inexperienced you are, etc...

The simplicity is in itself very instructive, as it teaches the actor that early straightforward goals are achievable despite vicissitudes.

Once an actor can be truly still, he is then ready for stage Two:

2. Can you feel yourself in the statue?

We urge the actor not just to hold a position when making a statue, but to really feel the statue he is making. This sounds obvious and axiomatic, but it is surprising how many actors will doggedly hold on to a position, in such desperation of 'getting it right', that they are effectively locking out any possibility of feeling what they are doing. We have a simple solution for this, by saying don't stop doing everything you are doing, but start to feel your arms, legs, body, etc, while holding that position. Immediately they start to invoke that suggestion, their statue gains greater density and resonance - it has much more inside it than if it were just holding a position; what is now occurring is that there is now the making (overt) and the feeling (covert) - the results of the making.

We also encourage the actors to consider that their stillness is not fixed, but feels as though it is increasing - that it is getting stiller and stiller. Not strictly possible in a living body, perhaps, but nevertheless an extremely provocative and **practical operational hypothesis!**

Believe it or not, that notion came to me when driving past an automotive brake repair business in a light industrial suburb, Woolloongabba, near where I live in Brisbane. It was called the STILLER BRAKE SERVICE, a fab moniker and cannot be bettered as the name for a company that helps to make cars stop!

Until an actor can feel himself in his statue, he is unable to apply creative use to the statues he makes. But once he can do that, he can start to use the statues creatively:

3. Is the Statue a portrait of your imaginative impulse?

As an actor continually revisits the exercise over months or years, statues must graduate from competent craft to inventive instrument. If training were merely a form of cathartic calisthenics, as is often supposed, then it could remain in the realm of grunt and clump. However, this is not so for us in Ozfrankia!

I encourage the actors to consider that their statues should be initiated by a creative impulse, and I neither stipulate the source of the impulse, nor judge the verifiability of the resultant. What is important is the instinctive nature of the trigger, and the visibility of the effect the impulse and statue has on the actors. We talk in terms of the statue being not just a position or pose, but a 'portrait' or 'sculpture' of a type of poetic impulse initiated by the actor's imagination.

The 4th stage is where the Statue sustains the actor, in ways both physical and metaphysical:

4. Can the Statue trigger in you a poetic process?

After dwelling on the Third Stage for quite a while, imagining how it might reflect some instinctive zones in my psyche, I had an experience which demonstrated how it might also work the other way.

I was doing a performance of one of Jacqui Carroll's versions of Macbeth, **Voodoo Macbeth,** in which, as Macbeth, I spend the whole time as a zombie, a plaything of the witches, who have been reconfigured as plantation slaves heavily into voodoo trickery. I spend a lot of time with my eyes shut which I found very pleasant.

At one moment in one performance I found myself walking forward to the audience, in a sort of zonked-out state, and for no

particular reason, I started thinking of David Attenborough's arm.... For real?.... Yes!..... Really!.... so as I walked forward, I followed that thought and began to think of myself as enacting an aspect of DA's arm, and it was very enjoyable as I felt it opened up a very different way of performing. Rather than trying to invent or recreate an emotion or a psychological situation and make it credible, I was following a train of inspiration, of feeling, and doing it as a public act. I had lost all trace of nerves and anxiety. I knew the play was going on all around me as before, but inside the play, I was, as well, going on a journey of discovery to find out where my feelings would take me.
I now recognise that I was following an unconscious impulse, for it was much more than a thought, and doing it in public amplified it even more. I have no idea what the audience thought - it wasn't a particularly climactic scene, and how could they know it had anything to do with DA's arm? Jacqui (the Director) said nothing particular about that moment, either for or against, but going from that I can assume it didn't stick out as being off the track.

That triggered an attitudinal shift in the way I approached the training as I began to see how I could enact such experiences and what exercises might be better.

On a subsequent training day I was doing a statue as part of a turn in the Tenteketen, and I realised that it reminded me of something I had done or seen before, so I decided to go with it, just to see where it would take me, and where it would go.

I explained it later to **Caroline Dunphy**, (see pic at back of book) Lady Macbeth, by using as an example the famous classical statue of the 'The Discus Thrower'. If you found yourself by chance in a pose approximating the famous sculpture, you would recognise it and think..."Hey, this reminds me of the Discus Thrower, maybe I'll 'follow its story to see what happens.' The operative phrase is 'found yourself,' because it indicates you didn't deliberately make the statue, it happened to you.

Caroline, one of our most experienced actors, has her own thoughts on statues and stillness:

On the subject of being STILL:
A transformative experience for myself as an actor with Ozfrank Theatre was during the rehearsal period and season of *Heavy Metal Hamlet*. Jacqui had directed me, as Ophelia into a pair of silvery ice skating boots which were bolted onto a lazy susan that swivelled freely upon a wheeled platform. Thus I could lean out, spin around, and be pushed around the stage, but I was stuck to the trolley – I was free to move in some magical ways, but heavily restricted in others. I was certainly on the road to learning many new things in this process (including unforgettable memories of working to THE late great Led Zeppelin's masterful music) besides that of relocating my consciousness for the heavy and somewhat dizzying episodes from Ophelia, and the transferal of core energy whilst in this confining contraption. Letting go to trust the weight of the moving trolley and my fellow actors who held it was one thing BUT the thing that seemed a true revelation to my body, was learning to *keep it still* – to be more specific *keeping my legs still whilst the upper body is free*. At this stage in my life, I had not yet been on a snowboard or a wakeboard, (let alone strapped in a trolley) and so the act of not being able to walk, run, kick or even stretch my feet was so foreign it was like torture to me. Many a day or night of rehearsal and performance, I would wait side stage standing or squatting and simply watching…for hours sometimes.

In the beginning, I would jitterbug around tensing, squeezing, pulling at my feet purely out of restlessness and frustration. I felt like a caged animal! …then, as time passed and the once impatient body settled allowing me to feel a tremendously pleasant *force of calm*.

"Ah, it's not so bad after all…maybe there's some sense to doing this for lengthy periods and feeling this way…maybe - that's it"!

My actions were a reflection of me and slowly I began to settle down and feel the true and grand essence of STILLNESS. These inside feelings of a caged animal were no doubt mine, and a part of me that could be utilized, BUT as the agitations subsided, there came a heaviness and everything including myself felt more connected and open. I could see clearly, I could feel more clearly. My voice dropped down into my centre and as I moved slowly through the air in circular motion with my feet firmly planted, I experienced a *live* drifting (as opposed to the sleepy kind) and was now full of imaginative energy it seemed. It was then I felt the atmosphere, the textures, the wheels beneath me, the floor beneath that, the earth beneath the floor, the spirits that lay deeper still…

"Our director Jacqui is a genius!" I thought," how could she know this was the way, this - this bolted booty contraption thing on wheels was to become my *mate*, my *revelation*, the key to my *imagination*."

Wondrous thoughts came in and out of me throughout that season from my position of the secured unknown. From Brisbane to Sydney to Japan, I flew with the notion of Ophelia's trolley as a magic carpet to a world of possibilities - all in the act of - or should I say ART OF STILLNESS (on wheels).
Caroline Dunphy

Like Caroline's 'Ophelia' stillness, both the DA's arm and Discus Thrower's impulses were instinctive. They all came through some unbidden pathway – via what Jung calls the Unconscious, the imaginative dreamscape of the mind. Previously, when I had tried to achieve similar states in a deliberate fashion, it always felt false and it was very hard to keep it going as it seemed to have no 'inner heart' to provide 'forward' story.

In ruminating on the implications of the difference between instinctive and deliberate, the instinctive statue is open and instructive. If premeditated, then it seems the result is much more of a fixed, mechanical experience that has nowhere to go. I assume that that is because premeditated is a prescription of the Ego, the 'I want'. Its intervention is such that it blocks the creative pathways of the instinctive, imaginative parts of the mind.
Given that the unconscious or instinctive statue is the creative option, the question then becomes: how do actors do statues in

A Devil Pokes the Actor

a way that are instinctive and therefore will have a creative impact on them.

Two facilitating devices that encourage this are:

1. The actors should try not to think in the millisecond before the movement, just be open to the potential and 'do' the movement - which means to react like an animal.

2. If they are thinking of doing a certain action, like looking at the corner, then they should make sure they do NOT QUITE look there. If they are thinking of lifting their arm straight above their head, then they should stop somewhere on the way. If they don't quite know where it's going to end up they are much more likely to create an instinctive statue

By applying those self interdictions, they'll never end up doing what they want to do, but something more elliptical. That something is a probe, an exploration, a question, and that keeps the movement or the speech alive and keeps the actors in a questing and sentient state.

The second interdiction above is inspired by a speech that Brando gave in the film *Missouri Breaks*. He plays an Irish bounty hunter, and he's about to dispatch some hapless horse rustler, when he waxes lyrical about the night skies. He goes on to say that if you wanted to see a particular star, you couldn't look directly at it, that you had to look a little to one side of it, and then it would become clearer.....As with many such 'Brando-isms' it's compelling behaviour, and it's also an interesting pointer to ways of shifting creative responsibility from the rational to the instinctive side of the brain.

A Devil Pokes the Actor

Top full of these seductive elliptical notions I dreamily focus on my devil's bony forefinger lazily waggling at me as if to silently say …'I'll give you elliptic'…..
After a drawn out sniff this devil turns into a 2 headed Antonin Artaud, one head the sleek sharp youth of 1928, and the other the tragic toothless inmate of 1946 – poor Antonin's 2 heads tell the tale: what happens after eighteen years of prowling the outer spaces of theatre potential, if you're too far apart and way too far ahead.

(Oh Lord, please don't let me be misunderstood…………..)

Somewhere between these two heads gives me a great idea…..

Meta Muscle Provocation #5
The day Artaud stopped the clock

In November 2008 Ozfrank did a performance based on Jacqui Carroll's prosecution of Antonin Artaud's frenetic and sacreligious 1947 Radio Play: **To Have Done With The Judgement of God (THD).** It had an all male cast of five, company members Glenn Taylor and myself plus company associates Noel Sheridan, Kieran Law and Donovan Holbrook, sinuously moving and talking alchemically for 55 minutes. It was an open plan 'body conversation' with one of the greatest and maddest theatrical pedagogues of C20. Key Comrade **Glenn Taylor** (see pic at back of book) wrote after he had performed it:

THD is an abstract piece to say the least and for some time difficult to relate to when approaching it from the conventional stagecraft/acting process. The director created an aesthetic and physical vocabulary within which the actor had to 'make sense' of the work. (I don't mean logical sense but a visceral feeling). At the conclusion of the first performance I realised that what I instinctively applied to the process was the idea that **the physical (and other sensory) experience of the performance WAS the narrative.** It was an experience quite pure and personal in that I was uninvolved with the other performers' experiences. There was a lot of trust at play, firstly, complete trust in the director's vision for the piece, and as well, letting go of the desire to tell a logical story.

After **THD**, the follow up question was: *What did that experience do to me?* I was quite absorbed in the piece itself, the dynamic between the work and the audience and was also undergoing, during the performances, epiphanies by making connections between snapshots of text combined with music and other sensory feedback from the space.

THD was significant in that it challenged me to think about the experience of the drama; the real visceral experience which allowed me to achieve real growth as a performer. No longer was the mastery of technical performance skills a yard stick by which success was measured, this points to a paradigm shift which values performance as

a transformative and instinctual process witnessed by an audience, rather than a display of a playwright's literary skill or the actor's ability to beguile the audience.
Glenn Taylor

Well put companero! In that way the Artaud piece set up an attitude for two works later in the year, the mediaeval miracle play **The Reckoning of Badengood,** and **Up Jumped the Devil**, based on the music and lyrics of Biblical Rockster, Nick Cave.

Now, your man Antonin was a pretty wild dude, for whom the biggest bummer was that with his ultra extreme notions of what theatre could be, even his hipster peers couldn't catch his drift. This spun him out even more and he spent a lot of time in the rubber room and this was not a good place to be in 1943 with Nazis down the road holding unhealthy designs on those deemed unhealthy in the bonce. In a sense he was lucky because he did survive World War 2 even though he lost his beatific good looks along with all of his teeth. He only lasted another few years when some kindly friends found him a garden shed where he whiled away his remaining time whacking at a block of wood with a tomahawk, wailing out his scatological screeds.

His work consists of lots of Weird and Wacky, interspersed with surprisingly astute observations about art and theatre - way ahead of his time, poor beatific soul! An empathetic Ozfrank friend, Sharmila Nezovic, once heard the radio play broadcast by the ABC in the 90s and suggested it to Jacqui, who was looking for a suitably loose and polymorphic text to intertwine with some atavistic movement. It turned into quite a turbid, toxic little piece with diamante skulls and real pigs viscera (which pass quite well for the human ventrihicle), and as Glenn suggested above, became very 'key' for future aesthetic fun and games.

One of the more outlandish Artaudian lines Jacqui used went:

> "The fact that the world is not yet formed, or that man has only a small idea of the world and wants to hold on to it forever. This comes from the fact that man, one fine day, STOPPED..... the idea of the world!"

One rehearsal Jacqui set the speech by asking the cast of 5 men to walk back and forth across the stage intoning away until we came to the word 'stopped', upon which we abruptly turned to the front and all of us held the stillness until one of us decided to start again by saying: 'the idea of the world', whereupon we all joined in and finished together. We repeated the sequence five times, I think, before we moved on to something else. This became one of the important triggers that inspired Glenn.

As I've said before, when we train before the show, we often use phrases or routines from the show, as it acclimatises us, getting us all on the same page, etc. This was one such exercise and we found it so Promethean that it has become part of the permanent Ozfrank toolkit. We use it at every level of the training from open classes for beginners to advanced company rehearsals and it has become very pivotal in cracking a performance problem that had puzzled me for some long time.

I have always wondered how the heck certain people could stand or sit on stage, stock still without blinking for extended periods. Suzuki seems to expect it of his actors, although I have never heard him demand it, but they sure as hell can do it. I've never been very good at it, and it always seemed that I was OK for a few seconds until I started thinking about it, then I'd have to blink. Which of course made me think: "Why did I have to think about it? If only I could do it without thinking, then I could probably sustain it!"

So, why do we blink? Especially when desperately trying not to... over the years I pondered ways to learn how not to blink, and eventually, as I watched more and more training, I ascertained that blinking was a form of release from tension. It became obvious from watching their physiognomy, that actors blinked when they needed a break from 'holding' a position - it was like an intake of breath. That was a big clue, but I wasn't any closer to discovering a technique for solving it. Not until we did the **Artaudian Stop!** did we get the tool!

The key to the Artaudian stop exercise is the greater awareness it occasions. When we first did it, we tried not breathing for the duration - really stopping! But that started to turn into a breath holding marathon, which is OK for the Guinness Book of Records, but not for much else, especially acting. Soon, I began to request that the actors keep breathing while maintaining the suspended animation and wait until somebody decided to make the break. And, when he or she started again, then everyone else would join in and we would all finish together.

Two aspects became crucial. One was that the actor who started up again had to make sure that he didn't leave the rest behind on the re-commencing. He couldn't just lurch off regardless of his partners. The other actors, as well, had to be similarly sensitive, extremely ready to join in seamlessly with the breakaway.

We stipulate that this stop period is entirely the responsibility of the actors inside the space. The director/teacher has no control over the duration of the 'stop', and this produces a unique feeling as the space is controlled entirely by the complicity of the actors, for a time they are outside the teacher's purview and are their own interdiction. The stop normally lasts some seconds, but on occasion it has lasted a few minutes (which feels VERRRRRY long!), and it could theoretically last for hours - an entire training session becoming one long acting pause.

This is not likely though, because the pressure to start again is compelling and increases exponentially as time ticks. It's reminiscent of a story once told to me by my sister, Sally, who was caving deep underground with a school group. In an underground cave there is **no**, and I mean, **no** natural light! Apparently the guide asked them to all turn their torches off which was OK for a few seconds... but as their eyes **did not** become accustomed to the complete absence of light, the urgency to turn back on the torches became excruciating, similarly, with the Artaudian Stop, the longer the pause, the greater the tensile quality of the 'stretched time', and the more 'mythical' the experience for the actor. There is no question that the actors look very involved and stimulated during the stop - even though they are very still, they look very much alive. As well their voices, when they restart, have a much greater degree of substance about them, possibly due to the build up of pressure in the hiatus

It's an excellent example of the Paradigm: **not** doing the thing is very propitious for **doing** the thing!

The Artaudian Stop is another **'operational paradox'** or **'instructive contrary'** similarly pregnant to the other Zen like tool **'Hold the stick/holding onto the stick'** that I mention in Frankly Acting, my first book. We have found that such 'invoke-able opposites', to be powerfully heuristic (self teaching) for any actors studying with us, and they are the practical working tools/formats that walk the walk that only exist as 'talk' in other forms of actor preparation.

We call such Parentheses **Codas** because they are rather like brackets around a routine - they are not the routine itself, but give the routine further definition by setting up particular reference points.

Another 'parenthetical' sequence that Jacqui has recently invented is the **'Return to Neutral'.** This involves finishing an exercise by returning to a neutral standing, sitting or kneeling position, Although we have had for some years performed exercises like **'Enka'** which finishes in a neutral kneeling position at the conclusion of the music, Jacqui suddenly started finishing the **Standing Statue** exercise with an 8 to 16 count dissolve to a standing neutral.

This has become another compelling example of 'Undoing' being even more pregnant than 'doing', and poses a very provocative question: why is 'doing the opposite' more instructive than actually 'doing' it?

Jacqui will often, during the training, structure an exercise around following a certain movement sequence, and at some stage exactly reverse the sequence. As you can imagine, it is very demanding and it took me personally some years to develop the concentration and recall to do it. Thematically, this forward and rewind forces the actor to re-evaluate his physical relationship with time, as he has to reconstitute his physical movements back in time. In so doing, he gains greater awareness of himself in the four dimensions. He can site himself quite specifically inside the space/time format of his environment, rather than being present in a general but amorphous fashion.

This idea of an actor aware of himself in the four dimensions (Length x Breadth x Distance x Time) prefigures the extreme molecular provocation: Provoc 23 **Spirit Speed the fifth Dimension.**

"Those last paras could make your head spin. Watch me spin Antonin!"

The twin Artauds disappear to be replaced by a diabolic boy bitten by a lizard! Ah! Caravaggio! The Baroque bovver boy who sold his soul to the devil so he could paint like an angel! The first man to paint an idea, to paint an action with invisible skill... But why show me this?

Thus spake this devil *"Actions speak louder than words - actually six times louder if you read further!"*

Meta Muscle Provocation #6
When Words get in the way

Given that the three constituents of speech as communication are:

a. The accompanying body language (**gesture**),
b. The sound of the voice (**tone**),
c. The meaning of the words (**words**),

What percentage of the communicable impact would you apportion to each?
If you answered, in order: 60, 30, 10, you would, surprisingly, be right!

When I first read those numbers a few years back I was bedazzled, but as I pondered deep and long, and after reading a smattering of info about such notions as conscious, unconscious and subconscious thought processes, I surmised it was not so surprising after all.

The confusion surrounding communication arises when the 'giver' imagines that the 'receiver' should accept the communication in the way the 'giver' wishes. In fact, the 'receiver' does no such thing! The 'receiver' digests the transmission in the way HE wants, and the interpretation may have little to do with the giver's original intentions. The 'receiver' may give lip service by nodding earnestly but, in the end, he can only ingest the information when it is filtered through his own thinking processes.

This may be direct and deliberate, as when the 'receiver' decides very consciously to shut the information out, but, in less obvious, more neutral circumstances, he will still absorb according to the dictates of his beliefs and character. In other words his own thinking patterns filter out the info he doesn't want and lets through the info he prefers. Just yesterday I read a newspaper article which illustrates the point: I shall paraphrase:

A family had a bunch of horses on a property abutting a road.
People stopped to feed them and left rubbish.
The family put up a sign that said: Don't feed the horses!
It got worse.
They put up a sign that said: PLEASE! Don't feed the horses!
It got worse.
They put up a sign that said: We only eat apples and pears.
Problem stopped!

This anecdote can be analysed in two ways:
1. The feeders thought they were being kind by feeding the horses, so that the prohibition didn't get through, even when prefaced with a please. It was antithetical to their mental through-line. But, when the request 'We only eat apples and pears' was aligned with their own attitude 'being kind by feeding the horses' it got through.
2. Another more con/uncon way to look at it: The miscreants wouldn't be told what to do by another human but they bought the story from the horse's mouth! And we all know that horses can't write. So they binned the logical (conscious) message and the message that appealed to their unconscious got through.

Another way of putting this is to say that the 'receiver' blocks out the Ego of the sender, parrying it with his own Ego, so his unconscious can grab the bits it wants. No matter what they may profess, it is everyone's desire to reconfigure info in compliance with their own preferences.

This observation stems from my personal experience, when I realised that people seem to find it easier to comprehend what I was talking about when reading in written form, rather than orally face to face. I suppose there is a remove associated with reading information as distinct from being told, and I assume it's because in face-to-face conversation, the receiver has to deal with the direct energy/Ego of the sender along with the message.
This is especially so if the sender is forceful (comme moi) and passionate (comme moi, also)......

What is telling here is the difference between conscious and unconscious relationships. Conscious against Conscious (Ego versus Ego) comes across as two battering ram energies head to head with no give on either side. Unconscious into Unconscious seems to be miscible, able to interpenetrate one another without disruption or resistance. This may be because there is no alpha supremacy issue – the unconscious functions on subliminal levels, and a bunch of gung ho Jungians could talk this through for a week under water, but the 'Why' matters not a lot.

Suffice it to say that with communication, Uncon is the way to go, apropos of which, haven't you heard it told that if you want someone to believe something, make them think they thought of it themselves? Surely that's connecting to their Uncon? And, if uncon is the doorway, what next?

 Back to the components..........

Of the three components two, **gesture** and **sound**, are lateral and subliminal, and one (**words**) is linear and prescriptive.

Of course both gesture and sound can be deliberate, overbearing and immutable, but in most speech, they generally match the words of the speaker.

The obvious, deliberate, conscious one is (c) **The Meaning of the Words.** I mean by this, the intellectual content as intended by the Speaker/Actor. The words are necessary otherwise the audience would be entirely without a context or frame of reference.

The words, such as the 'to be or not to be' speech from Hamlet, exist as eternal documents. They have been written down and they have existed before the current performance, and will still exist forever after. In that sense they are part of a continuing Collective Consciousness and are **known** throughout the world ..... as distinct from **felt**, which is the domain of the Collective Unconscious.

A Devil Pokes the Actor   137

The words are necessary to 'hook' the spectator into the zone, they open the door, so to speak, and usher him into the transformative space, but the words themselves offer no transformation because they are already known to the spectator. The spectator already has his own attitude to them.

And as for any other speech, even if unknown compared to Hamlet's big one, the English words are still 'already known' to the audience because they are part of an ongoing literary tradition. One could say that they already own the words......... and that the only way these words can be 're-known' is for them to be reframed, to be presented as unfamiliar so that the audience could perceive them afresh.

In our very conscious western society, our familiarity with English can be a blind to understanding deeper impulses in a performance. Often, while attending shows in other languages we don't understand, we can, due to our ignorance get a much more powerful sense of body language and through that, deeper insights.

Let me introduce **Kathleen Doyle**, a sometime member of Ozfrank, who is also proficient in Japanese and has worked with Suzuki as an intern:

The notion of the supremacy of the word in communication was smashed in my encounter with the Suzuki Method and more significantly Suzuki's performances.

I am by no means disputing that language plays a great part in communication, but clearly before my encounter with Suzuki's theatre, my understanding was that the word was the one driving force behind exchanges. In this schema, movement and gesture merely augmented the message delivered in the words.

My first experience of seeing a performance by Suzuki's actors was not unlike the experience I hear others retell: I was blown away by the electric energy in the air. It hit me on a physical level. I got immediate answers to my 'why?' question from others more familiar with Suzuki's work, with explanations like "the actors are highly energized". Surprisingly, this was enough to satisfy someone who was in no sense prepared to make any shift in belief about the word's dominant role in communication. I have since worked with Suzuki Tadashi's company as an actor (2004/2005), and I have had the chance to see his actors in rehearsal and performance more times than I can count. All of this, naturally, has helped me along this very long journey to accept, at a personal level, this notion that the body and energy can and do communicate.

For me, Suzuki's veteran actor, Tsutamori Kousuke, was one of the best examples of how the body comes first in Suzuki's work. Before he even speaks a word, his body shudders with the enormous mountain of energy he has stirred up (having been with the company years, he is a real master at rousing such energy). Only once his body is prepared, does he speak, and the words manifest as if a surfer were riding a wave; sometimes they hurl out with great force; at other times they roll and tumble supported by this huge life force. Tsutamori appears to be giving over to the energy wave he himself generated in his body. I imagine it takes years of practice to *trust* above the words spoken the power such a body has to communicate.
Kathleen Doyle

The pre-occupation with the words in our obsessively **conscious** theatre means that as the actors consciously try to impress the same words into the minds of the audience, they get blocked out by the audience's egos. They witness the performance as if watching exhibits at a museum, and no transformation occurs. It would be much more affecting to reframe the words with sound and movement that get past the audience's conscious gatekeeper to engage with their unconscious.
That would mean to beguile the audience with movements and soundscapes that intrigue rather than bombard, that suggest rather than demand, that provoke rather than prescribe. Two good examples of movement and sound that intrigue the uncon are dance and liturgical Latin.

Dance:
Modern Dance has historically been very good at generalised emotion and feelings, whilst not being very effective at conveying particulars. Dance can't do specifics, so that the mind of the audience takes the info in subliminally, in a non factual fashion through their uncon, and fleshes out the story by adding touches of their own history.

Liturgical Latin:
Ultra traditional religions such as the Catholic and Orthodox churches (bells and smells) have used arcane ceremonial language in their liturgy since year dot. For hundreds of years this has not been the daily speech of the congregation and the disaffected assume that it's because the nabobs want to keep the proles in the dark. Be that as it may be, one of the other outcomes is that the ceremony courts mystery. When the congregation is sitting through the service, their inability to understand the language means that they will fill in the details from their own psyche background. Paradoxically In that way it becomes more their own story - initiated from outside (the church) but completed inside (the soul).

Such is the potential, likewise, of theatre, for it is the mystery, entering the corpus of the viewer via the unconscious that transforms the viewer. And this is only possible because the conscious, which abhors mystery, has been bypassed.

As you can see words can often get in the way.........

A Devil Pokes the Actor

To see how those words went down with my devil I'd have to go by the look in his eye, the frown on his face or the curl on his lip. I steeled myself…..reeled around, ready to catch the glimmer of his glint……instead, a sepulchral sotto voce snort comes out from under an antique headmaster's mortar board…..he launches forth a poem in lisping sibilate, which even in such simplistic rhyming guise, challenged me to answer it:

"What do you do, on your martyred quetht,
 Unrecognithed, uncrowned, unbletht,
That'th tho much better than the lumpen retht,
And how do I judge-what'th the tetht?"

That speech impedimented scholastic air, perhaps a head of theatre studies at some august arthritic unifarcity…… the classic quatrain continued on, poking me in the conscience……

"You thay there is a quantum betht,
What'th the word, the key, the manifetht,
That'th written at mankind'th behetht,
A birthmark on hith opened chetht?"

The lispered, whispered question swishes about, a bowling ball bouncing around my perfervid brain. After several strikes, an answer comes:

"The manifest, the missing piece is……. Moral Imperative!"

He scoffed: "*Moral Imperative!*" **and scraped two scaly fingers across his peeling lips….**

"And I mean moral as in 'of or pertaining to character, disposition'
And this is not a sexless place of simple good and evil but an energy, a force, that propels theatre towards pioneer space and self discovery.
To draw a map and stake a claim there's a Triad of directors, Two Tads and a Jerzy too, that define this zone and Provoc 7 stakes its claim on the back of their beliefs."

This devil says *"Moral imperativeth beget the Way of the Migraine, you betta, you betta, you bet!"*

Migraine Provocation #1
The Two Tad Jerzy Club
Moral Imperative as distinct from Evasive or Avuncular Imperative.

'Moral Imperative' is a term which I have coined to describe the type of energy I perceive in the work of Tadashi Suzuki. I use the word moral in the same sense as in 'moral fibre'; that is 'to expend conscious effort in the quest to expand one's physical and psychic boundaries.' I sense it in both Suzuki's actors and himself.

To give some examples of the **MI** at work and play, **Fran Barbe**, a long time UK-based Ozfrankie and Butoh performer, has some insights to intersperse...but a little later

In general I would explain it as the manifestation of a 'supra human' charisma that emanates from ordinary men and women when they compel themselves to go beyond their own capabilities. In the particular case of actors: "They looked like they were about to burst out of their skin!" is an apt description.

Interestingly enough, you cannot sense this in actors who are exhibiting a lot of overt, frenetic activity. Neither can it be projected by actors who are proficient but also precious and portentous. Actors need to be still or moving simply, so that they convey a sense of 'contained energy'. This contained energy can be described as a combination of two opposite forces in isometric balance: 'Engine' (power) and 'Brakes'(restraint), and it is the way these opposing forces engage and interact that provides for this 'bursting out' effect.

The invocation of these 'paradoxical' forces occurs at several levels inside such work as Suzuki's, ranging from the physically apparent to the more abstract. By physically apparent I mean that you can easily sense a muscular

vigour – a sound, a 'smell,' a feeling of sweat. And by abstract I mean more complex meta-physical ideas such as good and evil in contest with each other inside the same body.

One sees something similar in sport when one watches athletes who, by extending themselves up to, and beyond their personal best, attempt to be the fastest, highest or longest. In sport, one might expect that it is only the 'engine' component that is required, but in fact sportsmen need to exercise restraint, as too much 'engine' would put their bodies out of rhythm and balance. One sees it in most forms of dance as well because they search for, and encourage, extremes of physical endeavour. But not, I might add, in post-modern dance, where the focus is instead on mundane movement that celebrates the quotidian.

Apart from Suzuki I have only witnessed this type of energy in the work of three other directors, Jerzy Grotowski and Tadeusz Kantor, and in Australia, Jacqui Carroll. The best works of these directors share two things with Suzuki. One is a semblance of disquiet - that something mysterious and unsettling lies just beyond the play's horizon. the other, which would be necessary for the first, is an affirmation of the necessary existence of the 'dark' - that good and bad co-exist in all of us and that a performance should in some way be a portrait of that.

I am sure there are other directors capable of this epic charisma, but the vast majority of plays that I have seen occupy a Kingdom of Niceness. One might term them as having an **evasive or avuncular imperative.** They may mention bad things, but only in such a way that totally lacks any sort of real threat - an empty 'whatever' reference, that by the lack of real belief, has all the impact of a fart in a bar.

Peter Berkahn, once said of a conventional 'nice' play, "even when they are being angry they are still being nice about it." One can only truly convey the import of evil if one, first of all, acknowledges a certain content of good and bad inside, and then to have them in oppositional conversation deep in one's soul. It is made truly manifest when an audience witnesses the contest.

I would like to compare the work of three directors: Kantor (K), Grotowski (G) and Suzuki (S) to elucidate how and why they each achieve this type of supra-human energy.

Grotowski (above)
Grotowski's work I have never seen in performance but recently, while a guest of the Grotowski Institute in Wroclaw, Poland, I saw some commercially unobtainable videos, as well as observing the work of those that are influenced by the thread left behind. When discussing Grotowski's work in this context, I am specifically referring to the Laboratory Theatre, as after he canned his theatre of productions, his interests ceased to be theatre in the measurable sense.

Suzuki (middle)
Since 1991 I have been associated with Tadashi Suzuki and his work. On several occasions I have been a guest artist with his company, the **Suzuki Company of Toga** performing both internationally and inside Japan. In my experience this 'moral power' evinces itself to a very high degree in his actors, especially when one considers how self effacing and modest they are offstage.

Kantor (bottom)
I saw a performance of *The Dead Class* by his company **Cricot 2** in 1978 and have studied it many times, in video form, since. It is an acknowledged classic, having had over 700 performances world-wide, and I have not met one person, who, having seen it, did not pronounce it one of their greatest theatre experiences.

If we relate the situations of each of the above three, the one process they seem to share most is a powerful use of **interdiction.** This describes the many ways they demand that their actors site themselves inside the director's aesthetic expectation, which is greater in vision than their ordinary daily actions.

In the following excerpt, Fran (see pic at back of book) describes what revelations may result when a willing actor is prepared to go the hard yards with a demanding but perceptive director, who is also prepared to go the passionate hard ask............

Look , Really Look at the Audience

Doing 'Moving Statues' with Frank Theatre, Jacqui followed me down the room screaming at me to "Look at the audience! Look at them! Just look at them!". After a few lengths of the room, something dropped in my solar plexus, something formulated in my centre, and I felt that I saw clearly through my eyes for the first time. It was about nine years ago, but I have never forgotten it. I felt my body light up. I felt more connected more whole. I felt a sense of authenticity that was purely visceral.
Pula, Croatia 2000. Fran Barbe

Part of a director's interdiction can be summed up as demanding the actor to be first of all believable **(self-defined)**, and then continuing to interest the director **(interpretive journey)**.
Believe-ability:
Believe-ability is another way of saying that somebody is self-defined, that they are very much 'themselves'.

For most directors and actors, theatre becomes a battle of egos where the director is trying to coerce the actor into conforming to some 'big' picture and the actor remains firmly convinced that his' personal picture' is more valid. This can be very obvious or extremely subtle, but seems to be an ongoing duel of prevarication – a theatre of evasion. Hence the expression: Evasive Imperative.
Theatre with moral imperative begins with actors who have believability.
An actor's believability in theatre is borne of repetition, where the very act of repeating oneself, under the pressure of demand, commits the actor to becoming more defined. The director's interdiction has to be astute and apposite, for the repetition to be worthwhile, for the actor must trust that the director is capable of perceiving the performative shifts that the actor makes.

An important requirement is the actor's acceptance of the veracity of the director's knowledge and methods. The actor's continuing trust in the director means that the experience takes the relationship beyond the 'Actor's Ego will vs Director's will' gridlock. The actor's Ego energy, when confronted by the director's knowledge, is subsumed into a subliminal space where it buttresses his sense of who he is.

Interpretive journey:
The actor interesting the director with his believability is the essential starting point. Continuing to interest the director means that the actor has to do much more than just be, 'very himself', he has to be 'growing' in such a way as to make the director feel he is seeing/hearing something anew; that the actor is not just repeating himself, but is renewing himself by discovering new and deeper levels in the material......we call this **Deep Play**.

From what I can judge of these three directors, real invention for the actor resides in mining the same dramaturgical material more deeply each time. This is quite a big ask, and only really possible when sited in equivalently powerful aesthetic landscapes. For it is only when placed inside the undeniable vision of a director that an actor has the possibility to amplify and enrich his personal 'story'. This is where the complicit trust between director and actor is the crucial axis, <u>because the actor can only enter this 'deep play' when he trusts that the director's attitude warrants it -</u> and the director needs to witness the actor's micro 'deep play' in order to pan back more effectively on his macro aesthetic.

The moral ask of the actor's 'deep play' imposes on the director a reciprocal moral imperative; he must work very hard at excavating and elucidating his unique vision, for if he doesn't, the actor is attempting his personal discoveries on behalf of a moral void. It is the 'inner' work performed by the director in responding to the moral challenge put out by his actors that gives the final product such a uniquely personal imprint.

This 'moral dialogue' between actor and director is highly symbiotic and confers a creative inter-dependency on these three directors and their ensembles.

If these directors share the 'moral' attitude in terms of equivalently making demands on their actors, what then are the aesthetic differences?

Kantor

I saw Tadeusz Kantor's *The Dead Class* in the Adelaide Festival in 1978. I was pretty green about the gills, but I do remember thinking: "This'll be one of the most amazing shows I'll ever see!" One of the things that set K apart is the fact that for his performances, he has not only directed the show in camera, but also conducts the show on stage in real time. This effectively means that he is in the act of building the show as it is being performed - it is in a state of developmental acceleration; the show is morphing even as it unfolds.

Of course, most conventional directors would exclaim that their shows are developing with each performance. And, to a certain extent that would be true. Most directors give a few perfunctory notes after the shows, eg "It dragged a bit there...or....you need more anger in your voice in that scene with X, etc.".... all very bland - rather like a kindly uncle giving you advice on where to get a good deal for a new car battery. Very different from K interdicting in real time on the deck! One can imagine the effect this would have on Kantor's actors; not only would they have to process through all the other functions that are demanded of actors, eg remember their lines, actions, etc., but they would have to be highly responsive to the additional demands of K on stage, in real time, in front of an audience.

I must admit that I have no real memory of individual aspects of the show that I saw in '78, only a general sense of wonderment. I certainly don't remember Kantor being on stage, but this is maybe because I was a very naive punter at the time - obviously he didn't stick out like the proverbial dog's ----.

K was also a highly gifted painter and an imaginative sculptor in his own right, and his works contain many sculptural elements, mannequins and anthropomorphic machines. Some critics said deprecatingly that he treated his actors as mannequins. He effectively spent his creative life focused on developing two great pieces: *The Dead Class* and *Wielepole, Wielepole* in a constant cycle of performances. In them one doesn't discern any principals. One could go so far to say that his actors don't even come across as actors. They are not 'pretty'- they look like ordinary people. It looks like the butcher, the baker and the candlestick maker have been co-opted into the play. One could term his theatre as a super-defined reality.

Grotowski
Jerzy Grotowski was almost the reverse of K in many ways. Whilst he also was Polish and had a highly gifted ensemble, the **Theatre Laboratory**, the focal point became his intense one-on-one working relationship with Ryszard Cieslak, G's principal actor. As well, while K had a painterly or sculptural approach, G had a dramaturgical approach that was driven by a spirituality - in effect a reconfigured religiosity. G's theatre canon lasted 10 years and also produced two masterworks of which *The Constant Prince* is the one I would consider has the greater moral impact (....... it must be admitted, I've only seen both on video!)

The other, *Apocalypsis Cum Figuris*, generally considered the ne plus ultra of all G's theatre works, but from what I've seen in a dutifully misconceived film, it has a laxity caused by G's whimsical inattention. Apparently G allowed the film director free rein to shoot the work in any way he saw fit. The director decided to film it with the same reductive style as the show itself, and consequently the film became a tautology of sorts, which makes it unwatchable. G was very unhappy with the result (his own damn fault!) and it will never be released for general public viewing; however, there is a suite of photos taken by an Italian photographer which are magnificent and go some way towards repairing the damage. But it is hard to appoint full marks to the combined filmic document in terms of moral imperative as it has a precious quality normally associated with more trendy avuncular pastoral theatre.

Using *The Constant Prince* as a benchmark due to G's better stewardship, the dynamic sensitivity of the entire ensemble bears witness to G's astute dramaturgy and acute interdiction. This peaks with Cieslak's performance which contains a transcendent sacrificial energy that is only possible by intertwining the 1st person emotional intelligence of Cieslak with the 3rd person spiritual penetration of Grotowski.

The moral imperative between G and his actors was enhanced by his spiritual attitude that had to co-exist in conflict/resolution with the political climate.

Remember they were operating in 50s-60s communist Poland; everything outside was the Stalinist pits so it was easy to keep them all in the room. As well the official censors only attended the final dress rehearsal which meant they could muck around to their heart's content in the interim. Consequently G used to spend up to 10 hours a day over many months working alone with Cieslak. This intense symbiotic relationship was the making of G as a director and Cieslak as a transformative actor.

Suzuki:
Unlike the other two, Tadashi Suzuki is still very active, with an ensemble that is basically stable. S's aesthetic, from my experience watching AND working with him, is borne of creating a distancing dialogue between himself and the Classic theatrical traditions of Japan; Kabuki and especially Noh. To serve this he has reconfigured their classic training systems to forge a contemporary acting method. Alongside tuning the actor's skills, the training also creates a platform of commonality, wherein the actors understand his directorial requirements by gaining knowledge of his attitude and style. So, his interdiction is understood because it is placed in a context that is determined by the training.

S and **K** have a lot in common in their visceral dynamic - where they differ is that **K**'s work occupies an essentially personal space, addressing a Judeo/Catholic/Communist/ East European/Wartime perspective. K made theatre about what made him.

S, on the other hand, in a long and continuing career has pitted his personal cosmos against any theatrical tradition he can find, from Greek and Noh to Beckett.

I very much doubt if **S** could sustain such long term interrogation if he didn't have a solid actor training that brought not only his actors onto his page but also grounded him in a practical routine during his imaginative inspirations. I believe one of the little understood aspects of his system is that he also uses it as a personal anchor and inspiration for himself as a director. It is S's highly formalized acting method that points out the different strike rates of the three directors in how they support their interdiction.

What makes this 'interdiction' sustainable ?

It could be argued that the director's interdiction, essentially a form of psychic energy that emanates from the director, must be reinvigorated by an equivalent energy coming in; in the form of imaginative impulses and ideas generated by experiences outside the director's conscious control. This incoming energy needs to be coralled and coded by a structure.

This structure's function takes the form of what I call in an earlier provoc, a 'teaching machine'-a **Machina Didactica.**

All great creators in any field have invented or discovered their own specific 'teaching machine' that suits their temperament. In the case of the football culture, the coach has such a machine which is the practice routines that he has invented or follows. He also has a number of assistant coaches that run the routines at an 'on the ground' level, while he stands off to oversee and 'read' the action. It is in this reading of the interaction between individual players as they unfold their skills against the 'landscape' of the team practice, that the coach devises new stratagems and 'plays'. In the following box Fran (Barbe) discusses how Jacqui Carroll, as director, combines with the training:

The Sensation of Really Standing -

Today I stood on my feet, really stood on them; it was as if it was for the first time. Well it was the first time that I had stood in that way! With that sensation of profound connection, and with that awareness of what happened to me as a result of standing in that way.

What is this training that can do that for you?

It is a training which uses movement, but that is not its goal. It goes beyond the movement to work on the connecting space between the mind (including fictive imagination) and the body between the consciousness and material, physical existence. It is a training that works on the potency of the performer's essence, and from there an audience can follow the performer's fictional life.

Without that training, no essence can become apparent, and the fictional life relies on the kind of 'standing' that I experienced today. This training, and Jacqui's approach, has helped me to access a deeper sense of presence, a real sense of existence, on which I can build my performances.

July 2006, London. Fran Barbe

In a general sense, such a 'machine' must be stand alone in that it must be able to function without the immediate input of the inventor, so that he can observe from outside.
Once he has set it up, his attitude towards their machine becomes one of 'listening' rather than 'telling'. This enables reflective states in which the unconscious processes occupy centre stage and the analytical, assertive aspects of the persona are temporarily shelved. Without such a 'machine', the conscious mind dominates by prescribing and initiating experiences, preventing the instinctive and intuitive inspirations that foster transformation.

In just such a way, Suzuki has utilised his training to not only teach him how to direct, but also use it as an aesthetic development tool, a type of **alchemical** chamber enabling him to perceive subtle and elastic directions he could take. I use the word alchemy for it denotes a situation which is not linear or rational, but a 'psyche space' that is 'outside the box' - to use a common expression for creative lateral thinking.

A Devil Pokes the Actor   155

It is interesting to surmise that **G** may have been unable to sustain doing productions because he had overstepped his inspiration zone, and he had no stand alone training **matrix** to come 'home' to. He is supposed to have a type of training but in video evidence I've seen, it was an approach, a dramaturgical attitude, the physical aspect of which was whimsical and un-formalised in the extreme - vapid peanut rolls and quirky handstands do not a 'training' make!

K's concerns were slightly different because he was continuously mining the same micro/personal landscape and, since he was already an accomplished visual artist, he had his own 'personal training system' - his experience and special knowledge as a sculptor.

Both **G** and **S** had more global visions to realize and this required a bigger machine. Who knows how many things may have affected **G**'s propensity to continue directing theatre, but it is quite possible that had G's 'dramaturgical machine' been of a more robust constitution, he may have been inspired to keep on keeping on. **S** has a more rigorous and structured machine, not dissimilar to that of a classical ballet class. This enables him to do much more than just support the Moral Imperative of his Interdiction. <u>Suzuki's system creates the Moral Imperative inside the actor even before the rehearsal process starts!</u>

The highly charged moral imperative between an actor and a director such as Suzuki, seems only sustainable if couched in a training landscape, formatted so all parties are in extreme common assent. I contend that Suzuki's use of his Actor Training Method as a vehicle for amplifying his relationship both with his actors and with his aesthetic has been a major factor in the sustainability of his art.

What makes a great Theatre Director?
Using these instances of Moral Imperative that define S, G and K, I began to ponder on what makes a great director. (I would include Jacqui Carroll as the Oz point-woman of the Two Tad

Jerzy club) When comparing those three with all the other directors I've seen, worked with and known, I began to realise that S, G and K are true directors and the others are essentially managers.

One of the reasons that Western theatre is so bogged down in a verbose empty realism is that most so-called directors consider their only duty to be a parading of the script with a shallow redecoration to distinguish it from any previous. In this sense, the so-called director is really a type of manager, manipulating and chivvying the various elements, such as actors, designs, script, into some sort of acceptable commodity, hopefully, in a good humoured (avuncular) fashion so that no elements would be disaffected.

It is noteworthy that any directors who exhibit definitive visions are labeled 'obsessive' by the commentariat because of their single mindedness, whereas in sport such focus is praised. I guess it is part and parcel of the fake friendly culture of conventional theatre.
    I call into bat a feisty East End Jew to back me up:

Steven Berkoff, in his book "Free Association" wrote:

"I'm not like those fortunate directors who say 'I'll plot the play in three days and then fill in the detail', since you can only do this if your work is naturalistic and you are copying life. Nothing wrong with this, but it means you cannot investigate other forms of communication. You cannot experiment with movement and rhythms. You cannot aspire to conceptions of anything but the norm; you certainly cannot investigate on an unconscious level. You cannot 'play' with the material or create surreal imagery..."

".....................many directors feel a little awkward with the idea of ensemble work: they don't want to get involved and hope somehow that it will be all right 'on the night'."

Isn't that a polite way to say they're managers?
So, what then are the hallmarks of a true director?

1. They must have a recognisable aesthetic,
2. They must have their own actors,
3. They must have their own creative format,
4. The developmental arc of their aesthetic approaches greater singularity.

The first three are inter-connected, for they form aspects of the same politic, and the fourth manifests as the journey produced by the combination of the first three.

1.   All the great theatre practitioners have a recognisable aesthetic that has a distinctly personal imprint. The look, sound and feel should scream out at the audience: "This is the work of X X!!!"
 A van Gogh painting, a U2 song, a Pina Bausch ballet, are all recognised by their faithful followers as of the same ilk as before and reaffirm in the followers' minds, that they are part of an ongoing journey with a unique style and vision that is readily apparent BUT also evolving. In commerce this would be called high level branding!

2. One of the most important components of the unique 'vision', is the long term complicity between the director and performers, and I mean long term! That complicity is built over time, and is borne of the actors understanding, then being able to realise the director's requirements, and on the other side, the director's 'reading' the actor's responses.
I have observed Mr Suzuki at rehearsal since 1992, and I have marveled at his ability to constantly renew his relationship with the senior actors of SCOT, many of whom have been with him for over 20 years. As I have stated before, the actor's loyalty places a great moral responsibilty on the director to reciprocate by taking them further on their creative journey. This complicity is compounded by time. Both the actor and the director have to re-'create' the relationship on a constantly recurring basis.
3. This follows on from no. 2, in that over time, great directors develop a functioning matrix, their way of conducting a rehearsal, consisting of their demands, expectations and the

tools with which they achieve their aims. By tools, I mean the devices or routines they may use as precursors or bridges.

In many cases, the main tool is stricture. This is in the form of a very tightly controlled structure. Under milquetoast western theatre polity, this is assumed to be very uncreative, preventing the actor her due emancipation, but as **Fran** indicates below, the opposite can occur.

Creative Restrictions:

Performing in OzFrank Theatre's Macbeth in Switzerland (2009) I was both frustrated and exhilarated by the tight parameters imposed by Jacqui Carroll, the director. The very clearly defined structures of the training are a preparation for this and not an end in themselves. I experienced these tight parameters as a launch-pad to creativity and to greater sensation.

In some improvisations I had the experience that I was following a thread, I was not planning, predicting, deciding or judging but following feelings that I could not locate clearly as either body/sensory or mind/imaginative.

It was this experience in the training that allowed me to have an insight into a moment of presence in acting in the performance of Macbeth. Playing the nurse in the sleepwalking scene, a single line gave me an insight into what I was searching for. I can never repeat that moment, but I can seek a similar sensation in all performance.

WHAT I was doing hardly varied at all between performances because of the tight parameters this training and directing style offers. It was HOW I was doing it that offered me endless variations and creativity. The fact that I could not change too much WHAT I was doing, helped me to focus on the HOW more deeply.

For me, one of the over-riding benefits of Frank's training is the access to greater creativity, the source of which is the fertile territory that links bodily sensation or experience with imaginative activity. The training places you under pressure in a way that asks you to respond spontaneously, creatively and kinesthetically.
September 2008. Fran Barbe

4. One can see in the big time painters such as Vincent van G, that, as they became more experienced, their paintings exhibited to an increasing degree, an inner cosmology. The narrative, decorative aspects gradually disappear and we are left looking at a distilled portrait of their interior world. The situation for directors is more diffuse, but I think this is the fundamental way of the artist, and although I haven't the authority to pronounce on S, G and K, I perceive the tendencies......how to tell a theatre manager, as distinct from a genuine, creative director?

1. Replace-ability,
2. Sanctity of the script,
3. Keen on superficial innovation,
4. Appears to be inclusive,
5. Distrust of the visceral.
6. Their soul has nothing to 'say'.

- The single most defining characteristic about the shows that 'managers' produce is that they look as much as possible like those in the rest of their club. We have in Oz, six state flagship theatre companies, and they are all completely interchangeable - in fact the directors even manage each other's shows, so it is crucial that they look and sound alike, so as not to upset the prevailing orthodoxy.

- The accepted mantra is that they are committed wholeheartedly to preserving the sanctity of the writer's words. This pretends to a lofty respect of the scribe's intentions, but in reality it's a prevaricative excuse for having nothing to say.

- They are keen that the shows pound the same pavement, but with a few bright knick knacks that give a nod to the modern. This harkens back to a mid seventies mythology, the baby boomer golden age of growing up in public theatre. The 70s is where they gained the foothold, and they are all still there, flying the class flag of anti-authoritarian leftism. These old fogies only foster young fogies, so there's not going to be much change there....

- They love to appear inclusive with all sorts of collaborators coming and going. They use the rollover as a pretext for hollow renewal, braying that it 'creates new opportunities' for everybody, whereas there has been no self interrogation, no revitalisation, and like good managers they are very much holding on to the spot, while their 'partners' have wandered off in search of another job, probably with other members of the club.

- They are very chary of any visceral elements on the deck that may interfere with their comfortable bond with the intellectual elements of a production.
  I have performed in many plays where the Director hired a Movement Director (most often someone with modern dance training) do the physical stuff. The D would absent himself for a fag and a cuppa while the actors would do a few non-demanding avuncular warm up exercises with the MD. After an hour or so of vapid 'senior citizen' aerobics, the D would come back and start the 'real business' of blocking the show. This shows no belief in movement as an integral part of the process, relegating it to a level of perfunctory fitness.
  I have also been a MD for many shows and I came to the conclusion that most Directors Hate and Fear movement, because it intervenes between their psyche and the script! Most of the time during these engagements the D was dismissive nay antagonistic towards the movement aspect of the show.

- But the big one is that your theatre 'manager' has nothing to say. Their deep psyches have no answer, no insight. Their minds, of course, are quite capable of supplanting this void with fashionable political catechisms, suffused with pleasant decoration that pleases their peers and their baby boomer clientele.

They have nothing to add, unlike the obsessive 'auteurs', who by their idiosyncratic tyrannical vision, have left indelible footprints and insights dotting theatre's longtime landscape.

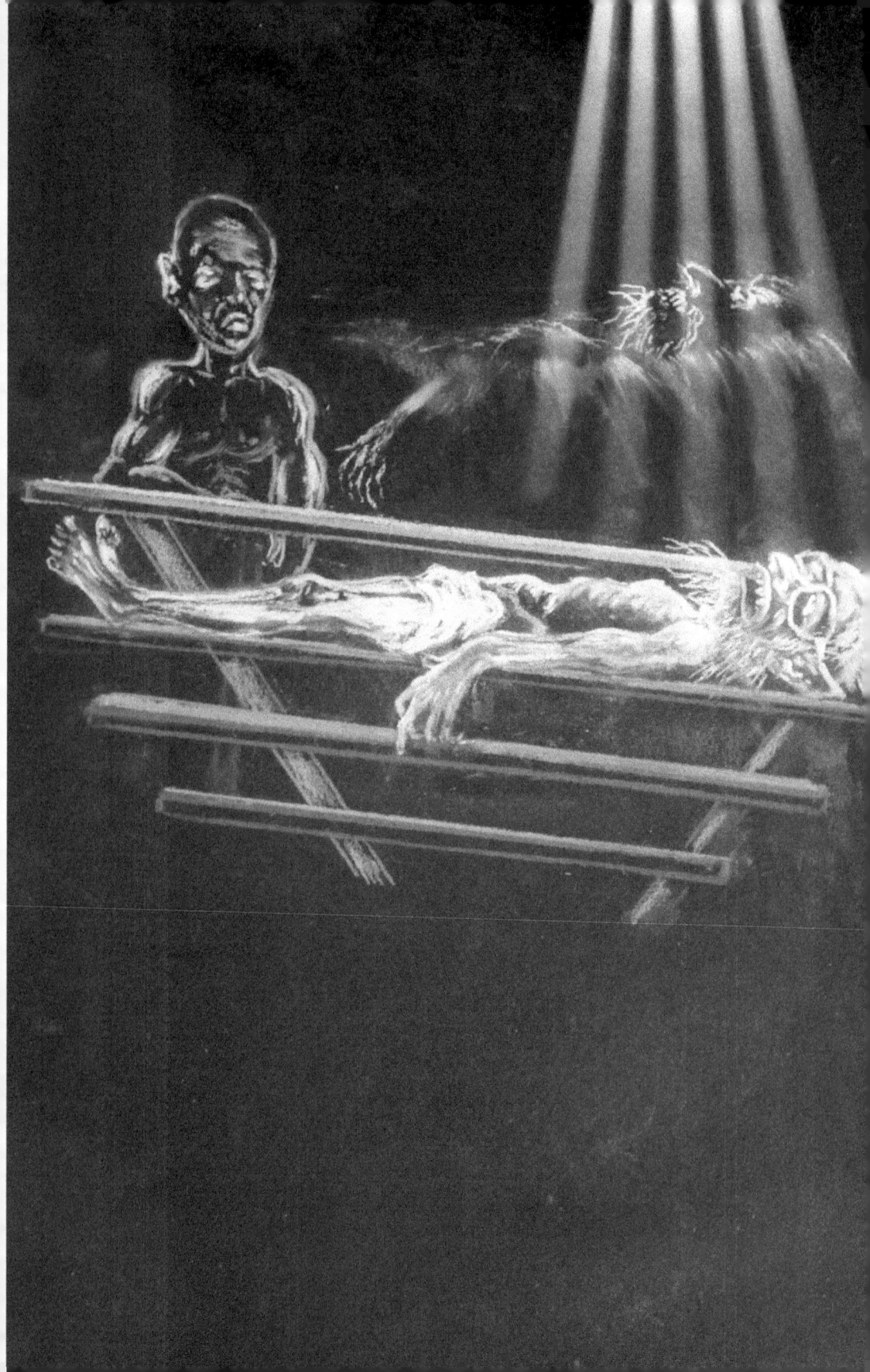

The temperature has plunged into cool, hard and mean – cut, peel...open up the spleen. He's now lying full length on the stairs, in a cadaverous spasm, skinny as hell... like Holbein's scarifying portrait of no hope, Criste Morte! But! With the head of Grotowski screwed on! In a reversal of the Holbein, the Grot's head is on the right and he's jabbing the bony, scaly second finger of his left hand onto the stair below. The effect is super spooky 'cos my devil knows that I know the Holbein pic. What's he going to tell me?
Each word blows away wisps of the dank, lank hair that always fell across Grotowski's later face:

"I'm bored and you've been too, too cordial! Let's cast around some discordancy. A transgressive essay that will prick a pap or two....apply no potions and rip a blister!"

"We are now walking the Way of the Migraine, and the next four provocs are lumpy indeed! Let's do the dance with the Grot's dead legacy."

Migraine Provocation #2
The Controvski over Grotowski

This is a short transgressive appreciation of Jerzy Grotowski (**The Grot**), written as a response to time spent in 2008 with the Grotowski Institute (**GI**) in Wroclaw and Brzezinka, Poland. This document is as transgressive as the Grot was, reflecting his dialectic of apotheosis and derision - probably the coolest tool he contrived.

My time there with his legacy amounted to three weeks, during which I had the opportunity to see several DVDs of his productions as well as a few more home movies. Later we observed a top drawer 10 day workshop run by the director of the Institute, Grzegorz Ziolkowski. Grzegorz is a Grot Swot, and if I am not mistaken these ateliers are designed to spread the Grot's hip and penetrating dramaturgy world wide.

The **GI** is devoted to sponsoring the research into the various aspects of the man's work as well as support gigs by some small companies that have taken up the traces of his legacy. At the moment these small groups are **Teatr Zar** based in Wroclaw and **Maisterne Pisne**, based in Lvov, Ukraine. The **GI** is not to be confused with The Grot's designated heir, Thomas Richards, who is to be found holed up in Pontedera, Italy, working on arcane actions. The **GI** does support Richards, although the relationship is somewhat testy as Richards is very preciously trying to keep the 'museum' virgo intacta. There are also other groups beetling away in Europe and the USA claiming that they are The Way of The Truth of The Grot, and word of mouth indicates that they are equally pretentious about their take on his legacy. And whenever they show some sort of result from their hermetic endeavours, it turns out to be very underwhelming - the emperor has no undies!

I have read about The Grot and recently had this concentrated period with his legacy, which doesn't necessarily qualify me for critiquing the game plan, but I am going to, notwithstanding,

because:
- I bring to the commentary box extensive acquaintance with Tadashi Suzuki, who is, in many ways, an eastern equivalent. Time with Suzuki has given me some clues with which to judge the game of The Grot.
- My other knowledge point is that I have considerable ken of the major dance techniques and their cultural history. I have used this know-how to dissect and articulate many of the aspects of Suzuki's work and this gives me the ammo with which to judge the veracity of The Grot's systems and their applications.

Grot's history can be separated into two main periods: early hipster Blues Brothers when he did his true theatre productions and the Beardy Wierdy hippy days when he divorced his company, morphed into a 70s tree-changer, bought the Erhard/Leary line and became mired in esoteric post theatrical mumbo jumbo.

The second period is usually broken into another 3 sub phases, but it's more pertinent to see them as a continuous drift off further with the fairies in the forest. But later on I will mention aspects of the first of these sub-phases, **Para-Theatre**, to show how inane you become if you believe your own PR and took yourself too seriously in the silly seventies.

The second and third phases became more progressively private and are called The **Theatre of Sources** and **Active Culture** - even more pretentious titles, whose putative claims are shredded once you see the pics, which look ever so earnest. (I might add at this point that I have earnt the leisure to lampoon this era, as I myself was doing similarly stupid stunts in Adelaide, Australia in the early Seventies – bounding around in brightly coloured but illfitting unitards to 'Earth' music. I know from whence I laugheth, because I know to whence it goeth – nowhere!)

The Theatre period:
It was very interesting being in Wroclaw checking out the videos

because the stuff that broke him internationally still looks really wicked, even on a crappy old video. The show in question is **The Constant Prince**, and one can easily see that the dramaturgy and the acting would have been a revelation to a bourgeois west. It would have been the first time in a long while that the West saw a show that wasn't another re-enactment in a faux-real setting by a disparate bunch of luvvies who preciously emote.

The Big Diffs that Grot and his band brought were:
- a. Mise-en-scene...he set the show in a cell with the audience watching down from over a ledge.
- b. Rather than do the whole play with all its padding, he extracted the themes he wanted to engage, and even added other dialogue which could add nuances of meaning.
- c. The band was a real team that had 'trained' and built their skills together as a pre-rehearsal process even before the show's development started.
- d. The performances had a **moral imperative** - the actors were working their rings off - they were 'sacrificing' themselves to the act.
- e. The actors' movements and voices weren't neat and bourgeoise - putting on an act with sham tears and gags. These actors really went for the doctor – gung ho, every show, every night.
- f. The main man (Ryczard Cieslak) was a St Sebastian figure, a sacrificial lamb whose inner transformation could make a man weep.

Crucial Factors:
From seeing the videos, reading the lines, and then reading in between the lines the separate factors that pulled it all together were:

1. He got the nod to put a small company together in a tiny little theatre in a dirty, dreary, regional mining town (Opole) in a commie country. Being tiny meant that

nobody cared too much. Being a country posting off the radar meant that the sexy actors weren't interested and a more committed artistically ambitious bunch was attracted. Being a dirty and dreary dump meant that life outside was so awful, that staying inside and rehearsing was a no-brainer. Being a communist country meant that everybody was getting paid as much as any other Pole prole and you didn't have to make a profit. But you did have to know how to talk the 'Comradespeak' and surf your way round the deadly shoals of the scary politics in the right way at the right time - which could be really tricky.
2. Poland, although communistic, was and is, a VERY religious country, and The Grot is an extension of this, being imbued with a densely spiritual attitude by his mom from a very young age. Later he read too much of his own gospel and tipped over the edge and morphed into an empty messiah. (I've got a tale to tell in a sec.)
3. Poland has a very classy theatre history dating from the mid 19th C with lots of cleva fellas all down the line. There was even a hip theatre ensemble called Reduta in the 20s/30s that provided a template and prefigured the Grot's Lab.
4. The Grot had a keen spiritual assistant in displaced Italian, Eugenio Barba (EB), a self confessed wide-eye, who put the Grot on the international map. Without Barba's preaching and bus driving, Grot would have remained unknown in the west, let alone hit the bigtime. There is a crucial episode in the saga that concerns Barba borrowing a mate's bus and hijacking an international theatre conference in Warsaw by snatching a bunch of influential delegates and zooming them off to a distant, unsanctioned Grot show. The visiting VIP's were gobsmacked by the demo and instant world fame followed pretty damn fast. Barba was the internationally mobile proselytizer - John the Baptist to Grot's JC.

Bringing up the name of our Lord also conjures up this telling anecdote told to us by Stephen Champion, an Aussie mate who went to work fulltime with Zibignew Zyncutis (ZZ) in the mid 80s. (Zyncutis was one of the original merry band who tried to keep the flame alive after the Grot left the building) Some little time after Stephen joined Zyncutis (in 1987?), ZZ carked in a car prang (some say suicidally-more of which later!) sinking the plan.

ZZ's tale goes something like this: Apparently, one day at work, the Grot asks the band: "Should I tell the world outside that I am Jesus Christ?" The band as one, looked at their toes, shuffled their feet, umm-ed and arr-ed, before suggesting that…. It was…er…maybe…. not…..err….. such a good idea!
It may have been a gag, but surely a tad predictive in the light of what happened later.

5. The Grot had a cluey Dramaturg, Ludwig Flaszen, and a handy designer Jerzy Guralsky. Flaschen actually got the Grot the artistic director job in Opole and acted as a devil's advocate, pressing buttons and prodding weak spots with sardonic wit. One could probably describe Flaschen as the Brain-iac behind Grotowski's soul. Guralsky was very quiet and very useful, especially in the early days, and he may have been the guy who thought up the 'setting' smarts.
6. Being soviet style there was tight censorship, but only at the dress rehearsal, so they were free to muck around and do whatever they liked, until the big day. Grot maintained this was KEY. That's not to say that life was easy! The whole game could be tricky and scary, though not as bad as Uncle Joe Stalin, who could end a chat with a bullet or a billet in the gulag. You had to be mighty quick on your feet and learn to pick the new shifts depending on which way the latest political wind was blowing.
7. Grot's elder brother became a Nuclear Physicist (didn't his mum do well to produce two such bright sparks on her own-some? Dad joined the free Polish

army, and after the war refused to come back while Poland was Commie!) and that may have given Grot clues re: theatre as labwork - it's also maybe the reason he was so shtumm in the anti-commie riots – big bro may have been delicately placed, possibly working on an A-bomb for the Russkies.
8. If you see footage of Cieslak going through his training schtick, or Thomas Richards and the Pontedera crew, the boys are all bounding around in their extra skinny speedos – the gals in all-over unitards.... Hullo Sailor!.... What does that say that nobody wants to talk about? That maybe Grot was a homoxual, although apparently the non practicing sort? And, if one checks out Cieslak's lap-lap as St Sebastian/JC in the Constant Prince, the sense of homo-erotica starts to stick out like the proverbial dog's genoculars.... Maybe Grot was never very active sexually, which means that the unconsummated energy morphed into transgressive spiritual éclat (something similar happened with Hitchcock whose unrequited voyeuristic impulses made ice-cold babes like Grace Kelly super sexy).
9. Apparently most of the time Opole and Poland was freezing and they were pretty much starving all the time. In all the pics they sure are skinny! This along with all the other trials and tribs of surviving in post-war East Euro Marxism meant that it was a hard life. This instilled in them huge chunks of Moral Fibre, which in turn gave them discipline and focus. The theatre space became a refuge where Grotowski could anneal all these factors into a rare delicate aesthetic.

After the international success of the 'Prince', Grot took another 3 or 4 years to put his final show together. It is a masterpiece and after two false starts, emerged as **Apocalypsis Cum Figuris**. A very good title for what was effectively an illustrated 5th gospel. To make this work it is recorded that he changed his working process. Prior to this his interdiction was one of relentless interpenetration – he was right there, inside the work with them, much like George Martin, the 5th Beatle. For **ACF** it morphed into an entirely passive response of saying a series of 'dos and don'ts'. He would sit in a corner saying one of four things: "I don't understand / I understand / I believe / I don't believe". This gnomic attitude of stony monosyllabic reticence made the actors work very hard at convincing him and at one stage he didn't even step inside the theatre for 2 whole months! This drove the actors spare and eventually they dragged him back in and made him face his job description. (It must have been bizarre being back in crummy old Poland after all the Western adulation in Paris, London and NY).

My sense is that after **The Constant Prince**, he felt under a lot of pressure to come up with something better; hence the blue funk. It was worth the wait though, because **ACF** toured the world very successfully for the next 11 years. It cemented his reputation and is such a key piece that even now it is the last word on western theatre as spiritual metamorphosis. It is classic like *Oedipus* or *Noh Theatre* because everything has been ablated or reduced to its essence, with minimal props, setting, lighting and dialogue.

Key Theatre Legacies:
Thus endeth his theatrical period. The key legacies from The Grot's theatre work as far as I can figure would be:
1. Return of theatre to spiritual event.
2. Let's have a real setting e.g. an asylum,
3. Actors who say what they mean and mean what they say and have the bodies to match it,
4. Writers are not sacred or infallible like the Pope and that there's going to be some dross that's worth dropping off and replacing with other texts more apposite. And it is this **other** information that can reveal deeper insights that lie dormant inside the original.
5. Transgressive acts: An early critic, one Kudlinski, who had watched G's work on the up and up, pinned it down in 1961 as a dialectic of '**apotheosis and**

derision'. The Grot turned these words into a manifesto, engineering a killer tool to shunt and shock the play (and by extension the audience) into abruptly facing itself.
6. Grot stressed an approach that he called at one stage 'bodymemory'. This indicated searching for cultural templates that exist in the body as a result of archaic or archetypical forces that continue to resonate inside a society or culture. The companies I have seen recently in Wroclaw, if their shows are a guide, have used this legacy as a valuable kick off. **Zar** and **Pisne** chant ancient religious songs for inspiration. One night in Brzezinka it was brought home to me when I was present at a compelling discursive chat by Jaroslav Fret, the artistic director of **Teatr Zar**. From what he said, it seemed that he used 'mythic hymns' as a metaphysical search engine for finding new unconscious data.
7. Lots of more street-wise directors than Grot have done a 'David Bowie' to Grot's 'Iggy Pop'. They have seen the commercial potential and made big names for themselves by
 a. dividing it by five,
 b. hiring some sexy ethnic types who speak LOTE (Languages Other Than English),
 c. dredging up a politically correct multicultural myth
 d. avoiding any Christian bits like the plague
 e. then watching the critical acclaim accumulate.
8. He left behind old fashioned concepts such as 'Character Development', as belonging to an earlier era of neo-realism. It would seem that he felt such shibboleths merely continued a culture, rather than engaging it anew.

Grot the Commune Leader:
Now, if those are his legacies, he's done excellent well! So far so good, but what's the next step?

After getting Apocalypsis on, and letting the guys do it by

themselves (A Bad Sign! Never leave the kids alone!) Grot went for a couple of wanderings, one back to India, where he'd been before and which had been inspirational in the past. And another across the USA on Route 66 straight to the heart of trendy Californian Counterculture. He went away a hipster and came back a hippie. Prior to this he had dressed in black suit and tie, white shirt, sunnies after dark, and liked to have himself filmed looking sharp, shady and inscrutable. Now he shuffles back into town vegan skinny, scraggly hair and beard, denim and sandals, carrying an off the shoulder fag bag. It was such an image shift that when he touched down in Bogota for a theatre conference in Colombia, many truly took him for a fake.

He dropped a bombshell by stating publicly that he would no longer make any shows and would devote himself to performance 'research'. Not only would this have been a huge shock for the arty world which wanted more of the same, thank you very much, but imagine the plight of the actors who had committed themselves to the Grot lock, stock and barrel? Now he was divorcing the very actors that made him as much as he made them, and leaving them to fend for themselves, scratching around for meaning like orphans in mourning - Bummer!!!! Some tagged along for a while with the Grot through his hippy workshops, while a few topped themselves when they realized that future play was to be wide and shallow, not deep as before. The team captain, Cieslak, slowly drank and smoked himself to death. The USA Grot Swot, Richard Schechner, recounts a dolorous tale of chatting to him as they watched the 9,500 (Yesssssss! 9,500!) gullible ferals cavorting ineffectually in the grass outside Wroclaw in the peak **Paratheatre** event of 1975. In response to a 'What are you going to do next?' type query, Cieslak turned his lugubrious brown eyes to Schechner and said something along the lines of "I hitched myself to the Grot for better or for worse". .....What remained tacit was: "It's a lot worse, but I can't back out now"

The Grot's dissing of his actors was a brutal act, fakely and feyly disguised as a 'need to be free'. It was monumentally self-serving, and typically emblematic of the indulgent seventies.

Many people felt then they had the right to break free from their responsibilities and do their own 'thing'. Imagine creating some of the most magnificent actors the world has ever seen..... then make them fart around with the tattooed and toothless, behaving with deceptive cruelty to the true believers, sacrificing them to the altar of his own myth. No wonder G's Karma never recovered! It's much less cruel to do what the other hard cases of the theatre do - make it so that your actors leave you – their decision! It sounds more brutal but it means that they take a part of you with them. When you leave them, as the Grot did, conversely you steal part of them forever.

Why the big existential shift? My take is that he was so freaked out by the success of **Apocalypsis**; it was such a killer testament that he could never surpass. Better to take his wand and go walkabout in the wilderness. There's nothing like fading to black on a big note to make people feel they are missing you already. When he divorced the Lab they lost themselves and that implacable act made him into a myth.

That was Grot theatre: now Grot the Guru, Space Cadet:
On his meanderings along Route 66 into the delusional clouds of 70s counterculture, he turned himself into Grot the Guru, buying heavily into the politic of nature worship. My thinking is that when he jawed with the likes of Carlos Castenada, Timothy Leary and the Gestalt Therapy crew he swallowed the 'no rules, no barriers' story, hook line and sinker and, seeing himself as a Messiah, proclaimed: "I'm going to do an open plan learning of my own and call it BEYOND THEATRE". He first kicked off with a scheme called **Paratheatre**, where thousands of people used to gather in fields frisking and frolicking, doing creative movement. These weren't actors per se, but wigged out hippies, mega-confused by the evaporation of flower power, and this was Grot's big chance to become messiah to the masses with dumbed down theatre as the Gospel. Of course the results, like most events in the 70s, were pretty dire and about as interesting as watching your sandals for six hours.

A few salient observations concerning **Paratheatre**:
1. Beaded, bearded pacifist commune-itis was very much a world wide epidemic in the early 70s. Australia had its versions too, and as I said before, I was at a few of them where temporary university arts festivals became live in communes where anti-establishment, anti-commerce, anti-nuclear family became the buzz and disaffected youth of OZ went to Nimbin to go feral and grow their own in 'non-structured' symbiosis with the earth. Smoking dried banana skins morphed into shooting smack... Goodbye paradise....Hello squalor....The Grot got sucked in too!

2. This philosophy of every body being equal and 'no hierarchy or elitism' meant that you had Eagles dancing with Chickens. Highly tuned and skilled artists such as Cieslak were forced to share space with unco bozos. Is this not like tennis great Roger Federer playing doubles with partially talented wannabes in the 'burbs? This is neither interesting, explorative or fair - its just plain dumb! And.... who wants to watch it? The real reason for making the experts such as Cieslak, Flaszen et al. move to the back of the line with the plebs was to make sure The Grot reigned supreme and alone at the top of the pole. More than a touch of Orwell's **Animal Farm** here: "Everybody's equal, but I'm more equal". (Funnily enough, hippie communes like this tend to throw up the same dictators as Communism).

3. Here is a quote from one Kolankiewicz dude about the Grot's paratheatre work in 74/75: 'I stand face to face with a tree. It is strong - I can climb it, support myself delicately on its branches. On its crown, a strong wind blows us both, on the tree and myself. With my whole body I feel the movements of branches, the circulation of fluids. I hear the inner murmurs. I nestle into the trees......'

Oh, Pu-lease!!!! Such self-important gibberish as you have ever heard......! Now, don't get me wrong, I'm a tree hugger myself, but I don't think such tree games are of intergalactic import. The wind, I hate to tell him, blows on all of us. Lots of ordinary guys and gals do it without writing an opera - it's called 'going camping'.

4.   More from Kolanks..... 'On some nights, we go, several of us, to the woods. We walk without any light. – I feel the quiet breath of the trees. We gather by the thick of the woods opening to receive us. The forest plunged into darkness lives in a different way than in daytime.....'

Oh! Really!! How Illuminating! Such tragic wishful symbiosis is made the more ludicrous when one realizes that other animals are silent and at one with the forest only because they are trying to **Kill** and **Eat** other furry little fauna.

5.   For guys that wanted to be so at one with the air and the trees, they were keen...one could say industrial strength, smokers!!!

6.   It peaked in 1975 with a giant be-in, where 9500 hopeful believers lobbed up from 26 countries, to undergo all sorts of workshops called very caringly, **Beehives**. It became a <u>giant show bag of the shallow soul</u> where the Roller-Coaster was replaced by Group Therapy, Meditation and Massage. Lots of luminaries like Peter Brook and J. L. Barrault turned up for the love-in, adding serious clout, climbing on board and making suitably clucky noises. But they found that unlike Grot's theatre phase, this time there wasn't much to purloin.

Journalists were allowed to be at the seminars but were excluded from the workshops. This was done nominally so as they couldn't contaminate proceedings by being judgmental but, in reality, so that they couldn't witness the waffle-dust.

The outcome of this self-important extravaganza had the long term impact of a burp in Bermuda! It disappeared down the sink with all the other 70s twaddle.

A few years of this and he was canny enough to figure this was going nowhere fast, and what's worse, outsiders could see too easily that there were no undies on the emperor. Thinks: "To maintain Guru status the smart move is to say I'm going further and deeper than any man has done before, shrink the numbers, and close the doors so the un-converted can't make harsh, uncaring judgements. You have to be a paid up member of the club that won't let you in unless you're a true believer". By pulling this stunt, the Grot can keep top spot because no-one knows enough to say, 'Hold the phone, Tyrone!'

So, in the last 19 years of his life, as he spun further out into deeper space, he had to become more precious and private. I can hear some say, maybe it has value; and some fellow space cadets will even buy the notion, but surely the analogy would be a tennis player who never plays a game but practices so.o.o.o.o well. Here he is, banging a ball against a wall every day, but is never tested, and never witnessed being tested. Surely he isn't a tennis player until his 'special talent' is measured as to how it affects other tennis players (try playing a game) and the crowd?

Holes in the system Let's cut through the charisma to dig some dirt.......

1) .There is a culture of denial surrounding Grot theatre's 'spirituality'. This is more than an unstated neutral it's double denial - his theatre was more than spiritual; it was downright religious, both in what they talked about and the way they did it. Both **'Apocalypsis'** and **'Prince'** were modern morality plays and if you put a Jesus Beard on Cieslak in both gigs, you're on the right track. But in the 60s, as now, the idea of God was submarxian heresy and you couldn't say you were religious in anything approaching a Christian sense – that would have been the kiss of death. So you had to rewrap the goodies, and brand them under Hindu or Zen. Witness the book; **Towards a Poor Theatre**. Should've been called 'Towards a Spiritual Theatre', but that would have been a No No in the slippery 70s

2) The spectacular irony was that the shows were a revelation precisely because they were religion repackaged! This was religious theatre for the 'devout agnostic'. It says so much about the climate of that time which continues through to the present. Under sub Marxian academia mention of things religious is still an unacceptable heterodoxy.
3) Grot wasn't really connected with his training. He was a brainiac, not a bodiac. Grotwork is not a training but a combo of spiritual interdiction and smart reductive dramaturgy. That it is an approach and not a training becomes obvious when you check out the video footage of Cieslak trying to teach the schtick to a couple of eager beaver Scandos. If anything it should really be called **Cieslak Warm-up Style**. As you watch the Scandos loping about behind Cieslak, it also becomes apparent that he's not a teacher- he can't pass his skills on. He was instinctively too good at it, to consciously know what he was doing. In no way is it a System in itself.
4) Due to the fact that there is no real methodology to hand down, the boys from Pontedera (Workcentre, Italy) and Akron (USA) have got nowhere to go. Grot has sold them a dramaturgical approach packaged as a method and if he's not there to run it, the results get precious and pedestrian. I don't know much about the Akron-ites though the goss is that their recent work is very 'how's-your-father'. What I do know is that if you spy the pics of the Pontedera Boys in their jockettes they look ever so much like a trio of part-time male models doing a 60s Lester Horton dance class.

The acid test is that if they actually performed and were any

good, we would have heard it through the grapevine. Instead, if you ask anybody who has seen them in the flesh, you get the shuffling of feet and mumbles....er.... well.... actually.... it's sort of interesting....
If that ain't damning with faint praise, what is?

The best test for any great theatre is the truckie's test. If you can get a bunch of truck drivers to watch your stuff, what's their reaction to be? If they say: 'Bunch of wankers!' Then it's all in your head, thespie-nerd! If they say: 'Shi-i-it, that's intense! Weird stuff, man, but they sure work hard.' Then you know it's a happening thing.

As I wind up, I'd like to comment on aspects of The Grot's deep interest in archaic or primitive customs used as tools in his **Theatre of Sources** phase. One of them was his long term infatuation with Haitian Voodoo.

Part of his 'Let's be caring in private' scheme is the desire to get back to nature and to hanker for an arcadian past where everybody lives a simple honest life, inside a perpetual 'nice' climate. While this is laudable in a notional sense, remember that people who actually live like that have pretty dracky lives and mostly die of some dreadful disease that the west has eradicated by inventing medicines that are only possible because they have been tested on nice furry animals that we should be kind to. Ergo, the locals are keen to get out of this 'natural state' Pretty Damn Quick!

Such a desire of return to nature is quite possible in our wealthy, comfortable western society for only one reason - we can afford to have such atavistic wishes because we don't have to live with them! People who have to scratch out a living in primitive, Arcadian societies are desperate to get a picket fence, a two car garage and air-con, ASAP! Witness Haiti where the transformational and transgressive voodoo comes from. While Voodoo is a good map of the other side of the soul, remember this is a country that's totally dysfunctional, giving rise to the psychedelic barbarism of the Papa and Baby Doc's. Here is a place where you'll see kids eating bits of dogs on the street - an Arcadian paradise - NOT. And Voodoo is a very big part of the whole culture, and a big part of what's holding them back.

Effete softies such as the Grot, love playing games like Voodoo, because it allows them the thrilling frisson of dangerous liaisons, as long as they don't have to do the long term wade through the daily squalor. So, after a few days with the Voodoo Queen, sitting on the dirt in Haiti looking dutiful, Grot takes them back to his place, which is like .... Really Nice. But of course now that the culture has been uprooted it must be treated much more preciously, because it only thrives in a dump, etc. Hence, the sacred attitude, the admonitions: the songs must be sung a certain way, they must not be sung without the Queen Bee, they must not be sung outside the space, they must not be copied... Ooooh!...... Freakout! To be 'Only sung truthfully with full sincerity from the heart,' etc. etc.

The spectacular irony is that back home the 'sacred' ceremony is a mad woman's breakfast of clattering pans, garish plastic tablecloths, chooks scratching in the dirt and wailing kids wiping the flies off their snot.... neither Sacred nor Profane – a Rabble!

This becomes crystal when one buys a CD of true Voodoo music. It's ...er... boring. It's much more exciting to listen to music inspired by Voodoo, e.g. Miles Davis or Perez Prado, whose Voodoo Suite is a lot more dangerous and transgressive. And check this out! After all these admonishments about purity, eventually the Voodoo Queen decamped, not back home to the shit and squalor, but to a nice civilized spot like the south of France. For her Voodoo was a handy little ticket to the good life! And guess what, the boys in speedos still sing the 'sacred' songs reverently and in the correct place long after the pure, original, genuine, sincere source has bolted, migrated from Haiti and taken up residence in the nice, clean, orderly French Riviera! ....Sheeeet!!!!!

So, from where I stand in the commentary box, if I had to give

marks to Citizen Grot for all he's done:
The Theatre of Productions: 9 out of 10, top of the class and an Elephant stamp.
For Para-Theatre, Theatre of Sources, Art as Vehicle, At work with The Grot on Physical Actions: a snowball's chance in summer.

End of transmission……………………………

This devil's horns now nestled in an unruly fifties flickover, a quizzical eyebrow cocked and locked and comical; back out, bum up and boxing gloves as feisty as can be:

"What sacrilege am I hearing? What sacred cow have you just taunted and T-boned?
Sell my horse I'm going back to Hell!!! What more have you got, pray Boy, to tell?"

"I gave you the drum on a dramaturg, now for a violent review of the divine right of the writer...."

Migraine Provocation #3
True and False and True....but how!
A Critical Supplement to David Mamet's 'True and False'

I read this book in 2008, and decided to critique certain sections I find contentious. DM is a successful and prolific writer and director for stage and screen, and is known as being feisty and opinionated, which might mean that he is a talented creep. I was interested to read what this Cantankerous Chicagoan Pedagogue might think.

Talk the Talk, but where's the walk?
There are many very good points and observations inside, but the book as a whole manifests a typical Western Theatre director's 'admonition with no back up' - namely: Talk the Talk, but where's the walk? One of our actors, Conan Dunning, once recounted such a scenario. He had a director say to him" You have to be more grounded!" Conan is standing in the middle of the room, deflated...sad eyed and arms slack by his sides, saying nought....but with a big question hanging in the space above his head: "And...... How do I go about being 'more grounded'? Can I pick it up in a shop like a new gearbox?" Of course, the director wanders off, very pleased with himself to have been so perceptive....The actor languishes tout seul, looking and feeling dopey.

Such fatuous admonitions fill the landscape of western theatre, and are facile and meaningless because they offer no bridging solution. This book is full of them.

Scripta Immaculata?
As well there is the obsession with the divine and immaculate truth of the writer. Scattered throughout are constant allusions to the text being some sort of sacred object, all dots and commas sacrosanct as they convey absolute knowledge.
There is another angle entirely, and I was triggered to think thusly, after Jacqui and I had taken a visiting German actress to a local Brisbane production of a lesser known Shakespeare. Her

A Devil Pokes the Actor

name was Antje Diedrich, and she was studying with us for a few months. Being Teutonic she was thorough and respectful of Shakespeare rather than cowed into literary submission. The play was King John and it had the usual clunks and gaps of an amateur production. I've seen worse, but it'd best be described as dutiful and artless. Afterwards I asked her what she thought, and she replied: "But they're just doing the play, they're not engaging it in any way!" I remember thinking at the time that that was pertinent thinking and well put.

Of course, at any one time, in your fair city, there is any number of companies, both Pro and Am doing the play, and like weeds, you can barely stop 'em. But! They are not talking to NOW. They are talking a then conversation, by way of Olivier, all the way back to the 19th C to Kean and Irving. If you want to talk to NOW, you have to interrogate the play, not pay it simplistic obeisance.

One does not need to slavishly reproduce the script as immutable, because the script already exists as a permanent document, and may be read as such, anywhere...... anytime. What a performance of the text does, due to the transient nature of live theatre, is place it in the immediate moment; the physical present. For that reason it must be provoked, interrogated, dismembered and defiled. It is only when such forensic transgressions have been performed on it, does it have the chance to become a great and lasting offering

All the weaknesses of analysis in the book result from this too, too conscious intellectual obsession with the rational faculties of a dramatic property, with very little grasp of the importance of the mysterious, shamanic, unconscious, unspoken energies that the human body brings to the text.

Reading books such as this make one realise that conventional western theatre practice still languishes in a Poetical Post-Shakespeare Prison. Any experience of the vibrant transformative work done outside the English language, shows that the adoration of the text is the genuine problem.

This pervasive rational formalism, rooted in the intellectual primacy of the text, has also meant that western institutions consider actor preparation as essentially attitudinal, and what passes for training is vacuous and deceptive, based on nostrums of puerile emotional and psychological mush.

I sent a hard copy of this to DM in mid 2008 via his agent for reasons of politesse and hoping for possible dialogue. To date, for whatever reason, I have received no response......

My responses are in **bold Italics**

TRUE and FALSE BUT HOW!

To the Actor
P3: I studied acting in various schools, and could understand little of what was being said. ... I knew that the goal was to bring an immediacy to the performance....but none of us understood, nor did practice reveal...how the school's exercises were to bring that about.
True! *He's 'lost' inside the confusion of the exercises. Although the institution makes him feel that way, it wasn't DM who lacked Clarity, Focus and Structure, but the exercises themselves that lacked C, F and S.*

Some Thoughts
P5: As actors, we spend most of our time nauseated, confused and guilty. We are lost and ashamed of it; confused because we don't know what to do and we have too much information, none of which can be acted upon ***(because information is not knowledge)***; and guilty because we feel we are not doing our job well enough... The good we do seems to be through chance: if only that agent would notice me, etc, etc.
True but How! *The answer to this comes in two parts.*
***1. It is because the whole scene is based on chance, both short and long term, that 'things will fall into place if I get a good break'. It's much like buying a lottery ticket and hoping you'll win the lottery - somebody will, but it's*

improbable that it'll be you. To take control over your situation (as much as one can), the question becomes: ' what am I doing to minimize the effects of chance?' Essentially all actors are in competition with their peers, and there is a lot of competition out there, and increasing all the time. If I'm doing the same things as my peers the chances are the same things will happen to me. Therefore, how am I preparing myself culturally, aesthetically and politically for all the challenges I will face? And it requires a lot more than just positive thinking- it requires implementation!
2. The existential confusion of most actors occurs because they are almost totally unprepared for the rigours of performance. While a lot of attention is paid to 'creative' approaches, almost no effort is expended on how these should be supported against the pressures a performance places on an actor, the instinctive "in the moment' responses, that are expected can only be fostered by the acquisition of undeniable skills and the confidence that goes with it. In any other discipline, it is acquired through training. The most important elements of training are: repetition, routines, formats and tools.
And since most acting approaches encourage actors to be terrified of all four as being stultifying and uncreative, they are automatically prevented from being prepared. Of course it doesn't dawn on the acting teachers that athletes and musicians are creative precisely because of their 'uncreative' routines. But that would be against their tenet of the sanctity of Actor Confusion, wouldn't it?

P6: The Stanislavsky 'method', and the technique of the schools derived from it, is nonsense.
<u>*True!*</u> *The so called Stanislavski 'method' is more an approach than a method. It looks at the creative aspects of acting without addressing how to methodically and practically gain the necessary skills.*

Actors used to be buried at a crossroads with a stake through

the heart. Those people's performances so troubled the onlookers that they feared their ghosts.
True! Actors used to be shamans – they used to summon up and confront the audience with its own shadows. Modern technology has flattened out real life experiences, and with it, expectations. Real shamans used to froth at the mouth, working themselves up, to not pretend to be the character, but to become the thing itself. The modern actor, much weaker in spirit, has devolved into performing the illusion of doing so. A surreptitious tear, a cracking voice are the civilized theatre's versions of such transformations. (This is a paraphrasing of a section from Martin Buzacott's 'The Death of the Actor')
This the only time Mamet's book touches on this magical potential of performance, and there is no attempt to decode and explore what is the real import.

Ancestor Worship
P9: The actor is onstage to communicate the play to the audience.
False! The actor is onstage to engage with the play in visceral, prismatic terms to 'real'-ise the play, that is, to take the words off the page and give them sculptural value so that they can be felt or experienced by the audience in a way much more powerful than just heard or read (which they can do home on their own!).

P10: Eisenstein wrote that the true power of film came from the synthesis **in the mind of the viewer** of shot A and shot B. Shot A: a judge clearing his throat. Shot B: a woman raising her head from a desk – the audience creates the idea: 'hearing the verdict'.
True! Referring to the synthesis in terms of the unconscious or instinctive, could one say that the audience creates their own 'experience' of hearing the verdict.

Similarly, it is the juxtaposition in the mind of the audience between the spoken word of the author and the simple directed-but-uninflected action of the actor which creates the ineluctable

A Devil Pokes the Actor

idea of character in the mind of the audience.
Half True! **The character also needs to be sited within an aesthetic landscape provided by the designer/director. This places the character in visual, sculptural and thematic relief, the combination of which adds nuance and depth, to complete a picture initiated by the text.**

P11: The actor on the stage, looking to create a 'state' in himself can think only one of two things:
1. I have not reached the required state yet..... or
2. I have reached the required state, how proficient I am! At which point the (**conscious**) mind, ever jealous of its prerogatives, will reduce the actor to number1.
True but How! **Neither of which are (in the moment), and that is because his ego is dominating his experiences and his feelings. All performers have and need Ego, for it is the Ego that strives for self discovery (the search that drives all artists). But, paradoxically, it is the Ego that also stands in the way of self-discovery, and an actor needs to corral his Ego, in order to progress. Easy to say...... Much harder to do.......**

P13: On the stage it is the progress of the outward-directed actor, who behaves with no regard to his personal state, but with all regard to the responses to his antagonists, which thrills the viewers.
False! **Surely, as well, the actor must be aware and react to the effect the others are having on him, as the viewers are primarily identifying with his feelings.**

P14: Similarly, on stage, the Great Actor, capable of bringing herself to tears, may extort our admiration for her 'accomplishment', but she will never leave us stronger.
True! **One of Tadashi Suzuki's well known observations are the comments he made following a viewing of a Broadway production of Chekhov's Three Sisters. He observed that at the close of the play the three sisters were able to cry on cue. He then noticed that the audience were impressed by**

the skill but noted that, rather than saying to themselves 'how impressive it is that they can cry on cue' the audience should have been crying in reaction to what was happening on stage. If that happened, then the actors would have communicated the 'sadness' of the play to the audience. As it was, the spectators were impressed but not moved.

P15:......but I suggest that they, the accomplished actors, young, vital, talented and hearty, succeed at the Actor's Studio and elsewhere, **in spite of** their training.
<u>**True but How!**</u> *A good point can be made that they are 'instinctively' talented, which begs the question: Can their abilities and exploits be approximated by some form of training? Also are there structured exercises that can take the 'non-genius actor' to a similar zone?*

<u>**A generation that would like to stay in school**</u>
P19: The audience will teach you how to act and the audience will teach you how to write and direct.
<u>**False!**</u> *The audience signs off on the completed production! It finalizes the process. Why not go past supposedly pithy but one dimensional didacticism to pluralistic interdependency - the audience is a witness and by extension, a vicarious participant.*

P20: The Method School would teach the actor to prepare a moment......
<u>**True!**</u> *It's absurd to even consider that one can prepare an <u>instinctive moment</u>. It is possible (and necessary) to prepare <u>FOR</u> an instinctive moment.*

P21: If the actor had simply opened his mouth on cue and spoken (even though he felt uncertain) the audience would have been treated to the truth of the moment........
<u>**False!**</u> *Easy to say, but extremely difficult to do. Aside from the Olympian fiat, how does DM suggest that yon callow young actor goes about it? It actually requires what is known as a technique.*

A Devil Pokes the Actor

P22: .....It is beside the point to have the actor 'undergo' the supposed trials of the character upon the stage. The actor has his own trials to undergo and they are right in front of him they don't have to be super-added - they exist. His challenge is not to recapitulate, to pretend.
<u>*True!*</u> *To pretend is to impose one's ego (the '<u>I want</u>') on a given situation. An actor has to undergo transformative experiences (a la DM's dramatique 'stake thru the heart at the crossroads') but cannot do this convincingly if he is pretending.*

Scholarship
P23: That is the mis-judgement of the method: the notion that one can determine the effect one wants to have on the audience, and then study and supply said effect.... Preoccupation with effect is preoccupation with the self.
<u>*True!*</u> *For, if an actor works in that way, it is prescriptive, imposing one's Will on the action and the audience. This may impress the spectator with its machinations, but will not 'move' them. The audience will only be 'moved' by witnessing actors being affected by experiences. Thus, the actor can only achieve such a state instinctively, by reacting intuitively and honestly to a real emotional and psychological experience.*

Find your Mark
P28: ... and then, rather than pretending, we can **discover** whether or not we are courageous.
<u>*True-ish!*</u> *Acting, at its most exciting occurs when it is an act of self discovery, both for the audience and the actor. The audience is having its own self discovery by witnessing the self discovery of the actor. Brando was without equal at this. He was adamantly against memorising lines, so that he could be more immediate. The result was that you felt, watching him, that you were witnessing him do whatever he was doing..... for the very first time! The camera allowed you to be there, to witness its inception!!!!*

P30: The magic phrases (arc of the character) and procedures (subtextual analysis) are incantations to lessen the terror of going out there naked. But that's how the actor goes out there, like it or not.
***True but How!* These incantations are attempts to ward off nerves by pretending they do not exist. This of course backfires because I'ts a double deception. It's easy to say things like: "Don't be nervous". This is deceitful authority, because it pretends to solve the problem but merely turns it back on the actor. A real solution would lie in: "What do you give the actor to subvert the anxiety?"**

P31: Actors like to attribute their feelings as it gives them the illusion of control over them. They are trying to wish away the unexpected.....
***Very True!* The actor has to think these deceptive thoughts to compensate for an awful void that exists because the actor cannot feel 'in the moment'.**

So wisdom consists in this: do not attribute feelings, act on them before attributing them, before negotiating with them....
***True!* This is another way of encouraging the actor to act instinctively before the ego distorts the experience.**

P32: ....giving oneself up to the play...
***False!* It is more appropriate to say here: 'giving oneself up to the performance' because the play exists as an extant document, but the performance of the play only lives for the duration of time that it proceeds on stage. The audience can go and buy the play (as a book) any time- they can only 'buy' the performance in the fleeting moment while they are witnessing it.**

Business is business
P41: I've heard of young actors, feeling constrained, speak of 'stepping out'. They want to invent, to mold, to elaborate, to influence, etc.... to be in effect, anything but themselves.
***True!* These actors want to dominate the role, to impose their egos on the role, rather than have their inner 'self' (or**

soul) experience the role.

It takes great strength of character- which is formed over time and in frightening times.....
True! *Time and adversity. It was Proust who said: "There is no knowledge without pain"*

P42: To serve in the real theatre, one needs to be able to please the audience and the audience only.
False! *A more holistic approach would be that you please the entire performance, which includes the actors, director, writer and audience. They are all stakeholders at their different levels, with different expectations, but linked inside a common event.*

Auditions
P44: Producers are not interested in discovering the new. They want the old- and if they cannot have it they want its facsimile.
True! *If you want to be successful commercially, you take something very old and make it appear new by adding some slight superficial changes.*

P47: As a member of an audience, I will tell you, it is an insult to come backstage and say to a performer "You were great tonight", only to be told: "No, I was terrible ! You should have seen me last week!".
True! *The audience comes for their own experience, which is not the same, but is predicated on the actor's – to disagree with the compliments is to repudiate the experience.*

P48: I have watched long runs over the years.... Generally the "I'm garbage" and the "I'm brilliant" were the same.
True! *The actor, by definition, is inside the performance, and so cannot judge it objectively (he cannot know precisely what the audience is getting). The audience is a witness and vicarious participant, so as well, cannot judge objectively – they only know what they feel about it. The*

only person capable of any objectivity is the director, and therefore they are the authority of last resort.

The purpose of the performance is to communicate the play to the audience.
<u>Almost True!</u> The purpose of the performance is to give the 'voice' of the play a 'body'. Until it is performed live, a play is really a book - a series of words and literary images, figments of the author's imagination. As a book it is a form of private communication. Once performed, it becomes a public event, a communal experience, where the audience bonds through sharing a ritual.

Such an idea of a ritual requires visceral energies that have meaning that can be felt as transformational (two that come to mind are Uplifting and Thought-provoking). For something to be perceived as uplifting, the movements and gestures of the actors must add sense and weight to the written words. This sense and weight add a mythic quality to the words, making them appear larger than life, affecting the audience much more powerfully than if they had come out of a daily or domestic body language.

P50: I knew a man who went to Hollywood and languished jobless for a period of years. He came back and lamented "I would have been alright if they had only explained the rules". But who are 'they' and what are the rules? There is no 'they' and there are no rules.
<u>True but How!</u> In fact you have to make your own 'rules' by making your own culture. Your own culture means that you must invent and invoke your own standards. This would determine that your culture is INTRINSIC- it belongs to you. Most theatre culture is EXTRINSIC- it is governed by rules imposed from the outside. In my country (Australia) this takes either of two forms:
1. *Your politic aligns itself with government arts funding policy, or,*
2. *You have established a certain clientele, who are happy to keep coming in the door if you keep delivering the same*

aesthetic
Both of these are extrinsic forces acting upon you and make you susceptible: If political fashions change, you're left high and dry. If you change the product, the punters may melt away.

Paint by numbers
P52: The only reason to rehearse is to learn to perform the play.....It is not to 'investigate the life of the character'. There is no character. There are just lines on a page.
True but How!* *Any character on stage is mythic or mythical - they are not real.
They are a combination of:
1. ***the writer's imagination,***
2. ***the actor's portrayal,***
3. ***the director's attitude, and***
4. ***the audience's apprehension.***
Even if the character is based on somebody real (eg Julius Caesar), the actor cannot pretend to be Julius - he cannot play Julius. The Julius of the play is a myth, a construct. The actor can only 'play' aspects of himself that may identify or align with the 'essence' of Julius.

P53: The use to which a gambler puts his or her money is: 'time at the tables'. And the use to which an acting student puts his or her time, money and faith is 'time at the school'.
True!* *It is an end in itself! Fascinating insight! Perhaps that is why actors, once they have left school, feel no need to train or to hone their craft. They have done their time.

P55: Actors must be trained to speak well, easily, and distinctly, to move well and decisively, to stand relaxedly, to observe and act upon the simple, mechanical actions called for by the text.
False!* *Sounds like a deportment class at a Swiss finishing school! This may be true for a conventional play, such as the old sepia standards, where the production recycles Macbeth in different period costume and décor (What! Mussolini's Fascisti this time!) Get Olivier's film of same

and direct traffic accordingly. Because these are competent re-enactments, they only require blocking.
But, what about a truly transformational piece of theatre such as Tadeusz Kantor's: 'La Classe Mort'. Works such as LCM stand above standard fare just as John Lennon's 'Strawberry Fields Forever', stands above pop. Works such as LCM or SFF, make you forget you are watching theatre or listening to pop music- they have shamanically taken you to another place. They redefine the possibilities of the form and open up new possibilities. This reveals new aspects of the audience to itself, of which they were previously unaware.

Work

P56: the text, finally, shields the actor both from anxiety about his performance and from the necessity of paying attention to his colleagues while on stage.
<u>*False!*</u> *Incomplete! Please add:*
- *paying attention to the audience,*
- *paying attention to the other actors,*
- *paying attention to the set and props, and finally (and even more holistically)*
- *paying attention to the performance as an experience.*

P59: The Fourth Wall: There is not a wall between the actor and the audience. Such would defeat the very purpose of theatre, which is communication and communion. The idea of the fourth wall is a construction of someone afraid of the audience. The actor before the curtain………may have feelings of self-doubt, fear or panic.
<u>*True but How!*</u> *The erection of the 4th wall is the negative 'in denial' response to those feelings of self doubt and panic. For the very act of performing to a public is a challenge to one's sense of self. The audience is there to gain knowledge from the play, the performance and the actor. Because the actor is their main point of contact, they place a great demand on his psyche - you could say that they are consuming his psyche energy. This challenge to his*

psyche energy is stage fright pure and simple.

As an actor, every time that I face the audience's energy, I am confronted with the shock: "I don't know who I am anymore". With training and experience that feeling ablates, but I do feel it initially, especially on the first exposure in performance. Once I understood it to be an existential shock, the issue simply became: How to acquire enough sense of myself (what I would call self-definition) to withstand the shock and protect the 'psyche' from depletion.

Oral Interpretation
P62: You have to learn the lines, look at the script simply to find a simple action for each scene, and go out there and do your best to accomplish that action, and while you do, simply open your mouth and let the *words* come out however they will - as if they were gibberish - if you will.
False! *That is a noteworthy proposal, but surely a big demand to ask somebody brought up on a standard acting approach? It is as if you thrust a guitar into a neophyte's hands and then say: "Just improvise, even though you can't play any music, don't know any scales, arpeggios, etc" Everybody would understand the absurdity of such a situation within a musical context. Why is such a demand so accepted in the acting world? Mind you, DM hits pay dirt with the gibberish suggestion, which intimates that the non-literary content of acting has tremendous value.*

P63: The best service an actor can do is to accept the words as is, and speak them as simply and clearly in an attempt to get what you want from the other actor.
False! *Again, this is a very easy thing to ask, but much harder to deliver as one of the great physical theatre teachers Etienne Decroux once demonstrate. He indicated a movement pattern and commented: Easy to see! Easy to say! Easy to do badly!*

However, the following line unwittingly provides the answer:

If you learn the lines by rote, as if they were a phone book......
True but How! *This is exactly how athletes and musicians train! Football players do routines that are formatted with highly defined time and spatial strictures. Inside these strictures they perform their drills by rote, repetition upon repetition, and they do this so that in the 'moment' of the game, they can react instinctively to any situation that may arise. If they had to resort to any sort of analytical process regarding a situation within the game proper ' how do I get myself in the right position to kick the ball', they'd be euchred! They would immediately have lost the moment (and the ball!).*

 For some strange reason (probably aversion to hard work) actors think:
"It'll be alright on the night!" Even though nothing they do remotely prepares them for the night. Actually most actors amplify the problem by avoiding training because it is supposedly uncreative, avowing: "It'll kill the moment, etc".

We do not embellish the things we care deeply about.
Oh so true! *Jacques Copeau, the grandpere of what has become gesture based theatre, once commented: "To be sincere, you have to move slowly". On first reading it comes across as too simplistic but on reflection it is most acute and it is a re-phrasing of DM's sentence.*

Most actors need to embellish, to fill the void so to speak because they care more about themselves than anything else. I am reminded of watching a documentary about a well known film actor traipsing across the Siberian wastes by motorbike. At one stage they were being carried on a truck when the driver saw a bear cross the track ahead. They stopped the truck, gave chase, killed and skinned the bear before resuming. This offended said moviestar superbigtime, even though:
1. The bearskin was probably worth a year's income to the

A Devil Pokes the Actor   199

driver,
2. It happens all the time, and
3. His reaction won't change anything.

What it did show was that his reaction; what it meant to him, was more important than the thing he was reacting against. Of course an artist's powerful feelings are important drivers for his expression, and indeed it may be that the need to express powerful beliefs is what defines an artist most of all. But the canvas for this outburst should in this case be the stage or film, not self important posturing in the midst of some muddy Siberian track.

... but the audience isn't looking for a person with a 'good idea' about the script. They are looking for a person who can act - who can bring to the script something they couldn't have learned or imagined from reading it in a library.
<u>True!</u> *They are looking to be 'moved'. This is to take them on a journey - on their own journey of self- discovery.*

Helping the Play
P64: Most plays are better read than performed. Why?
<u>True!</u> *Because most actors on stage are only reading the play, anyway! So when they are sitting down reading they are physically less distractive and more honest than when they are pretending to do more.*

Most productions are just speaking books because most directors are only interested in the dialectic between the script and themselves. (How often have you seen a director look at the script when they perceive a problem - they should be looking at the stage.... the problem is on the deck!)

Why are these interactions so less moving when staged by actors?
<u>True!</u> *Because the actors have no 'body' knowledge, power or poetry! They can add nothing to the words. At a reading*

it is no distraction because their bodies are silent and not exposed. But in most cases, as they begin to walk around their bodies become a distraction that obscures and fragments the audience's appreciation of the language - their bodies become an obstruction to the audience's experiencing of the play.

P66: What is required is not the intellect to 'help the play' but the wisdom to refrain.
True! *The intellectual, the 'I' is an impediment!*

Acceptance
P67: As if acting were not an art or a skill, but only the ability to self-induce a delusional state.
True but How! *Without a thorough and systematic training, acting is definitely NOT an art or a skill.*

But is this true of music? Does the musician devote his energies to forgetting that what is in front of him is a piano, and does the dancer strive to forget that she is dancing and endeavour to believe that what she is doing is walking?
False! *Because the musician/ dancer always need to know the notes/steps they are playing/dancing. That is in its deepest essence, them knowing themselves in the playing. Otherwise they would be as 'lost' as most actors are.*

If the actor had a similar 'physical score' he would then have the confidence to feel himself inside (occupying) his speech and actions and since the playwright cannot or does not provide the Physical score it is left to the director. He /she is the equivalent of the conductor/choreographer, the provider of the aesthetic landscape that frames and reveals the text.

P68: The dancer does not endeavour to create in himself or in the audience the feelings the choreography might invoke: he just performs the steps the most truthful way he knows how.
Not Quite True! *The dancer as well as doing the steps, must occupy the dance, must be on a journey inside the dance.*

The crucial thing is that these two aspects must even go beyond co-existence, they must interpenetrate and nurture one another by combining together. One must not dominate to the detriment of the other.

P70 Let us learn acceptance. This is one of the greatest tools an actor can have……
Too true! *Too many so-called acting methods prevent the actor from accepting himself by encouraging him to pretend to be something other than what he is. Unless you can face yourself and accept who you are, there will be no moving forward.*

Because the capacity to accept derives from the will and the will is the source of character.
False! *Subjugation of the Will is paramount, for it is the will (Ego) that stands in the way of acceptance. Will is the 'I want' which prevents the 'I am'.*

Rehearsal Process
P72: What should happen in the rehearsal process? Two things:
1. The play should be 'blocked'.
2. The actors should become acquainted with the actions they are going to perform.
   True but How! *Both one and two mean that the play should be structured so that the actors know where they are, and what they are doing at any given time and where they are doing it in the space. Whose responsibility is that? The director's since the actor cannot (can a violin write its own structure in a quartet?).*
P73: You've heard directors and teachers by the gross tell you :"Come to grips with your self", "Regain your self esteem", "Use the space", and myriad other pretty phrases which they, and you, were surprised to find difficult to accomplish. They are not difficult. They are impossible!
True! *They are impossible because they are only admonitions, they contain no practical suggestions. And why no practical suggestions....because, in the main, the*

teacher/director doesn't know any more than the actor and has to resort to unhelpful prevarications such as above. For that is the only way this type of director/teacher can maintain his authority - by shifting the goal posts rather than providing real information.

This is what makes a person with an objective alive: they have to take the attention off them selves and put it on someone they want something from.
True but How! *This is why somebody on stage really doing something is more compelling than somebody pretending to do something - their ego has been denied attention and authority, and losing interest, it metaphorically wanders off, leaving the body simply to get on with the job.*

The Play and the Scene
P76: The boxer has to fight one round at a time; the fight will unfold as it is going to.
False! *Too simplistic and reductive. Ali beat Foreman in the 'Rumble in the Jungle' by using a deliberate strategy of tiring him out over several rounds. In acting as well there is a long term action (the journey) and a short term action (the moment). A true performance is a compound of both, co-existing and interacting (interdependent) with neither dominant to the detriment of the other.*

Emotions
P78: The addition of an 'emotion' to a situation which does not organically create it is a lie.
Super True! *I think DM said either in this book or elsewhere that one cannot project emotion - emotion is something that happens to you. A rather brilliant observation! If the actor cannot project emotion at the audience, but only feel it, then it follows that the audience has to witness, feel or participate in the actor's emotion and by doing so, feel their own emotion. It can never be the same emotion, but the audience needs to be in the presence of the actor's transformational emotion to feel their own. The actor is the*

shaman that reveals the audience's psyche to itself, without the audience being aware of it.

P80: Emotional memory and sense memory are paint - by-numbers.
True! Emotional memory is fake because only the emotions you feel in the moment are real. The exhuming of them may create something attractive, but it is still fake.
Acting is a physical art. It is close to the study of singing and dancing.
True but How! Yes, but only if it has a comparable structure. Most theatre has no temporal or spatial structure and that is why the actors, production director and audience are most often psychically lost.

Action
P82: In a well written and performed play, everything tends towards the punch line. That punch line, for the actor, is the objective. If we learn to think solely in terms of the objective, all concerns of belief, feeling, emotion, characterization, substitution, become irrelevant.
False! And verye olde worlde! Surely a great and lasting work has several levels of perception, layers of meaning that allow the various spectators to extract their own personal 'stories'. It was Proust who said that "Everybody reads themselves into what they are reading". In a classic Commedia piece good and bad characters can be countenanced at a more subtle level as clowns of innocence and experience.

Guilt
P86: None of us is free of self-doubt and none of us is free of guilt. A guilt based educational system, which is to say most acting training, survives through the support of adherents who were guilty before they signed up, who came to classes and failed (how could they do otherwise, as the training was nonsense), and were informed that their feelings of shame - which they had brought in with them - were due to their failure in class, and could be alleviated if and only if the student worked

harder and 'believed' more.

True but How! *Under this attitude of learning there is no way out as the actor's guilt is folded back inside himself rather than allowed to be given expression. However, guilt can also be an important driver for gaining knowledge. Guilt is a natural emotion, a subconscious cry for self-betterment. It is self imposed psychic pain. It is easy to understand that there can be no physical knowledge without physical pain - all athletes would know this implicitly. But acting involves psychic and physical growth, and if you transposed the shifts, there can be psychic growth through physical discomfort. One can develop a training that combines the two, while still ensuring that there is minimal collateral damage.*

P87: Faced with nonsensical, impossible directions ("Feel the music with your arms and legs").

False! *And spoken by an unbodied nerdy intellectual! There speaks the rational man, unable to countenance mystery. Elite athletes, musicians and dancers would find no idiocy in that sort of directive. And your description 'nonsensical' is also inversely ironic as such directions are designed to increase the actor's sensitivity beyond the linear and obvious. The issue would be the context of the direction: is it just another bland admonishment with no practical backup? In most cases the answer would be yes. But if such suggestions were couched in contexts that were both poetic and structured, then the actor wouldn't feel that he was pretending. He would actually be feeling, following an unconscious train of thought that would have a similar creative, inspirational effect as though responding to his dreams.*

Nobody with a happy childhood ever went into show business.

False! *Too simplistic and not necessarily true, but it is true to say that actors seek redemption through performance - their soul's tonic through self discovery witnessed by an audience.*

A Devil Pokes the Actor   205

The audience, just like you, came to have it; anomie, anxiety, guilt, uncertainty and disconnectedness dealt with. Your responsibility is this: deal with your own.
Very true! *The audience, by walking into the theatre, agrees to a compact whereby they will, by witnessing you as a shaman deal with your own issues, come to a greater acceptance of their own issues – it's called psychic healing and has been the true purpose of theatre for millennia.*

Your fear, your self doubt, your vast confusion (you are facing an ancient mystery-drama - of course you're confused) do not mar you. At the risk of nicety, they are you.
True but How! *Fear, self doubt and confusion are part of the actor's armoury……waiting to be re-configured into positive agents which requires…….you guessed it! Technique!*

In rejecting a situation based on guilt (I can do more, do better, etc.), in beginning with a frank avowal (I am confused, uncertain, etc.), and proceeding honestly from one step to the next, you put yourself in the same position as the written character and can begin to bring to the stage the truth of the moment.
True but How! *I think what DM states as an ambit claim, is a very good starting point, but as it stands, it is only an admonition until the actor is provided with a highly defined aesthetic landscape (AKA a coherent training process) where he can progress through all these issues.*

Concentration
P95: The more a person's concentration is outward, the more naturally interesting that person becomes.
Partly true! *I assume outward means that he is attuning himself to receive outside information to a greater extent than he is expressing information. So that means he is in a heightened state of feeling, and one can push that a step further so he should also be feeling the effect it is having on him.*

We've all seen the 'vivacious' person at a party. What could be a bigger bore? It's not your responsibility to do things in an interesting manner.

True but How! *The issue here is: 'interesting manner'. Could you not say: to be interesting you have to be doing interesting things. Not pretending to do up you shoelaces - actually do them up, and the greater the degree of difficulty - proportionally the more interesting. And the more and different interesting things you are doing, the more compelling you become. Tadashi Suzuki once said: "True intensity on stage is borne of doing many things at once!"*

P96: The teenager who wants the car; the child who wants to stay up the extra half hour......These individuals have no problem concentrating. Elect something to do which is physical and fun to do and concentration ceases to be an issue.

Partly True! *Supplant the word fun with 'challenging but rewarding' as fun is the enemy of art.*

Here is a bit of heresy. Our theatre is clogged with plays about Important Issues; Playwrights and Directors harangue with right thinking views on many topics of the day. But these are, finally, harangues, they aren't drama and they aren't fun to do. The audience and the actor nod in acquiescence, and go to their seats or onstage happy to be a right thinking individual, but it is a corruption of the theatrical exchange.

True but How! *Plays about 'important issues', are invariably lectures delivered from 'superior' moral positions. In reality they are yet another example of Ego one upmanship, given lipservice to by the receiver, but indirectly repudiated after the event. Good art transcends time and circumstance by contending with the deep moral and spiritual issue of mortality.*

Talent
P100: A common sign in a boxing gym: BOXERS ARE ORDINARY MEN WITH EXTRAORDINARY DETERMINATION. I would rather be able to consider myself in that way than to consider myself one of the 'talented'; and – if I may - I think you

would, too.

True but How! *If talent, as you so rightly say, is so deceptive, then what can you have in your work process to stop its highs and lows corrupting you. You could argue, that like the other vicissitudes facing you as an actor, you need tools to stop the misleading highs and lows of success - intentions are a good start, but one needs a format in which to make those intentions real.*

Habit

P102: Put things in their proper place. Rehearsal is the time for work. Home is the time for reflection. The stage is the time for action. Compartmentalise and cultivate that habit and you'll find your performances incline to take on the tinge of action.... Be generous to others. Everyone tries to do their best....Yearning to correct or amend the something in someone else will make you petty. Cultivate the habit of only having aversion for those things you can avoid (those things in your self) and only desiring those things you can give yourself. Improve your self.

False! *Wonderful sentiments but they only flag an attitude or approach. To take that approach further, it has to be subsumed into a procedural doctrine. The most successful aesthetic movements inaugurate processes that corral and amplify those sentiments. What is incumbent on us as living in the 2010+ is to find our own versions of these processes, using as templates those ideologues that have gone before, and reconfiguring them to suit contemporary sensibilities and idioms.*

P103: Singing, voice, dance, juggling, tap, magic, tumbling. Practice in them will
perfectly define for you the difference between possession and non-possession of a skill.

True but How! *As well, see them as not separate and immiscible, but excavate them for their consanguinity - their underlying technical connections. Then assimilate them and transpose their attributes. For, if they are* *techniques, they are transposable - if not you are notching up un-connectible styles.*

Performance and Character

P110: If you decide to be an actor, stick to your decision. The folks you meet in supposed positions of authority- critics, teachers, casting directors – will, in the main, be your intellectual and moral inferiors. They will lack your imagination, which is why they became bureaucrats rather than artists; and they will lack your fortitude, having elected institutional support over a life of self reliance.
<u>True!</u> Essentially, they lack your intent - that essential deep moral imperative.

P111: An actor should never look inward. He or she must keep the eyes open to see what the other actor is doing moment to moment, and to call it by its name and act accordingly.
<u>False!</u> It is not possible to look outward all the time, just as it is not possible to hold one's breath forever. To look outward all the time is as fixed a position as looking inward. Perhaps it is better to look at outward/ inward in terms of energy balance. The energies coming into the body must be balanced by the energies going out – projection and reception.

P112: A word about teachers. Most of them are charlatans.
<u>Too true!</u> Most of them don't know any more than their students and that's because they never studied or worked with any one who knew more than they did – an unending circle of incompetence! it follows that they then have to resort to circumlocution and subterfuge.

Few of the exercises I have seen, teach anything other than gullibility.
<u>Oh, so true!</u> Most teachers, because they don't know more, have no moral authority and so have to resort to prevarication and obfuscation, maintaining their emotional /psychological command over their charges by increasing the gullibility factor.

The Villain and the Hero
P114 You don't have to portray the hero or the villain. That's been done for you by the script.
Partly True! *Or: The director's interpretation of the script.*

Acting 'As if"
P116: In none of these do we have to 'remember' how we are supposed to feel. We simply remind ourselves what we are about to do, and we are suffused with the desire to do it: we jump immediately and happily into the midst of the game………. We can make our speech to the tyrant time after time, and indeed we do, sometimes improving it, sometimes simply repeating it for the joy it affords us.
True! This perfectly describes the ideal instinctive state which is very special and the aim of every actor. It occurs at least once in any rehearsal situation, and it would seem that repeating it, or more properly, regaining it is the primary focus of ensuing rehearsals and performances. A la recherche l'instinct perdu!
The most practical way seems to be to repeat it so often that it becomes instinctive again.

What do we say of the actor who would wish it all away….. and substitute some shoddy counterfeit of emotion. We say that such a one is great, that he is a Great Actor, and that we have never seen such technique. What does this talk of technique mean? It means that we were so starved of anything enjoyable that we were reduced to enjoying our own ability to appreciate.
True! We were impressed, but not moved.

What would the word technique mean if it were applied to a chef or a lover? It would mean that their actions were cold and empty, that finally, we're disappointed by them. This is precisely what it means when applied to a stage performance.
False! Since when did the word technique mean cold and empty? When applied to a violinist it means effortless, and enables the music to be appreciated at its most sublime. The true aim of art is to sublimate technique so that the

audience's rational perceptions of time and space have been refracted - they have been transported to a dreamscape, where the usual conscious judgments are suspended. If they become aware of technique then they have dropped out of that magic zone and are back in 'I wonder if I turned the oven off?' everyday life - surely what theatre is NOT about.
The word technique itself is not emotionally loaded 'per se'.

Most actors are terrified of their jobs. Not some, but most. They don't know what to do and it makes them crazed. They feel like frauds.
<u>*True but How!*</u> *That is because they are generally lost psyches in a bland, ill-defined landscape. They don't know where they stand in terms of space and time and therefore have to fill the void with ' busy-ness', so that they don't feel empty. This means that they are not learning, discovering new psychic spaces.*
Instead, they have to trawl through their bag of tricks, their old habits, and put them on display as something new and exciting. They can't 'know' themselves in that false and empty environment, and that's why they feel deep down they are frauds.
Of course they can never 'know' themselves fully - that's an impossibility, but they can, when placed in a highly defined aesthetic, be on a journey of self-discovery, and that is a very exciting thing to witness.

They once Walked among Us
P121: Now, the great (acting teachers) are safely dead and cannot be quizzed, but we might safely assume that they brought something of passion and courage to their work.
<u>*True!*</u> *If you go back to the originals, they were made by the experience as much as it made them.*

P122: As we move further down the food chain, both the students and the teachers are attracted not to the new, but to the approved.
<u>*True!*</u> *The analogy can here be made with photo-copying,*

where each subsequent copy progressively loses definition. So too in acting….. as each generation of actors and teachers becomes further removed from the discovery/invention, the result becomes blander and more diffuse.

Scores:
True: 28
False: 19
True but How: 21
Oh so True: 2
Very True: 2
Too True: 2
Super True: 1
Partly True: 3
Almost True: 1
Half True: 1
True-ish: 1
Not Quite True: 1

I have extracted those statements that I consider valuable, contentious or wrong. The guy's got a good brain, no doubt about it! Needs to get out a bit more, gain real physical experience…..but it sounds as though he hates sport. If this isn't the case, then he has no idea as to how to interpose physical and intellectual realities…….anyway thanks Dave and Happy Trails.

"Damnit Mamet, why d'ya do it? That rancorous left hook let your left guard down, and........POW! A sucker punch to the elementary tract....."

…..having written to the writer now's the time for the teacher......

Migraine Provocation #4
A Soft Scrutiny of 'An Acrobat of the Heart'
by Stephen Wangh.

AAotH was published in 2000 and documents Steve Wangh's teaching processes as inspired by his exhilarating short time with Grotowski in 1967. The book was given to me by a young American actor whom I was teaching in Seattle in August of 2008. Just prior to that I had spent time in Poland observing one strand of Grotowski's legacy, where I had a chance to weed out some of the difference between the smoke and the fire.
As with a lot of pedagogues, there's a lot of smoke and that smoke somewhat obscures the fire.

Like SW, I have developed a training system inspired by my ongoing relationship with another great pedagogue. In my case my mentor has and continues to be Tadashi Suzuki, the still thriving Japanese modern master. I've been associated with him for 18 years of extensive training and working with his company, the Suzuki Company of Toga. As well, I am an actor with Australian company, Ozfrank Theatre. The training system we have developed is a translation and variant of the **Suzuki Actor Training Method**.

I am interested in how other second generation shapers have re-configured their 'exotic' inspiration. I come from Australia: a land of space and no culture: Suzuki comes from the land of time and culture that is Japan. Since the beginning of 1991 I have been intensely focused on re-configuring my experiences with him, and through that, to fashion a uniquely Ozfrank process and product.

Mr. Wangh is an American, well versed in modern theatre education ideology. Grotowski is the pre-eminent scion of the very rich religious, cultural and theatrical tradition of Poland. Like myself, Mr Wangh must have thought long and deeply as to how he could re-make his experience with Grotowski. The reason I use the SATM, is that from a point of view of a performer, whose skills have been developed inside the disciplines of classical and modern dance training, it is the only systematic actor training I can find. All the others I've come across are not systematic at all, and should more properly be called 'approaches'. From what I've seen so far of the work and legacy of the Grot there is no real training, only a very accomplished and elegant dramaturgy. With all this stuff rattling around my skull, I was asked by my director/collaborator/wife Jacqui Carroll to critique Mr Wangh's book, so here 'tis......

In tune with much of my other writing, I have taken the liberty of NOT being academic or 'fair'- in short I've been as transgressive as the Grot - the man who invented the device.

Hence, a **sharp scrutiny** it is.....
But before I continue, I sent my responses to Mr Wangh, who had the good grace to reply with a few responses of his own. I've presented them along with my responses to his responses!

The following consists of a relevant page numbered extract taken from AAoTH, under which is written my 'response' in bold:

P XIX. Cieslak for his part demonstrated 'impossible' exercises...which we tried to emulate....until we realised emulation was not what this class was all about.
Response: I don't quite get this? Surely if you get C. to get up and demonstrate his killer kit the purpose is to impress the yokels – what else are they supposed to do but try and copy him?

P XX. ... Grotowski **(G)** said: The real value of the exercises... is not being able to do them... For us schooled in the importance of success..........it was baffling and frustrating...and at the same time exhilarating.
Both the 'Success' based and 'Failure' based approaches, are dodgy psychologically - partial attitudes. They pay too much attention to the EGO. 'Success' based approaches

pander to the actor's ego, and 'failure' based, likewise, negatively impacts on the actor's reactive sub-ego. The exhilarating feeling comes from being very active and attempting to achieve a demanding requirement - rightly so.

P XXIII. His (G's) innovations have spawned 1,000s of experiments in textual deconstructing and environmental theatre. Yet his remarkable actor training has made only minor inroads upon more traditional acting techniques.
That is because his dramaturgy, which is his true legacy, is so powerful, that it blinded people into thinking it was actually a type of training! The reverse problem has occurred with Suzuki. Most practitioners have been so overwhelmed by his training that they think it is an aesthetic in itself, and they have mistakenly assumed that the training and Suzuki's aesthetic are the same thing. They are interdependent, but not the same.

If anything, what is called training when associated with the Grot is really based on Cieslak's extraordinary performative charisma. Judging from videos watched of Cieslak teaching with Odin Teatret actors, it was a personal style, and like many an instinctive genius, he couldn't analyse and transmit what he was doing and it really only flowered in a dialectic with Grotowski's dramaturgy.

P XXIV. Why (after G) ... are there still so many actors whose voices and bodies.......(are) so disconnected?
That is because the vast majority of directors don't demand these skills, couldn't care less and even more sadly.... the audience cannot tell the difference!
Directors as a rule are keen to get the show on the road with whatever actor technology they've got rather than upgrading the skills. That would take time and nowadays performances are so commodified that there is minimal preparation time.

P XXIV. (G) perceived that those who worked with him frequently became enthralled by the physicality of the work and

lost sight of the deeper acting values.
Once again, swamped by the dramaturgy! It has to be understood that the Grot was the prime example the West saw of a very strong Polish dramaturgical history, but with its Polish context universalised. The performances had so much moral power that those either involved or watching found it difficult to differentiate between the preparation and the result.

P XXV. G cautioned ... former students to not follow in his footsteps.
This is the old 'Life of Brian' admonition and a very clue-y way of maxing the Messianic Myth; 'Don't follow me, be an individual!' The classic response to which is: 'We are all individuals!' The smart way to make people follow you is to tell them not to!

P XXV. ...in the 'real' world actors rarely work with directors who are also consummate acting teachers.....
In the real world, most directors are glorified traffic cops making sure the actors open the right doors and don't bump into too much furniture as they obey the word for word directives of the writer. Management, not direction!

P XXVI. This political action (anti-Vietnam war activist theatre) seemed to me the most valuable thing I could do with my theater skills. G disdained such pragmatic uses of theater.
Good old Grot! He had his head screwed on with that! He knew that political theatre was for people who didn't have any thing to say in and of themselves. They think they should be busy doing something, but their soul has nothing to say - nothing to reveal.
If you've got nothing to say or display, you have to resort to polemic about intransigent issues. Find an issue like eg one legged lesbian dwarf ex-prisoners in the military and go hard and long with that – it's unfixable and you can always accuse the punters of not caring enough! Great and lasting theatre is about psychic healing – not social engineering.

Grot knew that art is about spirit and soul.
P XXVII. …..suddenly I was face-to-face with the gap between physical training and its applications to scene work...
That gap is filled by having a director who has both dramaturgy and interdiction. Part of the problem for most directors is that they still see the training as extrinsic to the rehearsal/performance matrix. This is due in part to the fact that the directors themselves are not connected to the training. They leave that to a 'movement associate'.

P XXVIII. …..it is not because I think there is any particular value in 'remaining true' to a teacher or teaching.
If 'remaining true' means slavishly copying precepts, then certainly there should be some degree of separation. One should have one's own world, using the teacher as template and mentor. And, with that idea in mind then one should, whilst <u>respecting the source</u>, endeavour to develop one's own style and strand. And this may mean using the systems of the teacher, and adapting them to more reflect one's own situation and culture.

P XXIX. Don't try to copy exactly another person's path. Use their knowledge, etc. etc. etc……you must discover your own path, but you can't perceive it if you are on it, only after you have travelled it.
This quote sounds pithy, coming from a great Japanese actor, Yoshi Oida, but empty. Very reminiscent of Coppola at the end of the doco 'Hearts of Darkness' when he came up with a wimpy homily, saying he was hoping the next great film would be made by some kids with a home movie camera…What was he thinking? That some stupid teeny who didn't know shit from a shilling would come up with a masterpiece on a mobile phone?

P XXXII. In 1773 Diderot said, "The actor who has nothing but calculation and reason is frigid. The one who has nothing but emotionalism and excitement is silly."
This is smart thinking, showing they knew a fair bit way back when.

A Devil Pokes the Actor

If we translate the statement into more psyche terms we would talk in terms of a balance between conscious and unconscious.
Conscious (Con): being those attributes that ensure control, time and space knowledge and other rational characteristics.
Unconscious (Uncon): being those attributes associated with transformational and non-linear thoughts and actions.
The Uncon is what makes an actor compelling, but the Con cannot be removed - it must be given a function that takes it out of the direct line of fire, by making it a witness to the experience of the Uncon.

P XXXII. The problem with Delsarte's system was that it tried to prescribe a fixed vocabulary of movements for each human emotion.......
True! He got a bit too rational there for what is properly a complex array of feeling and action. You can't really codify it too much. Rather better to talk about 'movement as allowing experiences to be felt' as distinct from 'movement as prescribing or representing feelings'. The issue then becomes how to corral the experiences so that they may work effectively but without overwhelming the feelings.

P XXXIII. In reaction to 'mechanical' actors, Stanislavsky (S) ....searched for a method that would depend on INNER psychological practices.
Stan the Man was on the money - going for the 'Uncon' side of the story!

When it was brought to the States....... it turned into what Lee Strasberg called 'emotional-memory' exercise: ....the actor is asked to recreate an experience from the past that has affected him strongly. The experience should have happened as least seven years prior. I ask the student to pick the strongest experience that ever happened to him, whether it aroused anger, fear or excitement.
Why seven years? Is that a 'statute of psychological

limitations' thing?
The error here is that when the con recalls some uncon experience from the past it automatically corrupts the recall. It worked best when done by Brando who didn't take it seriously (and would only rouse it at the exact moment as necessary) - he always maintained it was childish play!

The real problem with Emotional Memory Recall is that it's dredged up as a deliberate act by the Conscious side of the brain, corrupting the effect it has on the actor. If brought up unconsciously it can be genuinely transformative. There is a telling anecdote concerning one of Steve's students (P228 - Sandra) where she recounts just such a positive experience which led to some creative breakthroughs. In her situation it was serendipity, but the mission is how to create techniques that facilitate and enhance these experiences.

P XXXIV. Meanwhile, Stanislavsky had realised by concentrating so completely on the actor's mind, he had ignored the actor's body. In his later years, he developed a system of what he called 'physical actions' "In every physical action, unless it is purely mechanical, there is concealed some inner action". One of his actor's, Toporkov, described it this way. Diverting the actor away from 'feelings from psychology', he directed it toward the carrying out of purely physical actions. In this way the actor could penetrate in a natural way into the sphere of feelings.
Right on! So while Lee was Freud-ianising actors, Stan the Man went back to his estranged former mate, Vlesevod Meyerhold, whose Bio-Mechanics was a system for generating acting from physicality.

P XXXV. Stanislavsky.... had discovered ...that the body can provide a direct route to the emotions. G picked up the trail....."We do not possess memory, our entire body is memory...."
This is well and truly on the right track: Uncon/Con that talks and walks down the path of Jung and Artaud.

P XXXVIII. The external forms this book teaches include the Plastique and the Corporeal.....the exercises themselves are not a method, they are merely provocations.....
True! It is not a method (a matrix), but an attitude (a dialectic) – a dramaturgical approach. The dialectic is between the director and the actor. But that dialectic needs to work inside a matrix and the matrix cannot be a dialectic itself, as they self churn. Most so called actor systems are actually dialectics themselves and that is why, when they are mated to a directorial dialectic, they result in confusion and obfuscations.

P XXXIX. But as we grew older, most of us learned to suppress our emotions...
Is this the old Freudian blame game? The fact is, in daily life, if you want to survive, you can't possibly say everything you think because if you did you'd be dumped in the rubber room. As you get older you become aware that your actions have consequences, and so you learn to temper them - that is the etiquette of growing up in public, and it is called becoming conscious of the world outside. The problem in the West is that we cease to balance that drift to consciousness with a countervailing deepening interest in the welfare of the unconscious.

But for actors, emotional expression is essential to our craft, so learning to become an actor necessitates overcoming whatever emotional blocks.....
I think this is inherently backward looking. A more positive attitude is to use a training premise that looks far more equably on the human prospect - more Jungian than Freudian. Our version of the Suzuki training posits looking forward, accepting self as is, and opening doors in front, rather than closing doors behind.

P 7. ....While doing Yoga as a warm up: ... I was comparing my position with one of the other actors – and realizing my body would never be able to do what her body did. ....by the end of

the session my mind was as full of distress as my body was.
One can sense that the other Yoga practitioner was nicely put together, but nevertheless why was he doing an exercise where he was almost certain to think conscious thoughts like that - surely better to be doing routines that put the actor in a holistic state of occupation rather than negative comparison.
It also shows that Yoga is not performative. It is not meant to be observed! And, if it is not performative........it's time for the vertical file!

Theatre is a performative art - it is meant to be witnessed and in being witnessed, it is validated. This sense of being witnessed should begin inside the training, and exercises should be built around principles where the actor is conjoined to also be constantly aware of a potential audience's witnessing - he is not just thinking: "How do I feel?" But, as well, 'How is the audience apprehending what I feel?'

P 8. As I struggled with this question, I realized that the work I had studied with G.....was such a method of warming up the body and mind together, as if they were one entity, not two...... the essence lay not in the particular exercise.....but in an awareness of the connections between body, mind and emotions.....
In all this chat about body/mind together, where's the voice – yet to be mentioned! It is imperative to integrate voice from the start otherwise it's a mime and movement class, ain't it?

P 9. In the same way, when you walk into an acting studio, you automatically seek out a place in which you feel comfortable....
How precious. Surely you should be seeking out all spaces to experience their 'vibe'- such talk encourages the attitude of actor as 'precious victim'.

P 20. Slow Motion exercise.
Slo-mo is a very good idea, because moving slowly forces

A Devil Pokes the Actor 223

actors to really feel and occupy what they are doing, and, paradoxically they are also more in the 'moment'.
A very wise old frog, Jacques Copeau said that to be sincere one had to move slowly!!

P 24. One group is singing and clapping in rhythm, another is sharing shoulder massages in a circle.
Unstructured Ego massage for a sheltered workshop?

P 25. ...if your warm up comes before a rehearsal, the time you take for your warm up is time you no longer have for a rehearsal.
Surely the idea would be to see the warmup/rehearsal/performance as separate but integrated aspects of the same culture. This notion that 'warm ups' aren't the real thing, displays a non integrative mindset. That's why 'warm up' is a bad word and a bad idea. If you have a 'training' it is then a true preparation that <u>seamlessly segues</u> into rehearsal and performance.

P 31. "But my need", Aisha responds," was to keep working alone right then. It so happens that I had just gotten into something important."
Why encourage these 'Britney Spears' moments? The actors' attitude becomes more important than what they're doing. Acceding to this truculence only amplifies self importance.

P 34...L struggled with his chair and started to yell at it.
McEnroe Acting.........Theatre of the spoilt brat!

.....So even for the same actor there is never the right warm up to do every day.
A warm up (maternally bad word that is it is) is meant to be a stabilising routine that flattens out the bumps of the day and to put everybody on the same page. Musos and Sportsters do the same routines every day, although that may contain different vocabulary.

P 37 A warm up is not a regimen or a particular set of exercises.
Why not? If we look at Yoga - do Yoga teachers change the exercises each day to make the punters feel nice? No. They understand the importance of repetition, for only repetition creates the state for self reflection.

P 44 The vertebral column is the centre of expression.
This is an interesting temporary dramaturgical interdiction, but not tenable in the long run because it is applying a metaphysical impulse to a geographical place. Surely, if anything the CoE is the soul...and.... it is puzzling that the idea of a soul is not countenanced in the post modern world.........

P 44 Then G. goes on: 'The driving impulse, however, stems from the loins.....Every live impulse begins from this region....'
It may be poetic to make such coy sweeping statements, but such one track Freudian statements have limited value as they reduce everything to a simplistic idea. The point of a research based attitude like G's is to identify the specific loci and work on exercises that foster its development.

P 46 The undulation from the pelvis.
The above contains ineffectual information because there is no structure, no demand and no performative aspect.

P 48 When you are engaging in acting exercises, you may find yourself stumbling on material....... that is very new to you. And it is important that you take time after this intense work to let this information gel......it is important that you don't go into the hall to talk to someone, or have a cigarette, or drink coffee until you have digested your work.....
Very very true! It is during the immediate moments after an exercise that the uncon info is calibrated into the conscious body proper. Too often in the West we race on to the next exercise or event because we are wracked with anxiety whenever we are forced to stand still and dwell on what we've just done. This is because we live in a society that denies the value of unconscious feelings and experiences,

having spent centuries asserting the primacy of reason and technology.

In the East they are not so speed-freaky, understanding the advantages of meditation, and the benefits it brings in terms of feeling and occupying what you are doing. Having the smoke or coffee that he talks about, is a distraction from this crucial 'life' task.

P 49 The inchworm exercise.
Another of the 'therapy' type exercises that do not have:
   1. Formats in terms of time and/or space.
(In music and sport training there are time and spatial structures, wherein the participant truly 'knows' himself and where he is. Far from being 'repressive', this creates in the participant a landscape of freedom.)
   2. Interdiction/demands.
These are necessary external directives that impel the actor not to be self satisfied or idiosyncratic, but to aim for greater particularity AND universality.
   3. Performative aspect.
It has no injunction to incorporate an audience as an external partner, as a balance to the internal witness.

Such 'avuncular' exercises as the 'inchworm' encourage the precious solipsism and self-importance that has always been so prevalent in Western acting.

P 57 The Cat Exercise:
Here at last is an exercise that has the moral imperative that matches G's directorial attitude. It is very demanding and physically difficult. It seems to have achieved a mythical status, I suppose because it has a nifty name. Its one drawback is that it's very difficult for women to do, unless they have an extremely muscular upper body, which would exclude 95% of women.

Since it seems to be the only routine to have real moral dimension, I am surprised that over the years the Grotowsky-ites have failed to use it as a teaching machine and transpose its moral 'ask' into other exercises.

"Stephen Wangh:
It is true that many people, including many men, have physical difficulties doing the Cat, but very few really can't do it for at least five minutes. I'd say that 90% of my students (maybe 1,000 over the years) get a lot out of this……and that includes most women.
JN's response to SW:
Point taken! But you don't answer the much more important second para….."

P 62 The Forward Roll:
I am surprised that the peanut roll is so venerated! It is not performative and you can't speak while doing it and surely that should be the measure of the suitability of an exercise for an actor?

P 63 The Headstands:
Watching the '72 video of Cieslak with a couple of Scandos doing the headstand meander reminds me of the scene in APOCALYPSE NOW where Kurtz asks Willard his impressions of his 'methods', and Willard replies: "But Sir…… I see…. no method."
It was once worth a try, but since there is no rigour, there is no critique and it just seems to encourage un-mythic idiosyncracy and quotidian values.

P 68 The Kneeling Backbend:
Another semi acrobatic exercise with some benefit, but which divides the class into the cans and cannots. It is the sort of thing you either can or can't do, and if you can't you're either in a world of pain, or you wait for an exercise you can do. The definition of an appropriate training exercise is one that doesn't preclude any participant due to any particular personal un-facility.

"SW Response:
When I teach this, I'm very clear that the core of this exercise is opening across the chest the bending all the way to the floor is not the important part.

A Devil Pokes the Actor   227

JN to SW: Okey Doke."

P 76 **The Plastiques**: But as soon as you sense that lift of the shoulders is a 'jerk' or a 'slump' or a 'shrug' the lift is no longer simply an exploration of movement. It has become an *External* key to an *Internal* door, a physical way of asking an image question.....And that is not all. Each *Plastique* is in itself an emotive gesture... The feeling *inhabits* the shrug itself.
Even though the 'shrugs' are a little vapid, the idea of occupying or inhabiting movement is excellent and well on the road to genuine transformation. It's moving away from movement as an aesthetic code to movement as a tool for metamorphosis.
Such exercises would have much more import and impact on the actor, if they were given structure and format, by adding demands such as:" Do it standing on one leg!"

P 90 The Pushing Exercise:

Phase 1. Half the group begins as passive 'receivers' of impulses, closing their eyes and allowing the other half of the group to move their bodies......
Phase 2. ...still with shut eyes they permit themselves to 'receive' the impulses from *imaginary* partners....
Phase 3....they open their eyes to let themselves 'see' the imaginary forces that are moving them.
This is a very good device with which to make actors truly sensitive to external forces and ideas. It only falls down when its lack of format places emotional demands on the actors during the second and third phases, when they become frustrated and anxious with the shifting of the goalposts.
In the book this is very apparent with Carlos' reactions, "he yanks at my pull with cold determination...He grimaces at me with a vicious smile...."
One would have thought that after their time together there would be a modicum of trust, so either the actors don't trust their teacher as a teacher, or as I suspect, the

exercises place a great emotional strain on the actor, causing them to react like Carlos.

"SW response:
The Carlos character like many of the students is an invented one and a composite. I wrote scenes like this to make a teaching point in the book.
JN to SW:
That's missing the point. Carlos may be a composite but why, such childish re-activity? Answer: No real structure – disaffective admonitions. And how do you 'read the plasma' when faced with emotional smog? I wonder at the efficacy of exercises that have such emotionally loaded side effects. Proper training minimizes psychological confusion between the teacher and the student."

P 90 The pushing exercise:
…….The coaches move among the 'receivers', periodically giving them impulses…might lift an arm…gently touch the neck or push a shoulder….
It would be a really good exercise if it had a format. As it is the 'receiver' has to cope with all the 'games' the coach may impart. With luck they may be on the same psychological page…. But what if they're not? This shows that the idea of 'fun' is counter-productive. The reason for a 'training' regimen is to minimise idiosyncrasies and mood differences, not to amplify them.

"SW:
I disagree. After working with a real partner, the actor works with an imaginary partner. I usually say at that point: 'working with a real partner has advantages and forces you to really receive, but there are problems with a real partner, who has his own preferences and probably avoids risky things like working with your groin.
JN to SW:
Not sure what you're getting at here but why not see working with a real partner as a positive bridging experience, and carrying the memory into working without

**a partner?
As for the droll onanistic ending (working with your own groin?) hmmmm......"**
P 93 After this exercise I gather the group together to talk about their experience.
Asking actors how they feel about their acting too early can be counter-productive. The act of asking them to make a conscious judgment of their unconscious experience does two things:
    1. it interrupts the true feeling and
    2. it corrupts that feeling.

In such a situation they will say one of three things:
    a. they will tell you what they want you to hear,
    b. they will tell you what they think you want to hear,
    c. they will tell you what they think you should hear.

None of which they really feel! It defeats itself further, as it also encourages them to think that their judgments regarding their feelings are important, whereas it is their feelings that are important!

"SW:
You're right that there is some danger of interruption here. But one important lesson that comes out of this is that the actors become aware of two things: 1. Other actors have very different responses. 2. Everything they think and feel is OK in this class.
Here is a student response written to me after a recent workshop:
I really like that for every exercise, we get to sit around in a circle afterwards and are encouraged to share our questions and thoughts, as it's the perfect time to (sic) us to immediately think back on what we have just done and share it with everybody. Sometimes, the comments shared gave me a new understanding of what the exercise is about, and also sometimes there are comments shared on experiences that I similarly went through. It's strangely comforting to know that somebody else experiences some of the things that I have gone

through. Also, it was interesting to note that, whenever we have a question for you, the answer that we were given left me with even more questions that I had to mull over and think about it (sic).

JN to SW:
Of course you are a good teacher, and your student has written a coherent appraisal of the situation. But, both of you miss the point about the difference between thinking and feeling. The magic unconscious experiences of the student are not quantified by conscious chat, but are more transformational when in self cogitato – like you suggest back on page 48.
(Extrapolating that to your journey as a teacher, I suggest reading the collective unconscious of the group should also happen in the plasma of the exercise, where it is pure.)
In the chat after, it's too early for the conscious mind to have homologated the experience, and it is muddied by the saying of all sorts of 'I feels'."

P 104 The container exercise: ..... lying curled up on the floor... you feel your body is contained by something literal... your work is to discover the image by using your body, by pressing outward against the container, trying to find an exit.....
More mimetic work! Mimetic, because, if you don't involve the voice, this could be called mime and it's also prone to fostering preciousness. Indubitably it wouldn't pass the 'Truckies' Test'.

P 111 ...The work we will be doing is in many ways the same work you call emotional memory or sense memory work. The difference is that we do not do it sitting down **(good start....... Cut the chat!)**. We do it with our bodies active because memories are not encoded only in our brains they are trapped in our muscles, too. By working on your arms, you reconnect with a part of that memory, not as a past event, but as a living action. What we are doing now is freeing up our bodies to do that work.
Very, very good! The only cavil is the use of emotionally loaded words like 'trapped' and 'freeing up'.
P 117 After a 'bad' acting exercise: What made it bad was that

A Devil Pokes the Actor   231

its energetic gestures were not filled with emotional truth.....But we must remain aware that the task is finding strong emotional life with which to fill our powerful and expressive bodies...rather than cutting back on the power of our physical expression to fit within our shrunken sense of truth.
Very well put! Its crucial shift is the change of emphasis on *emotional life* rather than *emotional truth* - there's no such thing as emotional truth. That's trying to give absolute status to a transient and relative sensibility. So, searching for ET is an un-achievable task. Finding EL is quite feasible, as it describes a place in the psyche and its effect on the actor.

P 119 ... Many tensions arise in the moment as the result of small, self-protective physical habits. As we sit down in a chair, for instance, perhaps we cross our legs or unconsciously wrap our feet around the chair legs....What are these small obsessions?
It is true that we are all riddled with anxiety - they are a human norm, so why describe them in derogatory terms such as 'obsessions'. This is Marxian/Freudian rhetoric which ascribes negativity to human foible, conferring victimhood on the way. These MarxieFreudie loops are imploding spirals as no amount of discussion concerning the search for the seat of anxiety has ever made it go away. Far better to invert the negative, accept anxiety as a positive energy of the persona, and learn to channel it accordingly.

P 125 Bodily Emotions:
 Danish psychologist, Carl Georg Lange: "we feel sorry because we cry, angry because we strike, afraid because we tremble" This idea that our emotions are the result of our physiology, rather than the cause of them.......points to an important fact: that body movement can, indeed, trigger our emotional life.
Very good pointer to where the focus of a training should be - acting comes from the body! As an explanation, studies have shown that when a person apprehends a

speech, 10% is in the words, 30% is the sound behind the words and 60% is the body language of the speaker. This shows that the primary focus should not be the words of the actor, but.... how the actions affect the sound of the actor.

P 126 ...since many of us have undergone experiences of repression in our lives, many of us have built up similar muscular defense mechanisms....
More post Marxian victimhood looking for somewhere or someone to hook the blame - why create an attitude that looks back on a past that cannot be changed? Far better to forge a future that has potential.

Later: ...even now gestures of biting and kicking can stimulate the release of our anger.

No! It doesn't! All it does is make us think our anger is important, which it isn't. It's merely Ego asserting itself as reacting against not coming to terms with life.

P 127 ...Often a great deal of anger is stored in the lower body, so kicking or pushing with the legs... can be very freeing.
**Where is the evidence for that? I don't think it's feasible to ascribe absolute modalities to vague areas of the body. This is trying to define emotional qualities in quantitative terms - philosophically untenable.
Is 'lower body' a euphemism for genitalia? Why should the genitalia be the repository of anger?**

"SW:
No, 'lower body' means legs too. My experience is that many people who lock their knees in the work hold back anger, and that working with the legs is a release. Of course it's not everyone, but I've worked with enough people at this point to dare to generalize on this point.
JN to SW: Fair enough!"

P 128 The 'stomping' work taught by Tadashi Suzuki can also

empower the aggressive energies of the lower body to flow.
Respectfully said and a reasonable assumption if you see Suzuki training as a style of acting.

P 129 …and an openness of heart that most of us have learned to mask as part of that strange process of 'growing up'.
The above is another one of those '60s oppression' mantras. Why adopt such a pejorative attitude to what is a fact of life - it's called functioning as a successful member of a society! This immature, disaffected attitude is precisely what creates a theatre approach that is reactive and childish.

"SW:
Hmmm. I disagree. I think it's rather too easy in our world to act like a 'successful member of society'…..it seems to me that people 'growing up' is largely a masking process, which hides but does not eradicate the underlying 'openness' which is still available. Grotowski's Via Negativa would not make sense if this were not true.
**JN to SW:
To me this reflects a Newtonian reactive attitude more suited to the 19th century. It's a MarxiFreudie 'us-and-them' tennis match that should have died with Che Guevara. It's emotionally simplistic and one dimensional. We live in times made of wave/particle theory where assumption of paradox is the process – either/or morphs together. Surely modern acting should reflect that – not either civilized or primitive but both together in one compleat organism."**

P 131 In Search of Sorrow:
One place to begin is with the cat (exercise)…..the force of gravity itself will open your chest. Look upward and work with sound as you move forward.
This is Page 131 and it is the first time voice is mentioned! Surely if the aim is integration of voice and body, the voice should be there at the kick off.
"SW:

I agree......though Grotowski was very insistent upon our working in absolute silence at the beginning. The problem with adding sound early is that it immediately changes the privacy of some of the work. But you're right, that integrating the voice work is vital. I'm working on two books, one of which will address this directly.
JN to SW:
Interesting you should say that about G., as Suzuki has the same attitude for different reasons. S. believes that the body is not ready for speaking until it is really primed physically. The problem is that without voice at the start the Suzuki Method is seen as movement training. Without voice being prime it means that S & G are sidelined to the 'weird-side-of-theatre' ghetto.
For that reason I always start with speeches so participants do not assume that this is only 'physical theatre'. It's all about voice, but complicit with the body."

……..If you do have a hard time finding fear, try running hard, in place, while periodically looking back over your shoulder to see what may be coming after you.
Is this finding fear or making it up? Theatre as re-enactment, pretence?
There's a wonderful moment in the Peter Sellers film, AFTER THE FOX, where Victor Mature, in a wonderful self send-up trench coat cameo, is filmed running around a small Italian island, 'Antonioni' style. Asked what his motivation would be, he replied: "I'll be running away from myself!" After seeing this film it is very hard to take such 'gaming' seriously.

P 136 Only in acting are the creative personality, the material, the instrument, and the work of art itself combined in a single entity....
What about the dancer, the singer, the musician? However it is true, in one sense; that actors are uniquely different because they can forge their performative persona to a greater extent than the others, because unlike dancers, they are not prisoners of their given bodies. Ds, Ss and Ms

A Devil Pokes the Actor

require certain undeniable facilities to begin study, let alone continue....

P 137 The Paradoxes of Acting:
1. Acting is serious fun. **(I would say that Deep Play, (a phrase coined by hard-core mountaineers in Colorado, I might add!), would be more apposite).**
2. An actor must be both in control and out of control at the same time **(VERY TRUE!)**
3. As an actor you must pay attention to what goes on *inside* you and what is going on *outside* you **(also very true!).**

P 140 I feel: Sit in a chair........make eye contact... One of you says: "I feel"..........
The insurmountable problem with this is that as soon as you say: "I FEEL", you have unbalanced and de-stabilised the experience of feeling. To feel is an unconscious, subtle, amorphous experience that cannot be defined, and to speak of it is to make a conscious analysis of it by making some sort of 'rational' judgment. This undermines the purity and integrity of a special imaginative event.

"SW:
You're right. But this exercise is just a preparation for the physical stuff to follow, and it does establish the 'letting go' which is harder for people to find when active.
**JN to SW:
The problem with that is that the conscious mind has got there first, is now between the actor and the objective, and unless the actor is well prepared, its intervention depreciates the overall experience."**

P 141 In other words, in the first crossing, distance takes on an emotional quality, and emotion itself is felt and expressed in terms of distance.
Good start, to think of time and space in supra-dimensional terms, but to turn it into 'emotion' is too simplistic and

reductive. Why not leave it at 'feeling', and allow the subliminal complexity.
As well, emotions can only be felt - they cannot be expressed. A more accurate way to describe the transaction is to say that an audience is moved by witnessing an actor feel emotion.

P 141 The first Crossing:
Pt 7. ...to touch each other in a way the feels safe and comfortable, without breaking eye contact......
This becomes so subjective! One could just as easily say: "It felt safe and comfortable kicking him in the nuts." If you ask some one to make a subjective decision then you can't argue with the outcome. A true training doesn't countenance such ambiguous variables. It is not surprising that Carlos gets so delinquent and chucks a wobbly.

P 151 ...but then to make matters worse, we learn that we are to smile and say, "Thank you very much", even when we are not joyful at all.
YES! It's called being polite and, without etiquette, there is no societal structure. This is calling a cultural necessity a Marxian bad name. It's paradoxical that Americans should bring up these attitudes because they're the most polite people on Earth!

P 159 Grotowski helped actors expand their use of their vocal resonators by asking them to imagine that the sound they were producing was emanating 'mouths' in different locations on their bodies. In our 1967 workshops he would sometimes thump an actor firmly on the back, saying: "Let your mouth be here!"
Good dramaturgy on G's part. Notice how G didn't stand outside lobbing in ineffectual epithets, but was in there with the actor, in real time. It's called interdiction, and it imparts a moral dimension to the actor.

P 162 The Vocal Ribbons Exercise:
...the active partner pulls invisible ribbons of sound from parts of his partner's body, while the speaking partner permits his

body and voice to respond to the image of the pulls.
A Rainbow Moment! It's hard to imagine non-quiche eaters getting into such an exercise.

P 165 Every one is excited to be finally speaking words - 'acting' at long last. But in their excitement, most of them seem to forget many of the lessons they have learnt during the past month. While they yell yes and no at each other with great energy and conviction, many stand immobile, the physical and vocal variation..... forgotten.
Not surprising, because up to now, there appear to have been no exercises that integrate voice and body. The approach is bits of this and bits of that, like butterflies fluttering from bush to bush, unconnected and unresolved, and it all falls to bits when another issue or demand is presented.

P 166 ....let's return to the 'yes/no' game, but this time I want you to lead yourself into the words step by step. You will begin with the 2 person Plastiques, then add vowel sounds, and then consonants; then move onto gibberish, and finally, after making sure your bodies and voices are still engaged, move onto the actual English words Yes and No. Then, if you are able to keep your bodies and voices alive saying yes and no, try using other words to improvise arguments with each other.
Well put. That's putting a format in place, with a step by step structure and the use of tools - physical, sound, vowels, consonants, gibberish, words; having the tools and step by step structure means that the actors are much less likely to 'lose' themselves in the process. They have very clear objectives and subjective idiosyncracy is minimized rather than amplified.

The only caveat is the trainer/teacher's trusting of the actors to be able to judge whether they can 'keep their bodies and voices alive'. The vast majority of actors are unable to make this judgment because their body awareness hasn't been instilled! Even if they have an ability

to judge, it still requires the acute interdiction of a teacher/trainer.

P 169 I wish we could all read a few more plays and talk less about technique.
That's a major aesthetic issue! Quoting somebody that thinks plays are theatre! Theatre is NOT about reading and re-doing plays! It is about ENGAGING them, dis-membering and re-membering them!

I find it disconcerting that those touched by Grotowski's genius do not shadow his most important lesson for the West. He didn't do plays! He did works of theatre. Plays existed before G, but he showed everyone how to break the shackles of the written word and make engaging theatre.

P 178 "How was that", I ask when they finish. "Fine" says Joan. "I think these characters might even touch each other like that".
Why ask them about something they cannot really know. They are inside it – they may feel something, but ultimately they can't see, hear or quantify it.

P 181 For instance in the *Rimers of Eldritch* scene, Joan knew that something was wrong with a particular line, she was stymied by the opinion that her character would not act in a certain way.
This is proof positive why the teacher shouldn't ask the actor what they think! It only exacerbates the problem of making them think too much AND making them feel that their opinions are more important than what they are doing!

P 181 The basis of the technique we are studying here is that often your body will find deep, connected emotional logic without interference from your mind.
Beautiful talk, but where's the walk? This admirable proposal is countermanded by the lack of formats or routines that foster it! It always undermines the creative process if their minds are encouraged to intercede between themselves and the experience. Where is the exercise that

A Devil Pokes the Actor

puts their rational brain in back of the room?

P 186 Analogy with Sailing:
...it would be no fun or adventure if you could just go in a straight line. Its all that tacking that makes sailing fun...... Now please try doing the scene again as if you are sailing and you don't know whether you are going to get to your destination, right away or no, but there is a little time to enjoy the wind and the sun---- Allen Miller in Mekler...

It is compelling that he brings up sailing (I am a keen sailor myself) as it is the only sport where the person who wins is not the one who is fastest or strongest, but the one who's responded best to the variabilities of nature - the one who 'felt' and 'listened' most! In that it is very consonant with acting; as SW says before on page 137, acting is about relating to those around you (environment) as well as relating to your self.

P 187 ...Your character's intentions will arise within you, quite unconsciously, as you react to your own lines as well as your partner's actions and lines, without you needing to figure them out.

SW has put his finger right on it! Getting the conscious mind out of the way so the actor can genuinely feel what he is doing. It's very easy to propose, but how do you stop the conscious mind from taking over? How do you create a training simulacrum for that zone.

P 188 Alexander Tairov: While every other (visual) artist, both in the process of work and after its completion, being separate from the work he is creating, can at any moment physically see it, check it....... The actor lacks this important resource...... he must develop in himself an inner second sight; he must create alongside his own creative ego a second ego, unseen but seeing.

Spot on! Another way of articulating this is to say that an actor must develop an ability wherein his conscious mind is a witness to his unconscious creative processes - not

banished, but not getting in the way. It also means that an actor always needs a director, preferably a director with a strong personal vision and aesthetic landscape.

P 188 Blocking:
Blocking is incomplete movement direction. Why not go the whole way and provide fully defined structure? If you follow through your idea that you later propose on page 227, that true freedom lies inside discipline..... after all, discipline IS structure. The more structure, paradoxically the more freedom!

Nearly all directors are unable to furnish this structure, because they don't know what they want to see or to say. Most directors have no real point of view - no statement to make. They'd rather be vague and say 'they don't want to stifle the creativity' – 'don't kill the moment and hope it comes out alright' is the standard attitude. These are avuncular imperatives. To be more demanding of the actor would mean that they would have to be more demanding of themselves, they would have to look deep inside themselves for what they truly wanted to say…….

P 189 Viewpoints:

V/P's were devised as a post-modern dance tool, a DIY paint by numbers kit for choreographers that had nothing to say, but thought they should be saying something. As a professional modern dancer I was doing such stuff in the 70s so I know of which I speak.
It was developed by Mary Overlie who was part of the Judson Street Church post modern movement in the early 60s.
They set up the PoMo Codex :
    No story,
    No sets,
    No cossies,
    No sexual di-morphism,
    No hierarchical language,

> No start....no finish,
> No front...no back,
> No dancing to music,
> Actually... frequently no music.

There were probably other things they were against, but suffice it to say there wasn't much they were for. Having banned every aspect of imaginative content, they needed a compliance manual and Viewpoints is it. The name itself is an inversion because the VP's are for artists that have no point of view in Moral terms. They don't believe in anything except themselves.

Post Modern directors have picked up on it for the same reason. Real directors who have something to say don't need it as they have their own personal dramaturgy. Such directors that have something to say - soul speak, are as rare as rocking-horse shit.

P 197: Rehearsing on Your Own:
Mandatory.

P 200 How to talk to another actor (or: **how to get on with another actor).**
This is the director's job! An actor's compact is between his self and the audience - it is the director's purview to relate actors to each other, in physical, vocal, emotional and psychological terms.

"SW:
I disagree. I don't feel actors should need a director to talk to each other.
JN to SW:
So what's the director for? Traffic management? Is she a glorified cop?"

P 209 The Eyes:
Try telling someone about an event that just happened to you, and force yourself to keep looking at him while talking. Probably,

halfway through….you will want to look away… because while really seeing him you lost contact with the inner objects you were talking about….. while we talk we look intermittently at the person to whom we are talking……in between… we contact the inner objects we are dealing with.
Uta Hagen.
This is a very perceptive observation by Ms Hagen originating from a person who is highly aware of their actions and reactions and has been analyzing them thoroughly.

P 213 The scene has been affective, but the performance seems somehow reserved….I ask the actresses to tell us how they think the scene went.
Why ask the actors how the scene went? They are inside it, how could they know?

"SW:
I think that when you wrote 'another way of articulating this is to say that an actor must develop an ability wherein his conscious mind is a witness to his unconscious creative processes – not banished, but not getting in the way' you were 'spot on'. As you say here, an actor CAN 'know' from the inside.
JN to SW:
Touche! But not quite! I was saying that…..rather what I should have said was 'the actor can know unconsciously, but not consciously because the conscious corrupts, etc. etc."

P 214 "Were you aware that you were whispering?" I ask 'Sandra'.
"Whispering? No I felt like I was yelling all the time."
A telling anecdote! After several weeks/months of intensive work, she has no idea of what her voice is doing? Where has all the so-called voice and body training led?

P 217 Plastiques with Real Objects:
As I mentioned before, humans are *projective* beings. We fill the world around us with meaning. Not only do we fall in love with

A Devil Pokes the Actor 243

people who remind us of other people; we also endow objects (teddy bears, etc.....) with 'life'. In fact many ancient religions were based on the belief that every object had a spirit. Of course we modern, rational folks have banished the gods to the heavens, and we manage to keep our tendencies towards animism under control... most of the time, yet every once in a while our magical, animistic tendencies evince themselves. We talk to our plants, etc.........Each of these actions is a sign that we still retain our ability to see inanimate objects as filled with life- life that we have projected *onto* them, but that we experience as if we were receiving it *from* them.
VERY, VERY, VERY GOOD!

P 219. Working with Mistakes:
At the end of the run-through, 'Joan' is clearly upset: "I didn't want to start over; it was going so well, so it pissed me off when he stopped the scene for that line".
"And I didn't know that... all the moments we had set still worked....."
Are they so little prepared and so precious that they are unable to re-start a scene from any point? All emotion! No discipline and no moral fibre whatsoever!
Why don't they stop acting like spoilt brats and get on with it? Why the blame game? It shows that their Ego's emotional reaction is more important than what they are doing, and the process seems to exacerbate the problem. The true place for their feelings is the rehearsal, not the response to the rehearsal.

"SW:
Well, yes, but that's often something a young actor needs to learn. These lessons are exactly about that learning. Again, I feel my role is not to 'tell' actors this, but to let them discover it. My reasons for this approach to teaching will be made clear in a pedagogy book I'm working on now.
JN to SW: Okey Doke."

P 227 The true lesson of the sacred theatre, whether ancient or medieval European, Balinese or Indian Kathakali, is that spontaneity and discipline, far from weakening each other, mutually reinforce each other....Grotowski.

Very good summation of the purpose in configuring freedom to structure and that you cannot have freedom without powerful routine. It is interesting to conjecture why, when G. understood the purpose he didn't forge a training which fostered that.

P 228 Sandra describes how she was at home preparing a meal and in so doing she found some key elements.

........So I decided just to make myself feel better I would make some steamed vegetables and brown rice. Comfort food, you know. But then, as I was cutting the vegetables, the lines of the scene just started happening in my head.........

Excellent demonstration of moving into unconscious space and finding patterns and pathways that was foreshadowed in the response to P. XXXIII. How to transpose that and generate it in a rehearsal situation?

P 231 It is extremely difficult to repeat the same emotion over and over again. You are taking a big risk when you depend on your emotions as the basis for reproducing a scene when you have a long run. On the other hand you can repeat body details in exactly the same way every day. Working from body shape is useful for actors. (Yoshi Oida).
Very True!

P 231 What these students discovered is the strange fact that ratcheting up the demands for precision by insisting that their gestures be tightly co-ordinated with their text actually increased their experience of freedom and the strength of their emotional truth.....Once you have found emotional depth in your work external technical precision... can actually augment the fullness of your internal experience.

Oh so accurate! So why isn't that the core principle from which the training system should emanate? 'External technical precision' is another way of saying time/space formatting and if you are saying that such structure is highly beneficial, where's the simulacrum?

A Devil Pokes the Actor

P 233 To be an actor is to be an acrobat of the heart.
Why not go all the way and replace heart with 'soul'. Is it a measure of the pervasive influence of sub Marxian attitudes that soul has become a dirty word - a modern heresy? It's fascinating that G became a world wide hit in a godless society of devout sceptics by producing work of undeniable 'soul', yet even the mention of this word is an anathema by those very people who were blown away by 'The Constant Prince' and 'Apocalypsis'. Such was the climate of the sixties and seventies denial, and it still seems to be with us.

The proof of this denial-ism was demonstrated by the discovery (after his death) of a hoard of religious paintings that Andy Warhol had painted at home on his own. What does that say about where his brain really wanted to be? While he had warehouses stacked full of bric-a-brac, what did the King of Empty Popery really care about? And not talk about?

P 236 – 292
These 56 pages detail a way to approach character. This is essentially directorial, not didactic. There's nothing to critique here, as all directors have their ways of approaching actor and production preparation and one cannot critique a personal attitude or mannerism.

This section reads reminiscent of numerous other books, which slightly contemporize stereotypical clichés such as: "if you want to look old, practice walking with a limp". (These fuzzywuzzy little approaches date back to before electricity but that doesn't stop them being recycled).

My only comment is…… that was precisely what the Grot DID NOT do! He stood dead squarely against such sclerotic theatre and he became a superstar in the west due to his stance.
I think it becomes a moral prerogative that if your artistic sensibility is galvanized by something or someone, like G

or S, then you should digest it and attempt to somehow go further. I consider it an ethical duty to take the gift situation of working with a master, absorb the experience (which can take a LOT of time), and attempt to produce something evolutional. One cannot predict if it will succeed or not, but the 'attempt' contains an undeniable moral imperative.

This is theatre history that is accumulative, not continuum or even worse, devolutional. I accept that this is a resolutely extreme stance, yet not many people can even seem to regard it as mandatory, let alone try and live up to it.

P 298 Unlike singers and dancers.... Actors are asked to present real live human beings.
Surely the act of performing is, by its very nature, essentially a mythical experience. The real people are sitting in the audience, or walking around outside the theatre. Pretending to be someone other than your self, can't be *real*. Pretending to be someone real is a psychic lie, and must lead to existential confusion.

Stagefright – the eerie feeling that there are people out there watching you.

I would say that it's more than a feeling.... there are people out there watching - it's a truth!

Stage fright is simply the existential crisis brought on when an actor confronts an audience. When one is rehearsing in the studio, one becomes comfortable with the environment (be it the other actors, the director, pictures on the walls, chairs in the studio, etc). Suddenly, on the stage, not only does the environment in front of him change, it disappears and is replaced by a void - and even worse, there are eyes out there, hundreds of eyes, staring at the actor IN EXPECTATION!
This collective energy can overwhelm the psyche of the actor and, unexpectedly he doesn't know who he is

A Devil Pokes the Actor 247

anymore. His sense of self has been threatened and he feels lost and abandoned; but if you think about what he's going through, it's a simple issue. And once faced, not as an amorphous black magic cloud, but as an honest, natural procedural problem, it is not hard to counter-act.

Like all forms of anxiety, when they are faced square-on, they diminish considerably. The biggest step is to acknowledge them as a truth and proceed with: "How do I deal with it?"

There follows some examples of the ways many directors and theoreticians deal with stage fright, and all of them attempt to function under a culture of denial – all pretending it is something other than genuine existential crisis rather than acknowledge and accept it as anxiety, they try and shutter it out, denying it's there.
But like the elephant in the room that nobody talks about, it's there all right, and ignoring it is no way to handle it!

It's interesting that good old Lee S. gets the actor to pretend the audience isn't there- Well! Actually, the audience really is there! How weird is that? Pretend the audience isn't there?

That's not to say that these various remedies do not work, but let's face it, they are by and large negative and reactive, rather than positive and pro-active.

Postulating that the problem is 'others judging you', SW offers an exercise that asks the actor to anthropomorphize 'judgment', not necessarily a bad thing in itself, but a tad difficult. We at Ozfrank have created more structured exercises that use Teddy Bears as empirical role models. (Don't laugh too loud... it works!) Their tactile quality and anthropomorphic immediacy have been very effective at dealing with the separation of the judgmental and the experiential sides of the brain.

P 307 When you are depressed or burnt out or overworked, your mental and emotional processes are impaired, and that interferes with your art.
Surely, when times are tough, it's time to get back on the training track. You only build spirit by battling your way through adversity, and that's what a true training is for.
P 319.........and a bad teacher can destroy your interest, even in material you love.
In that case, you didn't really love it. If you allow a bad teacher to put you off, you were the temporary holder of a transient belief.

......But in the end it is not the technique that will sustain you. Any technique you learn will tend to fall away as you create your on way of working....

Try telling an opera singer or a surgeon that advice! This is another variant of the old chestnut that technique is somehow uncreative and kills the delicate soul of the thespian. Just over the page is a quote from Yoshi Oida, where he can't tell the difference between style and technique. Someone should tell him that style is personal idiosyncracy and technique is universal and transposable. It is so fatuous when genuine experts like Oida, who have buckets of technique and experience, mouth post-modern platitudes that deny the very factors that made them.

In closing, I was disappointed that the book couldn't demonstrate more of the 5 stage trajectory of creative growth that might be termed Inspiration, Interrogation, Ingestion, Inspection and Indication.

<u>**Inspiration**</u>**: Time working with a genuine master who is further and deeper along the track.**
<u>**Interrogation**</u>**: What were the constituent elements of that inspired the actor?**
<u>**Ingestion**</u>**: The process of osmotically absorbing these elements past the brain, into the DNA of the body.**
<u>**Inspection**</u>**: The time it takes to reformulate it as personal**

vision.
Indication: The expression of a new individual aesthetic.

Having said all this I am most grateful for Stephen's reasonable and gracious responses.

My devil's eyelids drop and twist as he, upside down and hangin' above my head, looks at me...... askance, the eyes narrow into golden green vertical slits...... suddenly, our spurts a torrent of vituperative verbiage:

"You're a clevva little fella, Johnny-come-lately ! How do ya do it, all those polysyllabic putdowns to render achunder all the temples of the toadies and put frighteners on the fogeys. Crashing and bashing up the pillars of their psyches, like Samson at the mill with slaves ! Let's see how you cope with columns cascading around your eyes and ears !"

Immediately my mind is assailed by my astrological trine and square, aided and abetted by toppled columns that triple toss and teeter.........maybe I augered too far......... too deep......
"OK OK OK now you want me to give some substance to my spleen. How's about a digress of matrix and dialectic to show the heart behind the horror."

Migraine Provocation #5
Agar Gel is not a microscope
The Complimentary Differential between Matrix and Dialectic:

In the last chapter whilst scrutinising *An Acrobat of the Heart*, I realised that few theatre people appear to understand the difference between an actor training and the dialectic between an actor and a director. They tend to think they are the same, and they believe that there is no difference in the way they affect actor preparation.

Matrix (definition): "an environment or material in which something develops".
I am using this word to describe the nature of a true actor training and to differentiate said training from a directorial dialectic.

Dialectic (definition): "to and fro 'dialogue' between two different positions leading gradually to some form of raprochement". In acting it might be put as the dialogue between the ideas of the director and the ability of the actor to realise them.
I am using the word 'dialectic' to describe the preceptive relationship between the director and the actor, where the director makes suggestions and observations about the actor's performance and the actor responds.

On Page XXXVIII of his book, Steve Wangh wrote:
'The external forms this book teaches include the Plastique and the Corporeal…..the exercises themselves are not a method they are merely provocations…..'

My Response was:
True! They are not a method (a matrix) but represent an attitude (a dramaturgical approach). As such, they are a dialectic between the director and the actor. But that dialectic needs to work inside a matrix, and the matrix cannot be a dialectic itself, as they would self churn. Most so called actor systems are

actually dialectics and that is why, when they are also compounded by the director's attitudinal dialectic, they become subject to confusions and obfuscations.

The important line is:
But that dialectic needs to work inside a matrix, and the matrix cannot also be a dialectic itself, as they would 'self churn'.

The Matrix:
Matrix is used in science to describe a structured environment that provides nutrition potential for an organism, and protecting the organism from destructive agents that would threaten or corrupt it. A good example of this is the **Agar Gel** used inside a **Petrie Dish** that scientists use to study and create chemical cultures. The function of the Agar Gel in the dish is to quarantine the material from contamination so that by lessening the variables and unknowns they are able to particularise the study.

If actor training is to have the same rigour it has to exist inside an equivalent matrix, erecting structures and employing formats to eradicate the maverick emotional and psychological elements. The 'protection' this offers is the cropping of the deceptive, delusional and destructive highs and lows to which the actor's Ego is susceptible.
Music and Sport do this by utilising clearly defined Boundaries, Way Stations and Signposts. The player/student is clear about what is required of them, and where and when they should be 'on the field' or 'in the song'. The basic craft work being taken care of by the Matrix, the teacher/coach is able to concentrate on the more sophisticated aspects such as strategy and nuance. These aspects would come under the heading of 'dialectic'.

The Dialectic:
Dialectic labels the give and take relationship between the actor and director. It is a circular 'dialogue' consisting of suggestions and interdictions given by the director, and 'answered' by the actor's ability to generate creative shifts. It is a dialogue because it has a continuous flow over the duration of rehearsals and

performances.

Its progress is very dependant on the character types on both sides of the fence and, as such, cannot be pinned down to any meaningful extent. Important determinants would include vision and perception on the part of the director and responsiveness and the technique of the actor. There are myriad other factors involved; personality traits, circumstance, time, etc., all contributing crucial components in the development of an actor's role.

Such a dialectic requires enormous psychic effort on the part of the director. One can understand the difficulty the actor faces as they attempt renewal, but that attempt places an even greater moral pressure on the director to enhance their perceptivity, so they can recognise the creative shifts that an actor achieves as they advance.

To sustain this psychic focus, the director needs a ready made, stand alone, landscape, that he can be 'inside' while working with the actor. He cannot be simultaneously 'inside ' the space whilst in the process of 'making' it. That would be analogous to a coach simultaneously giving instructions for a passage of play, whilst also trying to study the player in the passage.

Judging from reports of various situations like the ones described in AAotH, the director and actors are caught in a double dip dialectic, where the director is both running the exercise and trying to 'read' its implications. This causes the 'self churn' that I mentioned, and SW recounts several instances where the actors became frustrated and disaffected, due to the confused potential.

In most of the other books I have read that are concerned with teaching actors, this ambiguity and self churn would appear to be the rule rather than the exception. In AAotH, the mistaken belief that dramaturgical attitude is a methodology demonstrates the dilemma most clearly.

By self churn, I mean that the two dialectics in tandem erode each other like two sacrificial anodes, and the ensuing ambiguity in the 'room' makes the actors confused and emotional. In this the actors are reflecting the uncertainty of the director, because the director is caught between being a part-participant and a witness.

The matrix, to have its own inviolate structure, must operate as a stand alone event, with its demarcations and nodes formatted so that the actor can occupy them without the director's necessary real-time input. That is not to say that the director should be detached from the training, because that would mean moral abdication. The director must be separated from the matrix, but connected to it, so that he/she can stand outside it and re-enter on choice.

Without a stable matrix, the interdiction (demands) of the director is liable to misinterpretation by the actors because there is no undeniable structure within which to site the demands.

A Devil Pokes the Actor

"Enough of that stuff" **bellows from behind!**

Although I'm getting used to my devil's seismic shifts, this is bigger than before! Now my eyes are assaulted by Henry the Eighth in all his whiskered glory, waving half a chicken leg with his mouth spewing forth the rest.
As my mind tries to decipher the sputters, belches, and splutters it begins to dawns that he looks like Charles Laughton looking like the rascal Tudor Monarch. It may be that the old devil's a filmic buff………..

"Okeydoke! I submit a letter I recently wrote to an American actor, Nathan Sorseth, whom I had taught in Seattle in 2008. We had met in Toga some years before, when he had gone to work with Suzuki as part of a postgrad project for the University of Delaware. Amongst the Yanks he was the most temperamentally suited to the scheme and a coupla years later we set up a correspondence, after he bought my first book. This is one such. A forthright chap, of sincere and independent mien, we hope to work together again……….."

The devil adopts a wheedling, seeming sincere tone his conspiratorial mouth pursed and his spiny fingers in intimate play in front of his chin.
"My fwiend, this book has been far too weasonable! Let's wend the weader on The Way of the Molecule, whewein pewusal opens up a door to instwuctive abstwaction"

Deep breath……..now we'll take the left hand fork to the other margin of the mind, the shadowy borders of the brain, and open up wide to reveal the twilight world inside.

How do Butoh and Charles Laughton show us the refractive trails of more vaporous conceits, where the final provocations take us on The Way of the Molecule……

Molecular Provocation #1
BUTOH and Charles Laughton's attitude

A letter to Nathan Sorseth, an actor who lives in Seattle, USA.
March, 2008

Dear N8,
Your mentioning of KK (a colleague Katsura Kan - a Butoh practitioner known to both Jacqui and myself) has fired me up in another way. I know a little of Butoh, because I've been around a lot of it one way or another, and there seems to be many parallels between it and the sort of training we espouse.

As an example we use a lot of surfing music for the more improvisatory exercises. When giving suggestions, I would say," Rather than pretending to be a surfer, be the wave he is on, or the wax on the board!" or even on one occasion:" Be his underpants left in the changing rooms!" This is very parallel with Butoh as it concentrates not on outward appearance or structure, but identifies that which lies inside/behind, and then making it externally apparent. It is shooting for the deep essence of things and amplifying them rather than fabricating replication.

This attitude also refers back to the long term arc of doing the basic SATM exercises like number 2. The sequence starts by swinging the leg out prior to bringing it forcefully back into a high, bent position, on the second count the foot stomps into the floor adjacent to the bent standing leg, on the third count the stomped leg advances to a forward lunge with the back leg stretched and all the weight on the bent front leg. It repeats to the other side.

The movements are quite simple and require no exceptional facility – it is the way it is done that is paramount. As a beginner, one is concerned with getting the legs and timing and positions right. One then graduates to gaining strength, stability and stillness as one becomes more proficient. If it is continued, over the long term, one starts to move into a more transformative

zone where the approach moves away from purely athletic to more subtle, abstracted ideas such as:
- What is behind or inside the muscles and the experience?

If one doesn't approach the training with more elasticity and suppleness in the long run, it hardens into brittleness, and constipates. This change of field beyond the linear and obvious to the abstract and the subtle is also congruent with Butoh.

During training the other night I opined that that Butoh had become an inspiration for modern dance. Western post-modern dance had become so obsessed with the minutiae of vocabulary and had disappeared up a dry gully full of isms, e.g. minimalism, conceptualism et al, that one could say it had become fixated upon a sort of pictorial intellectualism. It is as though the pioneering spaces of broad movement invention had contracted into the dessicated obsession with esoteric minimal gesture.

Butoh's ideas of inner search have proved to be a window into a new world for dance practitioners as a way out of the muddle because it has foreshadowed a terra incognita to explore - that of context, ie that of exploring not the object (the dance sequence), but the performer's relationship with the object.

This attitude to context is where I have been leading the FSPA over the last few years and, I think I arrived at its objective articulation that night when I talked about the Butoh.

Within that move to greater abstraction we have also progressively applied more elasticity to our vocal work. We are applying Butoh-like properties to voice.

In the FSPA when we speak we use 4 major voice 'levels':-
1) Full voice (FV) – the body using its entire energy resources to speak as powerfully as it can,
2) Quiet voice (QV) - a standard full stage voice,
3) Super quiet voice (SQV) - the quietest one can speak with the vocal chords still resonating,
4) Whisper (W) - The loudest one can speak with no vocal chord resonance.

Actors are expected to sustain or switch the levels at command, with the proviso that the rhythm remains unchanged. Standardised rhythm is mandatory, because without it, group speaking would be chaos.

Full voice (FV) is the most often used as it is the best educator, because at full energy, as Jacqui once said '**nothing stands between the actor and the experience**'. With the FV being the primary learning point the other voices gradually learn to have the same intensity as the FV.

To make the experience even more flexible and fluent, I have recently added other voice zones:-
    a. Freeform - any level, own choice
    b. Change - switch to another free choice level,
    c. Crazy - any of the weirdest possibilities one can invoke,
    d. Different - the most interesting and most congruent with Butoh.

I might add here that all voice switches should be done as a completely instinctive action, as an animal might strike its prey. The idea is to 'land' on a switch-voice instinctively and maintain that choice despite any vicissitudes that may arise (such as shortness of breath). The actor shouldn't be concerned with the 'success' of the experience, whether it sounds good, but concentrate on the 'feeling' of the experience as it is being done. Of the four new zones, freeform, crazy are fairly straight forward, but, I hear you ask; "Aren't 'different' and 'change' the same thing?" I'll explain.

Another vector on this inspiration trail was provided when I read a biography of Charles Laughton by Simon Callow. Laughton would be considered by many people to be the greatest actor to ever appear on film and as far as I can see he is the inventor of 'Method Acting' in the late 20s in England, well before the golden period in New York in the 50s. Laurence Olivier, no slacker himself, said CL was the only genius actor he ever knew. The writer, Callow, is a very capable actor himself and so has forged a book full of pertinent eye openers into the drivers of

CL's achievements, and by extension opened certain windows into potential acting agendas. There are a stack of Bon Mots of the insight kind scattered throughout, but an earlier one in particular took my fancy. It is on Page 51 and goes like this:-

"......it's never the simple observation with Laughton though, it's never impersonation. He embodies both what he saw **and his attitude to it......**"

I found this very exciting to behold as it represents an intelligent actor's perception of a supreme actor's modus operandi, suggesting an approach to the craft that was pregnant with more potential.

If one could use the example of playing 'Richard III', using this approach meant that you could not only play the character of R3, but you could also invoke your thoughts about him, your attitude to him.

It is always difficult to play mythical figures convincingly, especially those with highly drawn character traits, (eg uber Nasties), as it is hard for actors to attain a transcendent zone where they can appear larger than their daily mannerisms. It is easier to have an attitude to someone such as R3, so if you can combine the character and your attitude to it, it could be possible to access deeper and more flexible interpretations. One way of looking at it is to say that your final version is the character multiplied by your relationship to it. As well, changing your attitude can be a prelude to changing yourself. It is easier to change your attitude to something than it is to change yourself viz: it's hard to **be** a nice person, but not so hard to **be nice** to other people. Maybe by changing your attitude to outside things, then you can evolve yourself.

Another piece of this thematic jigsaw.....
Whilst working with Suzuki as a guest member of his company, I observed how demanding Suzuki was and often found it difficult to ascertain why he became dissatisfied with certain aspects of

the play sometimes, but not at others, and how he would say a speech was good one day and denounce it the next. I personally could not perceive any differential and one could have put it down to his mood swings, etc. Of course as a director, he would be concerned with making the work constantly fresh and of continuing interest to him, so he could well have demanded that you say a speech differently. But Suzuki is rare in that he doesn't want you to change things for change's sake as he regards that as a weak and obvious response. So how could he expect you to be continuously interesting without changing elements such as speed, intonation, etc? I could never perceive any whimsy about Suzuki's attitude, so I pondered on this anomaly for a number of years (actually from 1994-2006), before realising that if he didn't want it to be the same , but he also didn't want it to be different; maybe he wanted neither OR both. Was he after what might be called the place between same and different? We generally expect 'same' and 'different' to be two separate experiences - perhaps they could be considered two paradoxical parts of the same experience (this is another Butoh thought pattern!) and it also mirrors Einstein's process (much more of which later).

Armed with this notional shift, I could look at how to introduce that idea into our training. Over the last few weeks during training the company actors and I formulated how the commands 'different' and 'change' would be interpreted. We decided that 'change' would indicate a pronounced shift away from the existing voice zone (full, or whisper, etc) to another zone, and 'different' would signify a different sensibility about it whilst trying to keep it the same as it was before. I wasn't quite sure why I wanted this or where it was leading, but I certainly felt that the frisson of energy in the room caused by this enigmatic state was very compelling. One night at training, the 'his attitude towards the 'subject' aspect of Laughton's craft came to me as we were doing a speech and the idea crystallised at once - " I don't want you to change the speech... I want you to change your attitude to the speech! ". From there it morphed into changing your 'relationship with your voice' without necessarily changing the voice itself.

Although I profess no deep knowledge of Butoh, proximity to it over a number of years has given me a nudge to be more ambitious and elastic about the exercises we do.
Cheers Big Ears John N.

All that 'other ether' talk brought about by Butoh has changed the space. The alien attitude has moved the mood of the room. As I sit at my desk, I begin to smell the shift. A slight whiff of unearthly halitosis wafts over: the bizarre opposites of hot ceramic and cool metallic ozone. I feel it on my neck, drift down my back, and..... turn.
As I turn I spiral up and up and up. My head disconnects from my bod and hovers over the stairs, devil at me back, a clouded beardy eminence slowly intoning into my ear:

"Speak of Jung and the big combo of con and uncon......."

My eyes glaze over for just above and far below, a couple of coal black angels spirit into view, echoes of another time, another life ago. A ballet called Black Angels. They shimmy unsuspended, a double from my dancing prime in '79. I left the dance, and left behind a shadow of my former kind.

As he brings it flooding back, is he trying to say that he's my other side, my other half of me……the unconscious, underskinny, undercurrent to my………..not sure what……in fact ! I'm trying to work it out.

"Loooooook I'm onto it!
Like harpies to a bag of shit
It'll make your wings flop and your horns split
Your fur fry to the last little follicle
As we go deep, down deeper into the Way of the Molecule......"

Molecular Provocation #2
Iggy's 'suctional' charisma
How to use the C and U words in acting

Now, before we go any further, this chapter will be full of references to the 'Conscious' **(C)** and 'Unconscious' **(U),** and I use these words in a way stimulated by some reading of material by and about Carl Jung, the dogma-lite interrogator of the mind. I am uninterested in the psychiatric academic blah blah blah surrounding the guy because I only want to use his attitude of 'working hypotheses' as an investigative process. So....please, no Jung freaks squawking that I got the third bit of the fourteenth chapter of the second book all wrong!

What really intrigued me about Jung was that early in his career he found that a female cousin had clairvoyant tendencies. He spent a fair time with her doing ouija board type trials before finding out that the whole thing was a charade - she was infatuated with him, and working her womanly wiles towards a wedding. What followed was very much the measure of the man and became a life long quest. He could easily have thrown the baby out with the bath water but instead he said: " Alright, she was fraudulent, but.....more to the point...What hidden part of the mind has she shown me - the state I could call the unconscious?" Rather than a blanket right or wrong, he saw it as a hypothesis to research. This makes him a lot different from others such as Sigmund the Freud who had one great notion and spent the rest of the time proving that everything can be squeezed into it.

Jung was a different kind of shrink. He didn't perambulate through the wards labelling the defectives in the mental institution with generalities. Instead he talked to them, one on one, to get their particular story. This pattern of augering deep into the **why** rather than being happy with the **what**, became his life's journey, opening a lot of doors for us all in the process. He was concerned with the C and U in terms of how it affected healing and he was most emphatic on many occasions that what

he was doing was **not art**.
I am interested in the opposite position and am purely concerned with their function in the production and reception of art. I see art as part of social healing - healing, not as repair, but as **unification of the divided psyche** in the actor and in the audience. To re-phrase Jung, Art is a vehicle for reconciling and balancing the conscious and unconscious forces: firstly for the actor, and then by using the actor as intermediary, for society as a whole.

At Ozfrank, we see the actor as a microcosm of the audience's macrocosm. The actor is a particular of the audience's generality, an on-the-spot Shaman undergoing transformative experiences on behalf of the audience. For that to happen, the actor's personal unconscious must connect with the audience's **Collective Unconscious**. And what stands in the way big time? Answer, the Conscious parts of both the actor and the audience.

Jung's C and U seem to be the most appropriate words that encompass psyche processes that have powerful qualities but are difficult to quantify. Because they are activities of the mind they have no definitive shape, but they trigger forceful influences in all sorts of ways in society.

Below is a list of the nuanced states and wider possible angles for C and U:

CONSCIOUS	UNCONSCIOUS
Analytical	Instinctive
Logical	Intuitive
Black or White	Varying shades of Grey
Linear time	Elastic time
Fully planned	Dreamscape
Tightly structured	Daydream
Reasoned	Nightmare
Rational	Mysterious
Know for a fact	Feel
Awake or Asleep	Half awake

Science	Alchemy
Jay walker	Sleep walker

All these words on both sides of the divide are 'for instance' synonyms, and their antonyms for **C** and **U**, to give some idea of the complexity and depth of field. Those on the left represent the search for reason - making sense of the world - being in charge - a position of control. Those on the right accept mystery - resign to fate - bend with the wind - deal with life's vagaries.

We are all a combination of both. Without a conscious mind we wouldn't be able to survive biologically - we know that if we don't eat we'll die of starvation and if we don't Look Right.... Look Left..... then Look Right again at the school crossing, we'll get king hit by a milk truck! <u>But we also have an inner life: we read.... watch art.....enjoy sport....... none of which is necessary for survival, but ironically, is what life is actually for!</u> Every society has to both be in touch with itself (soul) and also be prepared to progress (science), U covers the first and C governs the second. Our Western society in general is very good at the science and progress and seems to have junked the soul and replaced it with 'nice'.

As you no doubt have had it drilled into you by anything and everything you read and hear, we live in a technologically advanced society and we have sacrificed some things to get it. An example: I was called for dinner the other night, at the time I was writing this chapter and listening to some music on another laptop. I pressed one button to save and then left-clicked the media player and immediately the sound stopped dead.........instant silence!

I had a full frontal thought: "How easy is it now to kill music!" .....and a follow on: "What does it do to my soul to be able to kill music so easily?" Even in the old days of record players, you had to reach over, lift the needle off the LP, put in its holder, clip it in then replace the cover. The whole event was slower, more mechanical - you didn't kill the music so much as put it to sleep. If you go back further, unless you were personally making the music, the time it took to either get into or out of music was longer - the further back the longer... 150 years ago, to get access to any sort of music meant sacrificing time to go and see someone play, and you couldn't just turn them off and abruptly sever the access to your soul (for music talks directly to the soul). That time of approach and the time of receding are important because it is during that time that the soul, having imported the transformative effect, diffuses it throughout the entire body. As we speak, current Ipod technology has made it possible to hold an entire music library in the palm of a Paris Hilton hand and listen to 'like whatever..... like....... whenever'! I'm sure that soon, you'll be able to get waterproof ones, with a shampoo attachment, that work in the shower.

What little must it really mean to said punter when they have to make no sacrifices, clear no space in their brain for it to occupy. Paradoxically, it fills up their life, yet it doesn't mean anything, because it is both ever present but no particular psyche space is apportioned to it.

So there is a price for techno-progress. All the helter skelter means loss of contact with soul, and the only way to get it back is to beef up the unconscious, because as one of our associates Jor'el Mitchell proposed: "The Soul is the thinking place of the Unconscious".

Art is the secular matrix wherein people and society have intercourse with their soul, and in our field the audience has a conversation with their souls by witnessing actors who are in dialogue with:

1. their own soul,
2. the soul of the 'space',
3. the souls of the other actors,
4. the souls of the play and playwright,
5. the souls of the present audience,
6. the souls who have witnessed the play throughout its history.

When the audience pays their shekels, they contract to have both an individual and a collective experience. For us that means both the Individual U and the Collective U of those present and past, and by extension, humanity in toto. At Ozfrank the actor's vocation in complicity with the audience as refractive mirror is to discover or reveal a new 'soul value',. The actor opens and exercises the instinctive aspects of his mind (unconscious), and the audience intuitively 'reads' this emanation in similar fashion to a pre-cognitive culture witnessing a shaman performing psychic 'healing'.

I first thought like this while watching a video performance, **Kiss My Blood**, which is footage shot of **Iggy Pop** in Paris in the early 90s. Iggy is a genuine rock and roll shaman - poetic, sacrificial and eternally interrogative. He spends most of his time bounding around chaotically in his unique antic way, with occasional moments of breathtaking poise and stillness. One of these 'stillnesses' occurs half way through a chunky version of 'China Girl'. He'd been maniacally leaping about facing the back of the stage, when he suddenly crouches.....goes quiet.....turns to the audience, puts his finger to his lips and whispers: "She says Shhhhhhhh".

It was very compelling, because the unexpected quietness suddenly sucked you in to what he was doing, whereas immediately before you were 'standing back' marvelling at his spastic acrobatics. I called that a heavy dose of **'suctional' charisma**. I realised that all his gestural mayhems were to get himself into instinctive unconscious states - they were preparations for a series of shamanic moments.

Some time later I thought of an important corollary to that. On going over in my mind what he had done, I further realised that possibly Iggy hadn't meant to do any thing of the sort - maybe he was just singing a song, and that I had invented the whole story, maybe it was all in my head. But then I thought: "It doesn't matter how I got it, it's such a great notion even if it's all my own invention". I eventually surmised that even if he hadn't intended it, I couldn't have received the idea without watching Iggy do his own personal 'schtick'. In other words: I had my own transformational idea by watching Iggy go through some sort of personal transformation.

Even later, I realised that his manic provocative movements were possibly a deliberate act to take him into chaos, so that his conscious mind would be distracted. For the conscious processes cannot abide physical confusion, pain or exhaustion. The conscious rational processes retire hurt, so to speak, and go back to sit on the bench and wait out the rest of the game.
In Iggy's case, this opened the space to allow his unconscious, imaginative self to elevate him to a transformed state. Those watching are drawn into this dream time zone. Each watcher is taken to their personal dream zone and, because it was shared, it became a collective dream zone.

Who knows where these zones may lead, but that's really what the people pays their money for. <u>Effectively they are adding to their unconscious experiences to balance out the enormous overburden of the conscious which fills their daily lives.</u> For the 'magic' experience to continue, the audiences' minds need to remain in unconscious mode, with the power of their rational 'critical' faculties suspended, observing from the side, to later re-assert for homologation.

(**Homologation** is a term that refers to the approval of design/structural developments in motor car racing). I use it here in a similar fashion to describe the way the conscious part of the brain amalgamates and incorporates all the new experiences that the body undergoes. It is the responsibility of the Conscious to de-cypher, categorise and prioritise the wide variety of sensations so that the mind as a whole may learn how to use them effectively for navigating the springs and shoals of future life.

Homologation is the term that describes the process whereby:
Information morphs into **Knowledge,** and
Knowledge morphs into **Wisdom.**

It is what links the three stages of learning:
1. **Inspiration** - the taking in of new information,
2. **Digestion** - the deconstruction and reconstruction of it to suit the body, and
3. **Expression** - the portrait of its new individualised configuration.

Without the critical categorising of the Conscious, all incoming information would have equal and equally chaotic value. It would be pandemonium up there in the brainbox! It is the conscious that allocates responsibility and relative importance - the usefulness of any information and how best to apply it, in order for the survival of the organism. During the ingestion of new information the Conscious mind should temporarily be given a subsidiary role; that of witness, to observe without interfering, until the time when the mind as a whole has gathered in all the information through the gates of the Unconscious. Once the information has been assimilated and digestion has begun, then the Conscious **needs** to become involved to turn information into knowledge then wisdom.

The audience's primary experience at the coal face should be predominantly unconscious, and later, possibly much later, should the Conscious work its homologatory act, archiving the discoveries into their preferred zones of influence. Thus the magic of theatre enters through the gates of the audience's Unconscious, while the Conscious takes a back seat for their transformational ride, and the ride only continues while enveloped in a cloud of Unconscious 'plasma'. If, during the experience, the audience's critical faculties become dominant, the game is up and the enchantment is over. I've lost count of the times I've heard a punter intone after trying to watch a piece of earnest, boring theatre: "I couldn't understand it!" Translation.... the actors, or the script, or the story, or the direction, or the design, or all of the above, didn't engage my imagination, so I **had** to resort to trying to make some sort of **logical** sense out of it.

This is an example of the audience members being pulled back into their daily thinking patterns because the show couldn't feed their imagination, and most often the biggest contributor is the actors' inabilities to remain in their Unconscious zone. In my experience, when actors revert to conscious daily mannerisms, the audience similarly reverts, and resorts to thinking about such mundane matters as coffee breaks and shopping lists for the supermarket. If you've been to the theatre and found yourself thinking quotidian, that's the reason! For the solution turn to another provoc and a Teddybear!

Not surprisingly, after their mention, my private devil has transmogrified into a Teddy Bear! A Bubba Diabolic! Downgraded from mad, bad and dangerous to know to the comparative safety of naughty cuddly.

All furry fun and very true…..but still…..but still…..there's alchemy in that physiognomy……

Molecular Provocation #3
Teddybear: Concierge to the unconscious

Question 1: What do teddy bears have to do with Unconscious? ...and Question 2: Why do they work so well?

We have been using the Teddy Bears in our training for several years now. They were first introduced in a short theatre piece that I made for a demonstration. It was called **"The Brotherhood of the Sacrificial Anode"** and was devised for 6 men. There was a section where they had to crawl on stage and change nappies on their respective Teddys whilst engaging in good natured fatherly barbeque badinage.

During performances I was amazed at how easily the men related to the teddys. They seemed to have no inhibitions, as they might have had with dolls, and the whole ambience was very confident, despite the relative inexperience of some of the players. This ease was surprising as it is generally very easy for women to access their emotions performatively and, while men have greater strength, physically and vocally, they often find it more difficult to engage the nuanced, softer parts of their psyches.

The **SATM** and the **FSPA** have a justified reputation for defining the actor by building focus, self definition and body charisma. These lie on the moral imperative side of the spectrum and I am always looking for tools and formats to integrate the softer, more emotionally fluid aspects of acting.

Given the success of the Teds with the men of the group I introduced teddy bears as training partners and I began to collect any and all the soft teddy type toys I could find, especially if they were super-size, second hand and super cheap!

The tremendous value of the teddys was fully brought home to me in an experience I had when Jacqui and I were conducting a series of workshops for the **Satori Group** in Seattle, USA in

August 2008. They are a group of young but well trained actors from the Eastern Seaboard who formed a company and moved west to Seattle to work. They are a co-operative, sharing all the artistic and administrative roles between them.

One of them, **Andrew Lazarow**, confided in me half way through the 10 day session that he had congenitally bad feet and was never able to feel comfortable on stage, but after a few days with Jacqui and myself, could feel the floor for the first time and was able to 'occupy' the space like never before. It was obviously a revelation for him and gratifying for me. **My revelation** came the next day when, in discussion during a break, which followed a two stage exercise called **Stomp** and **Prelude** (the first section highly vigorous and focussed, the second, more contemplative and measured as a reflection on the first). The first stage uses an up-tempo, workmanlike Kletzmer style instrumental, and the second is usually more reflective, using music such as Handel's **'Largo'** or **'Pipeline'** by The Chantays. The poetic second music invokes more meditative slow movement forward whilst experiencing the music's visceral heart.

That day I had asked the Satori actors to do the stomp holding onto the Teds in such a way that the Teds would be watching them stomp for the duration of the first stage. I can't remember making any suggestions for the second stage. It worked very well in both stages, but the real illumination came when Andrew and I were chatting later. He told me he had found it amazing, because, during the second stage he felt the teddy bear was giving him a critique of all the aspects of his stomping experience: "This aspect was successful, but so and so aspect was not so much, etc, etc". On hearing this, I was suddenly struck by a think-bolt from the blue! He had bifurcated his mind and managed to temporarily devolve the role of the conscious self into the teddy bear, freeing his imaginative centre to occupy the experience, unencumbered by his own criticising faculties. I'll let Andrew continue:

I am not a performer. I am a director and projection designer who has always had a cerebral approach to my work. Though I valued the usefulness of demanding physical training for an ensemble, I used to be too self-conscious to benefit from it myself. I never felt at home in my own body, and rarely confronted the intricate and complex facets of my own emotions. I mainly thought through the way performances worked rather than feeling them.

A major breakthrough came for me while training with John and Jacqui. Through the week we worked with small teddy bears. One particular day they had us hold the teddy bears to the side on a flat palm, with the teddies watching us stomp. Because of an issue with my feet, I am at my most self-conscious during exercises with the stomp. But that day was a unique departure.

Before we started, I thought through how I was going to use the teddy to test my work. I decided it would be an external extension of my center, (showing if I was able to maintain steadiness and stillness during the stomp). Once the exercise began, the teddy stopped being what I expected. It was an external part of my center, but also of my mental and emotional state. I imagined it critiquing my journey during the exercise: telling me not to ease up on the stomp, to keep my center from bouncing, to keep up the rhythm, etc. My imagination almost split during the experience. I compartmentalized my tendency to over think which freed my body and emotions to take in what was happening. I remember feeling myself breath for the first time. The space became active and alive. I felt the floor underneath my feet, and also felt it supporting me. A well of seemingly contradictory emotions swelled up inside of me as I

A Devil Pokes the Actor

opened up to myself. For the first time I felt like I was aware and fully present.

John and Jacqui's teddy exercise has become a microcosm for how I work. I come into rehearsals craving the unexpected. The unthinkable. I listen to a piece and what it needs at every given moment. I steer away from the 'accepted' choices that have the correct connotations. Instead I hunt for the choice that makes the audience feel what a moment needs. That demands that I stay open to what I feel, and what surprises me.

I set my critical analysis aside, next to me, so it does not impede my ability to experience what happens in the room. At the same time, I make sure it is awake and present. The challenge now is to determine how much weight to give that voice as various points in a creative process. (How close do I let it sit? How loud do I let it speak? How do I use it to create with intricate specificity?) Every rehearsal I strive to maintain a rigor that is physical, emotional, unobstructed, and even intellectual.
Andrew Lazarow New York 2010

In acting, most particularly when learning the craft, much use is made of the expression "self conscious", especially in admonitions such as "Don't be self conscious....just be yourself," etc. It is a most deceptive turn of phrase, as actors must be highly aware of what they are doing to a certain extent, otherwise they'd become too immersed in what they are doing and become lost, ie they'd forget their lines, stage directions, the other actors, etc. Instead the admonition should read: "Don't be so conscious of what you are doing that it impedes your experience!"

So the expression **'Self Conscious'** should be replaced by **'Too Conscious'** as it more accurately describes the problem. This expression also goes to the heart of how to address the issue. In most acting situations the teacher/director will proffer platitudes such as "Don't be nervous...just act naturally....." This is about as useful as saying you should be six foot tall with a face like Marilyn Monroe. Not do-able! All it does is reinforce a sense of inferiority, yet another way for the teacher to stay a step ahead of the student.

Nervousness is an honest human feeling, an apprehension that the future may not work out as planned. It is a conscious judgement loaded with doubt and self criticism. Its most extreme manifestation for an actor is stagefright, where all self belief is lost entirely and there appears to be no future. Apparently **Sir Laurence Olivier** had it as a mature actor for over five years, which shows it has very little to do with talent, as one might think. So, to say: "Don't be nervous!" is to ask that the Conscious be turned off, like a tap, as though one could shut a door on it. The FSPA attitude is that, rather than it be ignored or denied, nervousness should be embraced, accepted as an accessory, a by-product of new experience. We suggest that doubt is a necessary adjunct, and that the crucial premise is to not let the doubt overwhelm the experience. By accepting his 'nerves' as a positive, the actor's energy is transmuted positively to enhance the experience.

It has only been recently that I have realised that nervousness is a negative manifestation of the conscious self-critical process. As Andrew L. related the role that he had given his teddy bear during that sequence, I realised how effectively soft toys could be used as tools for corralling the conscious part of the mind into less obstructionist zones. I knew from before, that trying to shut out the conscious is not an option, and what Andrew had done was to ask the Conscious mind (in the form of the teddy bear) to metaphorically 'sit in the corner' and witness the process, rather than be a 'first person' participant. The function of the conscious part of the brain became to observe from outside the experience, and later, while at a more contemplative remove, to fulfil its proper role which is to catalogue and critique as part of the digestion phase.

Whilst I have been mulling over Jungian attitudes the last few years, it was the Andrew/Teddy exercise in Seattle that showed me both the issue and the tool with which to engage it. The issue is that the roles of the U and C must be initially separated, with clear functions for both. After they have fulfilled their functions separately, at some later stage they are reconciled, homologated into the body proper. This is the unification of the mind and body of the actor, and a very good tool is the teddy because it has unique anthropomorphic properties. When I observed my performers those years ago with their nappy changing badinage, it began to dawn on me that people in widely different situations have special relationships with Teddy bears.

I believe there are many reasons:

1. **They are not human**. They are more like an animal. Dolls, which could be considered equivalent, are not, because they have human connotations eg one thinks of having to nurture dolls in true biological fashion, like feeding. There is a conscious perception of a doll's physical vulnerability and the ramifications that follow. For instance, punching a teddy can be funny - punching a life-like doll is somewhat more macabre.

2. **They are not animals.** Although they are sourced from a bear, they have human characteristics. Teddys date from the first few years of the 20th century, an efflorescence of the golden age before World War One. It is a rather interesting story as it is also an example of international collective unconscious convergence, as it originated in the US and Austria in much the same year - separate but connected. One origin stems from a hunting episode in the life of Theodore Roosevelt in the year 1902. He was out bear hunting in Mississippi, when he was offered a tied up bear to shoot. He sportingly declined and a political cartoon resulted. A toy shop owner in New Jersey related to the story by making a stuffed bear which he called Teddy's Bear (Roosevelt's nickname).

At the same time, but with no connection, in Austria a toy

company called Stieff started producing a stuffed bear of almost identical design. Very quickly, all over the world teds took off, becoming a phenomenon continuing unabated to the present. It also prefigured anthropomorphic children's stories such as 'The Wind in the Willows' (1908) and 'Winnie the Pooh' (1926). It is, I believe, the first 'soft' toy and the original DNA of Micky Mouse, Bugs Bunny and all other cartoon 'animals'.

3. **All humans relate to soft toys**. Regardless of age, sex, creed, culture or race, all humans seem to empathise readily with teddys. In 2008, within the space of a month, we did Teddy exercises with groups as wildly disparate as young American actors and Nepalese amateur theatre troupes. Even though they came from very different situations, the attitudes, emotional responses and results were very nearly identical and equally as profound.

4. **Teddys seem to connect people with their 'lost, golden' childhood**. Many adults can recall a special soft toy they had as very young, and not so young, children. This was a companion, often inseparable, a confidant, the repository of all the special dreams and wishes that we all had in our pre-conscious life before adulthood. It was the emblem of our innocence, our own childhood Partner of Eden before we had to grow up, gain knowledge and compromise our ideals to deal with the world at large. That innocence is the 'lost time' that Froggy writer Marcel Proust and much other art searches to regain. In that way it seems to connect actors with their own personal pre-cognitive myth, the search for which may be the reason we actors do theatre at all!

5. **Teddys have a dual manifestation, as individual and collective unconscious**,
Individual, as in personal childhood and collective as there is probably nothing as universally empathetic that one can hold in one's hand.

In our training we always encourage the teddy's use as crossover tools for bringing the Conscious and Unconscious into balance. Their main function is to facilitate access to the imaginative/emotional zones. We do this in two ways:

- Within a routine we ask that the actors engage the audience for some time and on a music cue, transfer their gaze and concern to the bear that sits between themselves and the audience. This may not sound very impressive, but the resultant shift in expression that passes over the face is quite profound. We extend this into vocalising by saying: talk to the audience/ talk to the bear and feel the difference between the two.

- At the end of an improvisation we'll say a speech 3 times:
    The first: **You** speak....Quite straightforward
    Second: **Teddy** speaks... Speak any way you like as if Teddy is speaking.
    Third: Join the two speeches....The third speech is an amalgam of the first two.

The directives are:
a. All speeches may differ as much as possible with the one proviso that the rhythms remain identical, so the actors can stay together and be heard (otherwise a descent into chaos would result).
b. Whatever decision is made as to type or style of voice, the actor should aim to stay on that 'voice' for the duration of the speech.
c. The 'voice' decisions, as much as possible, should be totally instinctive. Do not prejudge or prescribe.... the actors should go for the first 'voice' that happens to them.
d. Think of the third version as a compound of your 'own' voice and the extreme 'teddy' voice. We are not asking for alternations between the two voices. They should be combined in an alchemical fashion, integrating with each other. The resultant should sound unique - you've invented a new voice for yourself.

In our experience, if all those directives are adhered to, over time the actor can accumulate a myriad of voice levels, intonations and pitches. These go to round out the actors vocal palette and he acquires expertise that is natural and empathetic.

Using the teddy bears for voice discovery follows a classic alchemical program: separation, distillation and re-integration and their affectionate temperaments totally trash precious diction and 'naice' elocution.

As I trail off with the teddy talk….. an apprehensive glance to the upper right hand side, and what do I spy with my nervy little eye, furtive tear softening the side of the devil's sad dog face? The last provoc has thawed the icycules of this devil's cold heart.

Ah ha! As the watery tear drops down the dial, it morphs into the sorrowcast
head of Carl Gustav Jung, the man who invented Uncon and went on to make it mean even more.

His moustache quivers as he pours out his plaint *"Vot haf you done? Zese teddy bearen bringz me back to my difficult dayz. Pleez not to dvell on zis, but talk more about vot I got out of Africa……"*

Relieved I exclaim righty-right-right!
"Let's swing into another speccy observation that can serve an actor's inspiration…….."

Molecular Provocation #4
We make the world and we make it now!
Jung's heuristic 'moment':

Heuristic: (definition): Enabling a person to discover or learn something for themselves.

While on a trip to Africa in 1925, Carl Jung had a mystical experience as he gazed on a section of the African plains, host to countless herds of antelope, zebra, wildebeest and giraffe. As he observed the innumerate wildlife from a low hill, it suddenly came to him that their 'reality' was guaranteed by our observation of them. He thought that this meant that consciousness had a cosmic purpose and that Man was indispensable for the completion of creation. It further occurred to him that such knowledge could provide a humanist 'myth' that could supplant the discredited certainties of Christianity.

In his book **"Memories, Dreams and Reflections",** He states on P 255:

'There, the cosmic meaning of consciousness became overwhelmingly clear to me....Man, I, in an invisible act of creation put the stamp of perfection on the world by giving it objective existence. This act we usually ascribe to the creator alone, without considering that in so doing we view life as a machine calculated down to the last detail. In such a cheerless clockwork fantasy there is no drama of man, world and God...... man is indispensable for the completion of creation; that, in effect he himself is the second creator of the world...'

That is one hell of a way to view the Man/God matrix! This will of course appear sacrilegious to some, but it does in truth ascribe to mankind a dignity and with it, a responsibility in his dealings with spiritual issues.

One of our exercises consists of a series of Walks across the studio. There are some 10 or 11 in total and they are all done in a group Indian file in a straight line to and fro across the stage. The feet can be turned in, turned out, or stomping as well as many other types of challenging gaits. They are challenging because they are all very extreme ways of moving, and even though the 'choreography' is simple, it is difficult maintaining energy and clarity for the entire duration of the crossing, no matter how experienced you are.

The walks are one of the major routines we use that derive from Suzuki, and we have been doing them as a staple since 1992.

As with all our exercises, it is not so much the vocabulary that is important (getting the steps right), but......what the challenging movement does **for** you, and...... **to** you.
The Walks are mostly done to music with a strong rhythm and we encourage people to really FEEL what they are doing. To that end we stress that they should not be just 'moving' to the music, but rather see the music as signpost and structure; moving as quickly as possible between the beats and stopping for as long as possible in between the moves, to stay in time. One of the reasons for encouraging this **move quick/stop long** attitude, is that the actor, by dwelling on the stops between, discovers each stop anew, the music anew and himself anew, which is what this provoc is all about... read on...

In one of the nine types of walk, one is with legs held almost straight and feet on tiptoe, so that the body doesn't rise and fall and during the moment of stillness, the weight is evenly distributed between both legs.

One session, some years ago, I was halfway through one of these 'tiptoe" walks across the floor when I suddenly had the feeling that not only was I stopping but, as I stopped, I could also imagine the world stopping. It was as if I had stopped the universe for a nanosecond, before it started up again, and I moved on. Looking back over it, of course, it wasn't the universe that stopped, but **my** universe that arrested for a second.

To be sure, it is absurd to contemplate that a solo Homo Sapiens can stop the world, and in our world of artifice we are not advocating anything like that. I wasn't sure at the time why I found it so provocative, but it certainly has proved useful in terms of unlocking acting capabilities.

That subsequent reading of Jung's musings corroborated the earlier idea, and added another twist during our December 2009 intensive......
We generally finish an exercise with a speech, because even though there is much physical vigour in everything we do, it must culminate in speaking otherwise it would be perceived as a movement class.

In order to make the actor more highly aware of the surrounding space and to make him more 3 Dimensional, we often do the speech rotating about our axis, invoking the idea that we are filling the space with our voice as we scan it. Normally to give an imaginative impulse, I might say something like: "Your voice is like a beam from a lighthouse, scanning the space and filling it all the way to the edges as you rotate through the space!"

But this time, I said: "As your eyes alight on the space... sense that you are discovering the space for the first time ... that in a sense... you are creating the space!" Parallel with this, is the idea that your voice can also 'create the space'. This may at first glance seem arrogant, that an actor should have the hubris to imagine they can control the world. But keeping in mind that the actor's world IS artifice he must employ such imaginative constructs as they empower his acting either overtly or covertly.

As well, if looked at more practically, it has a double imperative;
1. The actor has to make his own world. It would appear that for Jung, the equivalent experience made him realise that man was no mere pawn of an omnipotent God.
2. He has to assume the moral responsibility that comes with the knowledge. A self- imposed discipline about his conduct.

Recently, following a trip to Toga in 2008, we developed a deep phase version of these 'stopping' exercises called the **Wop Wop.** We had seen Suzuki's actresses doing a demanding routine which involved short sword strikes, with stillnesses followed by intermittent speeches. All done to the extremely silly Chubby Checker song: "Let's Twist Again". This was, as usual, most impressive and had an added piquancy because Suzuki's actors suggested that he was inspired to create this exercise after visiting us in Brisbane in early 2007.

Back home we developed a variation on it. In order to de-Orientalise the exercise we decided to replace the small swords with Badminton racquets, and use, as background, an equally vacuous song "Simon Says" by The 1910 Fruit Gum Company.

The premise is that a solo actor has to say a medium length text (of her own choice) during the run of the song, but she is to interdict herself by making big swipes with the racquets, initiated from her centre, but with huge variations in height, rhythm and body structure. It should involve moving across and dropping to the floor plus large changes in direction and focus. As such it has the similar elements of chaos (but more self impacted by the actor) that are invoked in many of our advanced exercises.

Each swipe or strike is to be accompanied by saying 'Wop' delivered with utmost intensity. And in that arrested moment when she decides to resume the speech, she should remain perfectly still, and speak a short section of the selected speech to that 'moment' that she has just made. The speech proceeds in this continuous/discontinuous mode until all spoken where the actor starts again at the beginning until the music is finished. These 'moments' are more heightened versions of the 'stop moments' as described in other exercises – even more heightened as they occur with great rapidity and interruption. The totally instinctive cataclysmic affects of the actor's body on herself!
The voice for the speech sections should be quite distinct in style from the 'Wop" sounds.

Mostly, the actors get two runs of the speech during the song, and once the music finishes they speak the same speech at whatever speed and with whatever inflection they may desire, whilst maintaining the very last 'Wop' position. It is very demanding and, with the dynamic interceptions, most of us forget the words to some degree and need prompting.

The ability of the actor to perform the interdictions and the text during the song is not as important as the affect it has on the actors - invariably they sound transformed and compelling when delivering the last freeform text.

In February 2010, one such moment occurred when company actor **Glenn Johnson** (see pic at back of book) was saying the speech after he had finished the song. He had done the 'Wop-Wop' a number of times before, but this time, his free form speech was ear-catchingly different. A voice emerged which was powerful, grounded and resonant.
In his own words Glenn continues:

The body's calm, but on fire!

At 44 years of age and having not acted for 15 years, when I walked into an Ozfrank Intensive 12 months ago I didn't have any major goals which I hoped to achieve. It was more on a whim than anything else, and a sort of curiosity, having heard only a little of what Ozfrank Theatre was about.

Well, 12 months on, I am still attending Ozfrank Intensives plus, on invitation, the twice weekly company training and rehearsals and my curiosity is continually being reignited. Furthermore I feel more 'ready' to act now than ever. By ready I mean prepared.

I've always been of the opinion that actors were an odd bunch in that unlike other artists such as musicians or painters, writers, dancers etc, they felt their craft required no ongoing attention other than ticking off on a number of 'acting workshops' every so often. With Ozfrank I found a discipline I hadn't come across since I'd trained with Richard Hayes-Marshall in the early nineties.

I've also thought that in order for an actor to be 'ready' to act they needed some kind of framework on which they could rely to hone their craft, just as a pianist sits at the piano for hours on end or a writer goes to the computer each day. In Ozfrank, I found this fundamental work ethic to be rock solid, and around this ongoing discipline opportunities to develop and create flourish. And now after 12 months training I'm beginning to see the potential to 'act'.

An example of my feeling of this 'readiness' to act (which by the way is something that needs to be addressed on an ongoing basis) is a recent experience I had at an Ozfrank training session. The exercise is an advanced version of a routine called Wop Wop. It goes roughly like this – interspersing responsive movement to music, stillness, the sounds 'wop wop' and text, you follow the givens of the exercise until the music stops, when you remain still. All that has gone before this moment has been priming or gearing you for the next moment it's part of the same journey but at the same time the constant creation of something new. Physically exhausted but energised you then speak a piece of text with no restrictions placed on you. I'd done this exercise a few times before but this night produced something quite arresting for me in that I felt I had seized something, or something had seized me, that I hadn't felt before.

As I began the speech, motionless but alive and alert, I had no thought to where the words were coming from other than my body as a whole. It wasn't a matter of saying a speech I had practiced in a certain way. I didn't know what words I would stress, where I would pause or speed up, what pitch or tone I would use; it wasn't a concern: it was just happening unencumbered by psychological distractions. It was as if I were a tree, rooted to the spot but alive to the elements of time and space. I was aware of being watched by the others in the room but it felt more like a conversation than a display. The speech was coming from some place I'd never been before. The body was calm but on fire. If I think about John and Jacqui's teachings I would say it was coming from the unconscious. The conscious mind had been sidelined by the concentration applied to the framework of the preceding exercise and when it came to the moment of 'acting', the unconscious was given reign. Quite a blast! Of course, the next time I did the exercise the results weren't quite the same –but that's a work in progress.

Even so, I suddenly realised that there were a 1000 ways to say a speech and that each performance could be different as long as the foundations had been laid, provided the roots of the tree had taken hold and were full of nutrients. As Jacqui says it's only on reaching this point that you begin to discover the immense potential open to you: it is just the beginning.
Glenn Johnson

As Glenn intimates above, the Wop Wop creates a great number of instinctive 'moments'. It is an accepted truism of acting that an actor has to be in the moment, and this holds for any style of acting. It is also well understood by those who try it, that it is damn difficult!

This is mainly due to the intrusion of the conscious mind (Ego) which tries to interpose itself between the actor and the experience, and ends up having an adverse effect.

One way to subvert the Ego is to make it a witness to the event, giving it a secondary job that prevents it dominating the experience. (**See the Provoc. "Teddybear: Concierge to the Unconscious"**).

We have also found that 'universe stopping' imaging during exercises like the walks, provides the actor with another attitude that enables being 'in the 'moment'.
When I reflect on the source of the FSPA exercises, it always seems to work out that they evolved instinctively, seeming to create, of their own accord, very compelling scenarios in which actors make breakthroughs in their skills and confidence. At some later time (often years later!), I have a revelation about the aspects of the exercise that trigger the transformations. This most often occurs when I have an epiphany whilst doing or watching the routine. And later still, when I get access to some form of analytical information I can rationalise or homologate that revelation into some form of neo-scientific 'map' of the experience.

This happened to the 'universe stopping', when I read that 'Man as Second Creator' excerpt from Jung's book.

I continue to be intensely interested in the explanations to things, and being a performer from a family of scientists means that I have applied the curiosity blowtorch to Dance and Theatre. I am very fortunate that Jung has been brought to my attention, because he is likewise a very eager beaver learner. He did the early psychic mapping hard yards pretty much tout seul and never became bogged in academic dogma like those on the other side of the psychiatric fence.

By judiciously reading the easy bits, I can lever wisps of his knowledge to winkle out the give and take vis-a-vis the acting game.

Thuswise the sudden interest in the conscious and unconscious workings of the brain. In other, earlier chapters I have explained why they fit the bill, but the **'universe stopping'** aspect of the walks or any of our other routines seems to be a very pronounced way of emancipating the unconscious and coralling the conscious.

The 'universe stopping' is an approach that really addresses **Time** for the actor and by that I don't mean the 'Let's finish at 6 o'clock!' time. I don't mean daily time. I mean both highly particular time (the nanosecond time of NOW) and universal time (The Cosmic time of Infinity).

The conscious mind can only deal with daily time in fact it is entirely locked into the quotidian (what time do I need to catch the bus?). It can't understand either NOW or Infinity, because it can't deal with paradox.
But the unconscious can, because it transcends time...... so... the invocation of 'your' time and the 'universe' time is yet another way of subverting the Ego's meddling, which enables being 'in the moment'. This is also heuristic, because every moment on stage for the actor and the audience, should feel like a 'new'

moment, a new moment discovered by the actor, and witnessed by the audience.

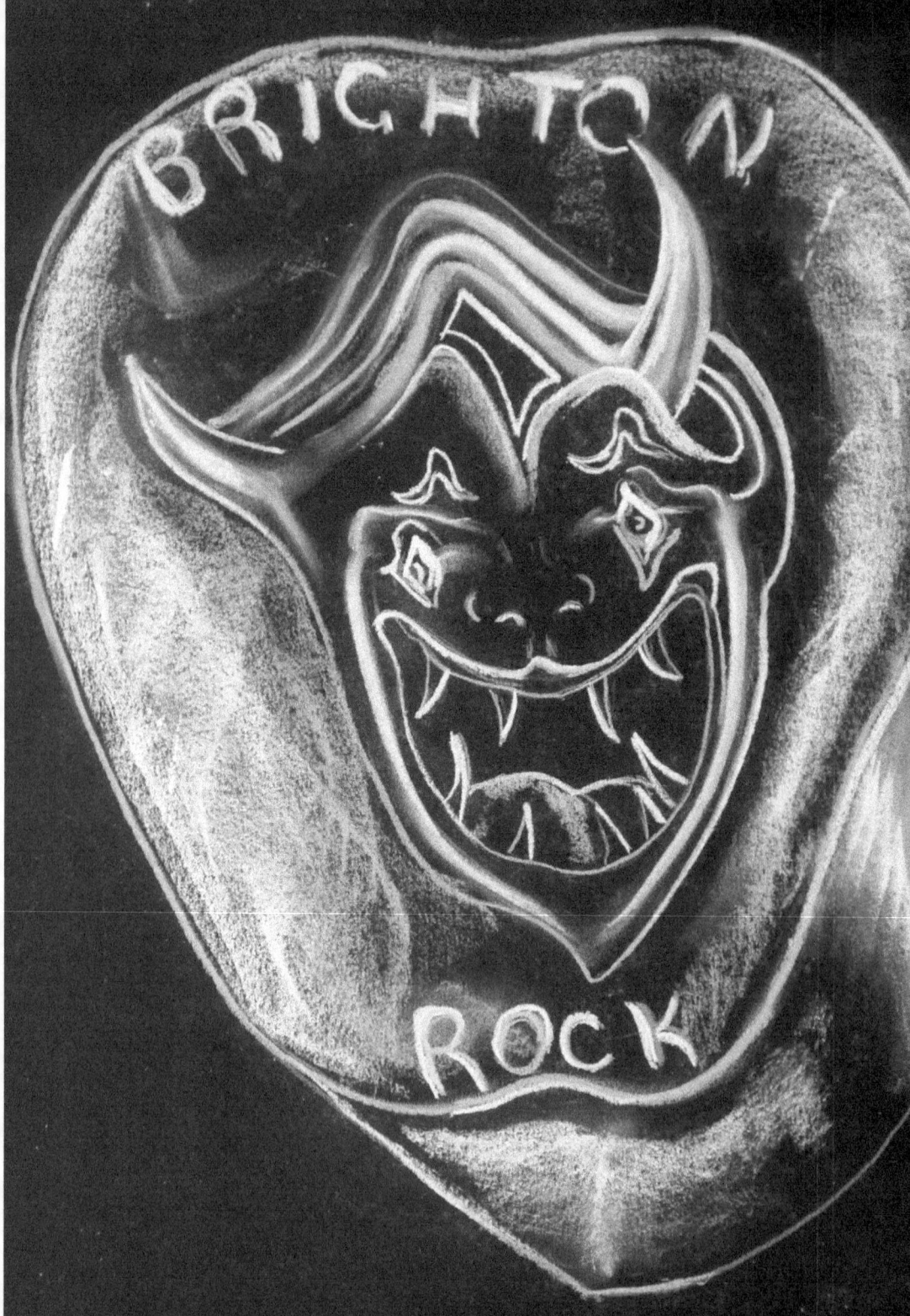

A Devil Pokes the Actor

The smell mutates again. Over my shoulder comes the slightly puff of peppermint…… the devil is sucking on a Crown Mint! In his case, must be TripleXXX! He brushes past and around, his face once scarifying, now almost benign……hesitantly he offers me a Mintie in his thin bony paw.

Haltingly I accept……as I gaze on the familiar chalky white disk, I hear a whisper that recedes in the dark: *"Watch me ! Watch me ! Watch me……"*
He is evaporating, disappearing into the ether while his face slowly etches into the front of the Mint. This is Wild, Weird and Wonderful!……for as I hold the Talismanic Sweet it stretches out behind, growing into a Shiney Stripey rod…..the only rod you can sweetly suck…..Brighton Rock!

Head down, prop up the feet and start Molecular Provoc. Number 5.

Molecular Provocation #5
Brighton Rock: character imprinted back into the soul:
King Lear: Act 3 Scene 4: "You are the thing itself",

Quintessence: A central and intrinsic aspect of something, from the Latin: Quinta Essentia, meaning the 5th substance in addition to the four elements, thought by ancient philosophers to compose the heavenly bodies and pervade all things.

In England there is a certain candied sweet called Rock, which is named after the seaside resorts where it is sold, the most famous being Brighton and Blackpool. It is a close cousin of the Candy Cane; an inch thick column of pure sugar with the name 'BRIGHTON ROCK' embedded in the ends. Impossible though it seems, the name continues all the way through from front to back so, no matter how much you chomp or lick off, the letters still appear in relief against the white background.
Apparently it can only be made by hand, and it takes a good ten years to master the technique, both of which are noteworthy for being rare these days.

We were in a training session in late 2009, when I made an observation that related to the Brighton Rock stick. The observation arose out of a discussion during the previous session. In that session I had posed the question: Could charisma be defined as looking as though one knew something special, which the observer would like to access in some way?

One of our newer actors, Glenn Johnson, commented that posters of our actors displayed on our walls suggested the affirmative, and in contrast, he had recently seen photos of an actor that did not display this inner knowledge. The pics he mentioned were of an Aussie film actor performing live in the Big Apple. Glenn thought the pic unconvincing and as he wandered down the page reading the crit....lo and behold, it was borne out by the reviewer. I was reminded that personality is skin deep, **but character is etched all the way in**, and for some reason

the image of a stick of Bright Red Brighton Rock snuck into my synaptic centres. I thought that one's persona or character doesn't or shouldn't lie just on the surface, where it can be swept away by the slightest malfunction, but still be there, radiating out, no matter how many layers are stripped away. First of all I saw it as indelible all the way to the back of the brain, but eventually worked out that it had to burn bright, back to the seat of the soul.
A succulent metaphor if ever there was one - now for the provenance:

For quite a few months, I had been intrigued by a recurrent image I had in my mind: that of a charismatic actor sitting in a chair, whose presence was so strong, that the essence seemed to reverberate out beyond his body, both backwards and forwards, not only in space, but also in time. As you looked at this actor his **quintessence** seemed to send image pulses, both into the future and out to the observer, as well as backwards in time. I believe that the 'pulse' that lodges in the mind of the observer, converts into an archetypical memory unit that lives on, acquiring greater proportion as time passes. It's as though they've become an archetype that has always been there and always will.....

This idea of a type of mythic energy pulsing out in ways beyond ordinary thinking, brought to mind notions of **Quantum Wave Mechanics**. In the early 20th century QWM was developed as an explanation to make sense of the recently discovered electromagnetic radiation. Quantum is pretty much Latin for blob (of light). Wave is a beam (of light) and QWM was designed to bring the idea of blob and wave together. More of which in a few minutes, but next is the 'wave' part of the story....

I had noticed the other day, one of our actors, **Kate Lee**, (see pic at back of book) doing a voice/movement improvisation and she gave the definite impression that she was more than what she appeared to be. She was, of course, herself but she also seemed to be something else.

I'll let her continue, as her thoughts corroborate my perception:

We have an improvisation we do to Cher's 'Bang Bang', done with a long stick. The improvisation is combined with various cues for particular actions. We begin standing in a neutral position with the stick by our sides. When the music starts, we move only the stick and when the lyrics start we begin our improvisation. We then speak (not sing) the words to the song. At one point we are required to only move the stick and at another point we raise it above our heads and shake our hips as fast as we can whilst still saying the words to the song.

I was doing this improvisation when I had the sensation of feeling my actions slide between the music of the song and the way I was saying the lyrics. It was like the song was giving me a platform on which I could place myself. Here, I was able to create meaning, a character and a context. I didn't do it deliberately or with any contrived idea of who I was and I didn't go into the improvisation wanting to create something. It was like I became an *idea* or a *feeling of* myself. This feeling was separate to the 'me' in daily life and to the song itself whilst being inherently linked with both.

For me, the actual effect of the song was that it did something like double my energy. Not in terms of physical output, but in terms of making a bigger me. Or to explain another way; I felt as though I was both joined with the song and the energy of the song whilst also standing on a platform where I created a completely separate narrative that, should the song not be there, I would still exist in that narrative - just as strong as if it were there.
Tennant Creek, Australia, 2010 Kate Lee

The aspect of that anecdote that I find compelling is that, while she was having that inner revelation, I was witnessing an external manifestation of it – what was 'inner' was also 'outer', which is one definition of performance. Kate, being 'herself' as well as the 'role' brought to mind descriptions of two very different but equally outstanding performers, Rudolf Nureyev and Henry Fonda. In two books I have read about them, their writers are emphatic that they were always very much themselves, **BUT** they were also very much the role they were

A Devil Pokes the Actor   303

playing, whether it be ballet in Nureyev's case or film in Fonda's. Quite independently the writers described the same sensation: whilst one was always aware that one was watching Fonda/Nureyev, one was also completely absorbed in the role they were playing. These are examples show that the 'greats', no matter what the field, convey an expansive sense of dualism in their performance - they are both **very much themselves** and in combination with that they are inextricably involved in the thing they are doing - **they have also become the roles they are playing**.

This is of course a paradox. Normally one would think that they would be one or the other; either themselves OR the character. How can they be both? And of course in most acting preparations they are told they have to completely become the character, that they must subsume their whole being, sacrifice their ego to become this 'other' thing.

This 'subsuming' to become the character led to many great performances, but if one considers exemplars such as Marlon Brando, I believe that there are really very few credible roles he played: being Waterfront, Streetcar, Last Tango, Godfather and Apocalypse Now. In the other films, to my eyes and ears, he appears quite 'lost' and the acting is bizarre, mannered and entirely unconvincing (viz. the 'Friends, Romans and Countrymen' speech from the film Julius Caesar and I believe that that is because there is no Marlon in there, only the pretense of being someone else). His great roles only happened when he was playing someone very close to himself when his self definition came into alignment with his role.

What could articulate this dualism, and what format could cultivate?

To open the oyster, I needed a gimlet.

To hand was a winklepicker.
I had recently been handed a book by Peter Berkahn which

studied the parallels between Einstein and Picasso as they separately revolutionised Science and Art in the groundbreaking year of 1905. It's by **Arthur I. Miller** and is titled *"Space, Time and the Beauty that Causes Havoc"*.

I knew Picasso's trajectory, but was only vaguely aware of Einstein's creative approach that led to the breakthrough in formulating the fantastical theory of relativity. I say fantastical because it is pretty daunting for the average punter to comprehend - most people are in love with the idea, rather than know what it entails.

Up until the invention of electricity, the 3 Newtonian laws of mechanics were quite OK, thank you very much. Simple equations such as Force equals Mass times Acceleration, gave us all the answers we needed from horses and carts to steam and Steel
Electromagnetic induction, with its complex interaction between optics, electro magnetic theory, and mechanics, blew Newton's linear explanations out of the water. These little things we can't see called **electrons**, have, upon their discovery, introduced several shattering 'Please Explain's' into the goulash, and it needed a funny looking little Cherman living in Switzerland to tease out the fondue.

Einstein is probably the most famous cute and cuddly person that everybody loves and nobody understands! In the 60s with his crazy professor hair style, he was a hippie poster boy alongside James the Dean and Jimi Hendrix!

Physics had become stuck in third gear, as to what described light best. Was it a wave (continuous) or a pulse (particle)? The problem was that at different times and in different places it was one or the other. It could bend around the earth like a wave, but it could also travel through outer space, which was empty! That meant it had to be a blob of energy - a pulse. These seemed to be massively contradictory. Surely, it had to be one or the other, and scientists in their desire to make sense of the mutual exclusion, came up with all sorts of almost solutions like

Luminous Ether that supported one side or the other, some of the time.

Einstein, figuring they were trying to straighten out a paradox, went back to basics and said: Hang on a mo, boys! It's not one or the other it's the same answer from two different points of view! The same answer from different questions about the same thing. He looked at the polar opposite explanations of light: Wave and Particle. He didn't try to make them the same, to make sense of them, or try to make them agree. He wasn't trying to straighten out a paradox. He, instead, accepted their paradox and allowed them to co-exist in the same idea. He said it's not either/or..... it's both! They are complimentary aspects of the same story. One doesn't exclude the other and they cannot exist without each other.

This is also a very productive way of approaching the acting dualism thrown up by the Fonda /Nureyev paradigm.
The two opposites are:
1. Classical Acting - be yourself and say the words... and
2. Method Acting - give yourself over to the character

In most acting approaches they are viewed as opposites and mutually exclusive. Nearly all directors adopt an old fashioned approach which is to see them as impossibly antagonistic and therefore, such directors are only able to countenance one or t'other.

Classical acting has been developing over the last few hundred years and probably reached its apogee with Olivier with his WW2 films. It places great importance on discipline, tradition and technique.

Method acting, most exemplified by Brando, is about behaviour, emotional recall and entirely giving oneself over to total immersion in the 'character'.
Well, why not do an Einstein and see them as complimentary forces, which when compounded, combine to create a much

more elegant transformational vehicle?
As an introductory reduction, why not see the particle aspect as the self definition of the actor (his sense of who he is) and the wave aspect as the thing he is doing (the role he is playing)?

A Devil Pokes the Actor

"A portrait of the actor in the grip of a revelation"

A quantum provoc later and my devil's no come back! Is he on the dunny, doing whatever devil's do, that passes for defecation? But I'm on a roll here and won't need him for a while. The quantum's got me thinking of plasma and taken me back to a time much closer, and back to the beach as well..........Sunshine Beach High School that would be.

Molecular Provocation #6
Death comes to Sunshine Beach
AudioPlasma - the Audience as Multiple Mirror

In 2008, Jacqui and I were again in Japan to see Tadashi Suzuki and his most recent work. While there we had a meeting with Suzuki and he invited Ozfrank company to perform a new work at his 2009 festival in Toga village in the Japanese Alps. Jacqui, the director, after much rumination and consideration, chose to do an upgrading of the English miracle play "Everyman" which was subsequently named **The Reckoning of Badengood.** Jacqui organised the scenario and I hipped and primped the dialogue to be attractive, coherent and amusing to the modern ear. Our costume designer Marysia Aves added some simple but effective outfits (long black red-lined coat for God complete with top hat and finished off with a large red sash with gold writing spelling out GOD; black pants and T-shirts for all with simple writing on the T-shirts spelling out the players roles, eg. Sis, Bro, Best Mate, Badengood, Death, Good Deeds, Goods, etc).

Before we took it to Japan, we did an 'out of town' tryout at the Sunshine Beach State High School 100k North of Brisbane, as we were offered free use of the theatre due to 'God', Glenn Taylor, being a teacher at the school. It was a low key event to iron out a few inevitable bugs in front of a small but extremely appreciative audience of some Pals and Ma's and Pa's plus a few walkups. I played Death, and came in and out of the show, herding Badengood (James Anderson) through his various trials. Consequently I had a fair time between my short speeches to do some thinking about what was happening between myself and the audience.

Somewhere about two thirds through the show, I had a very powerful realisation. I felt the audience had become a type of multiple mirror, reflecting my speech back to me, and, by doing so, had shown me something else about myself through my speech. It meant I had reached the fourth stage of performance;

that of interdependence with the audience. I had projected the speech out as a kind of 'audioplasm' hovering above the spectators. They then absorbed it in their own fashion, digested it and then answered it by re-projecting back up into the same ether, which I would then feel as the completion of my speech. I envisaged that this whole sequence would happen almost instantaneously, even as I ended the speech in question. **This 'instantaneousness' I leave for the next, even more extreme provoc!**

What I'm proposing here is not so much an attempt to define an unprovable absolute truth, as to offer an operational proposition - a course of action that might prove profoundly productive. When I conjecture that the spectators are functioning in a certain way, I am not suggesting that I know exactly what they are thinking, but that I'm apportioning a trust in them, asking for their input, their covert 'collaboration', which would manifest as their 'instinctive critique' of the speech that I proffered. In a way I'm asking them to 'finish the speech', because their reception of it is the final instalment, and their interpretation of my saying the speech would be the speech's completion or closure.

The formal veracity is not really important, but the fact that I'm asking it; is in itself a provocative performing attitude; one that's bound to produce stimulating results – it is a question that doesn't need a formal or definitive answer. The spectators do not respond in any overt or demonstrative way, but with their individual unconscious impulses which conjoin to build a collective unconscious mirror. As I've said elsewhere, this can only happen if I occupy and reveal my unconscious zones while performing for them.

The reason I could conceive such a proposition comes, like many another, directly from our training. As the FSPA has become more and more sophisticated, in order to make more lateral discoveries, I invented more abstract and oblique exercises. In addition to that, during these exercises, I gradually interdicted more indirect and inexplicit commands, in order to see what would transpire when our advanced actors reacted instinctively.

As an example, half way through an improvisation to a surfing instrumental, I might say, "Surf like a surfer with his leg half bitten off by a great white shark!" They would, of course, hop around pulling some pretty unconventional moves. At the end of the song, I could create an even more bizarre potential by asking them to say the standard speech as though they were the severed leg!

I might add here that this is very different from the Lee Strasberg 'Pretending to be a Teapot' exercise that the film actors such as Brando and Dean used to whinge about. Quite right they were, too! Pretending to be anything is puerile and futile, and as Brando was wont to say: "Just childish games!" We remove that jejune emotional pressure, by setting the context more in a third person remove. We would rather suggest that the actor: Speaks with the attitude of a teapot, or as a teapot would speak, if it could speak. It helps too, to go past mundane daily images to ones which are more mythic and provocatively surreal, (such as sharks and severed legs). The effect, as the actors would do the same speech with a very different, instinctive sensibility, could be remarkable. There would be a frisson in the air, a change of barometric pressure, a semblance of some special feeling hovering over the room.

After watching, I'd always exclaim to myself: "Wow ! WTF....was.....that....??? " I need to add here that the shift in sensibility would be from the entire group, not just a few exemplary individuals, and this is crucial - it had to be connected and communal. Any other witnesses present plus the group itself could confirm that something special had transpired!

It took many years (and a fair bit of boning up on neo-Jungian know how) before I realised that I'd been witnessing **a shift in collective unconscious by the group**. For a long time, I couldn't figure out a way that I could make sense or use these ideas, until it dawned on me that all I had to do was simply to 'feel' the plasma or 'ether' that the actors had produced, and let it osmotically enter my own psyche and drift to the back of the brain. At some indeterminate later time, these ideas would re-emerge as a transformed creative impulse.

These experiences, as a result of teaching the training, gave me the template for what I could sense later during that ***Reckoning of Badengood*** show up at the Sunshine Coast.

I've said before that this situation is the highest level in a quaternary of stages that relate to an audience, and the four stages are a series of graduated levels of sophistication concerning the complicity between the actor and the audience. One cannot proceed to the next stage until the present stage has been achieved. Each stage also denotes a progressive shift from the **particular** (the actor's concern with himself) to the **universal** (the actor's inter-dependence with the audience). Each stage also contains all the previous stages, affirming that the gradient is accumulative.

Each stage can be summarised as:

1. Can you hear and understand what you are saying - Do you know yourself?
2. Can you be understood by the audience - Does the audience know you?
3. Can your speech tell the audience something - How does the audience know you?
4. Can the audience augment the speech for you - Can the audience tell you something about yourself?

Following each stage, I've asked **Tracy Shoemaker**, (see pic at back of book) a very assiduous Swiss actress, to comment on her journey through the 4 stages.

I am a Swiss-American actress/teacher and first met Jacqui Carroll and John Nobbs in 2003. After having participated in five of Ozfrank's annually held intensive training workshops in Europe, I was invited to join the company in Australia for regular training. During my time in Australia I acted in 3 different shows including "The Reckoning of Badengood". I would like to share some personal experiences I had with the 4 stages John has described……..

Stage 1: It may seem self evident to ask if you can hear and understand what you are saying, but, in fact, it takes a long time and quite a lot of training before actors can truly hear what they sound like. We augment the actor's training visually, by using hand held mirrors which give the actor a good sense of what the audience sees when they are saying a speech. The actor's hearing and understanding what they are saying is a further manifestation of self -definition - this requires much repetition and inside that repetition; self inquiry which can be "What is the effect that the words/actions are having on me?"

TS: To me, stage one is comparable to building the foundation of a house. Only when the base was solid could I begin adding to it without *falling apart*. The first few months of training were very hard because I did not trust my body; having never really worked with it, I did not know it. I recall understanding instructions on an intellectual level and not being able to translate them into my physical being. This was very frustrating at times. Neither my body nor voice understood me. In my own mind, they lacked the sensitivity to listen to what I wanted them to do, while, in reality, my mind lacked sensitivity to listen to what they could, and would naturally do if I just relaxed. Jacqui and John often told me to calm my mind and *feel* more. This simple instruction helped me tremendously. The moment my brain "backed off," I suddenly *felt* my feet. From then on, they were no longer just things at the end of my legs; they became my friends, and I began to appreciate them as trustworthy tools.

This trust was gained through endless experimentation with them, during training. Once I trusted my body, the trainings became much more than just "getting the steps right" or "speaking loudly – quietly – whispering". It became important *how* I did the steps to make them *mine*. (As Jacqui Carroll says: *"It's not what you do it's how you do it!"*) With every training, the feeling of "owning" my voice and body grew.

Stage 2: Stage 2 is the state where the actor is highly aware that his performance is reaching out to the audience. He is not selfishly immersed in his own world. At the same time as he is speaking or moving, he should be aware that the audience is a realtime witness to the speech or action. Incidentally, this sensitivity grows out of an awareness in training that he is also a witness to what he is doing - he is both first and third person.

TS: As body and voice knowledge developed, I gained the necessary confidence to include stage 2 in my circle of awareness. **Acknowledging that there is an audience watching** -- and that they may have thoughts on my performance -- entails having enough skills to feel secure in being observed. Performers who do not have a training system which provides them with solid skills may consider it more pleasant to simply forget that the audience exists in order to overcome nervousness. In my opinion, the fourth wall is a tool for actors that do not yet possess sufficient skills to feel secure on stage. It was the absence of this barrier between the actors and the audience, (which I first witnessed in a performance of "Macbeth -Crown of Blood," in 2003), which first interested me in the Ozfrank training. I could somehow sense the performers' expectations of me, as a witness to the magic they were creating on stage for my interest and pleasure.
Some years later, while performing as Lady Macbeth, in Switzerland, I found myself experiencing stage 2 as a performer. I remember having to remind myself continually that although I was speaking to Macbeth, I needed to hold my head toward the audience so that they would hear me when I was not speaking at full voice. I recall being very concerned about what the audience was receiving and whether-or-not I could maintain everything I was doing while still raising the audience's level of awareness.

Stage 3: This goes further than conveying something to the audience, the 'what' is replaced by introducing the 'how'. Not just telling the spectator, but..... what are they getting? How are they perceiving you? Not...... what do you want them to get? But what do they want to get from you? You cannot, of course, have the question answered - it is enough to pose the question inside the speech.

This 'How' involves a shift from independence to partial interdependence, as it confers on the audience the responsibility for interpretation - that they are no longer passive observers, inert sponges, but actively ingesting incoming information.

TS: Shortly after my performance as Lady Macbeth, I performed in "The Reckoning of Badengood" in Japan. I shared my role with Glenn Taylor, a more experienced actor. Our characters of *best mates* had been compared to Lewis Carroll's "Twiddle Dum and Twiddle Dee." Knowing that the predominantly Japanese audience would not understand what we were saying – I tried to provide meaning via body language and the tone of my voice – this shifted my attention away from *what* I was saying and made me think more about *how* I could deliver the role. I wanted the audience to get a feeling – to understand unconsciously, from the type of energy I was radiating, what the character was all about. It being an audience of hard-working professional actors, (who I knew would be very actively ingesting the incoming information) I wanted them to feel that I was giving them my very best. Between lines, I was able to look at the audience and found myself asking them in my thoughts, *"How is this coming across? Do you feel the essence my character? Do you feel I appreciate the fact that you are here, and that I am thrilled to perform for you?"*

Stage 4: The audience graduates from interpretive observers to participants. The audience comprises a catholic group with diverse backgrounds and attitudes and will interpret any performance eclectically. Once understood that the audience will have its own 'take' on the experience, the actor can escalate the sense of inquiry, expanding from the idea of 'How are they receiving the speech?' to 'What responses might they have?'

TS: The fourth stage is the magical "audioplasma" which I had heard John speak of, and believed to be true -- but had never had the experience. I thank our director, Jacqui Carroll, for creating a perfect situation in which to experience this phenomena. In "Up Jumped the Devil" my character was a Pierrot Clown that had no spoken text to deliver. I entered the stage by appearing out of a magic box. The scene was so staged that the focus at this particular moment was completely on me. Before appearing, the lights went up inside the box, I started to whistle a song and then my head appeared over the edge of the box. And then it happened.

I "felt" the whole audience watching. I could sense the questions flying at me – some 300 observers now trying to figure out what I was and what I would do next. It felt as though the audience had become one, giant organism, with many eyes, and it was completely with me for a brief moment.

After a few performances, John suggested I try an experiment by making some pauses in my whistling. So, the next night I stopped in the middle of my whistling, thereby stretching the moment of suspense in which all were involved. It required a lot of courage, but also taught me an important lesson about *owning* my space on stage. It also showed me that the audience is silently requesting to become a part of my journey and can be trusted to respond to the questions and challenges the performance presents.

This is unconscious feedback, unspoken and instinctive, totally different to realtime interruptions, such as clapping and cheering, etc. This can and does happen of course and represents total complicity.
Switzerland 2010

Regarding the total complicity of the 4th stage I remember once, when I was a modern dancer, I was playing the part of the 'Godfather' in a pretty frothy ballet about an Oz-Italian suburban wedding. It was a cheap mafioso skit, where I had to beat up some misbehaving punk, then did a solo dance with sunnies, black pants, white shirt, thin black tie, etc. As I was performing the solo dance the audience started clapping as one. It was an incredible moment as I knew the **whole** audience was totally with me! Thinking back on it, I guess it was a rare case where the combined conscious and unconscious came together. I knew who I was and the audience knew who I was. I felt something and the audience felt the same thing. There was a complete match between myself as particular and audience as universal.

This only happened once or twice in a 15 year dance career of some 1200 performances, but it was a clear case of total rapport between performer and audience, and some sort of overt precursor to the discovery I made at Sunshine Beach.

As I write this I realise that those infrequent experiences as a dancer some years back gave me insights into the sporadic special complicity that could occur between a performer and the audience. Dance, by its mute nature, communicates with the unconscious of the audience, unencumbered with rational and prescriptive patterns. So it is perhaps not surprising that it sensitised and stimulated in me a quest to discover and articulate in general theatrical terms, which on winding forward, I could reconfigure, as a type of audioplasma when, as Death, I came the Sunshine Beach.

"The very picture of a pedagogue groping for a locum cogitato"

Molecular provocation #7
Spirit Speed: The 5th Dimension

I was talking with **Ross Hobson,** (see pic at back of book) a young opera singer who was performing with us in Jacqui's music theatre work, **Up Jumped the Devil,** in 2009. He was the featured singer, playing the central role of **Walker**, and he was with us for a number of months training and rehearsing. Jacqui and I had taught him the FSPA while he studied at the Queensland Conservatorium many years before, so he was very au fait with the Ozfrank aesthetic.

I was recounting my recent experience up at the Sunshine Coast playing Death in The Reckoning of Badengood and the 'Audience as Plasma' revelation (Mol Provoc 6), and, as I mentioned the part about the reaction of the audience to what I was saying and my reading of their reaction, he suddenly blurted out with: "It happens instantaneously, doesn't it?"

He'd beaten me to it! When he connected spirit with instantaneous, he came up with **Spirit Speed!** I'll let him take the floor in his inimitable fashion……….

As I entered the training and rehearsals the only motto I held true to, was to take on board everything and anything the training had to offer a "visitor" to the transitional performance state between this world and another - that "moment of clarity" state.

In this state, language - of body, mind, soul and sound, is the mist in the space, translated instantly by any who are present, whether it be the viewer or partner. The fifth dimension 'spirit speed' exists on this platform moment of clarity. Spirit Speed is the comprehension between the actors and the audience - instantaneously ping-pong-ing between the two.

It's like being lost in the desert with only a mirror as your means of survival - getting the angle of the mirror right is essential. There are varying degrees of "getting it", but hopefully getting the sun's rays smack-bang in the middle of the mirror, so you can use the mirror's full potential.

When it is recognized, accepted and reflected back by your rescuers (the viewers) you get what John has called "spirit speed". This can go for a nanosecond or last for many seconds...... outside factors come into play - the sun's rays, the time of day, the survivors and rescuers!

The more this state is revisited in a performance, more mirrors align the spiritual forces to refract, and refract again the full beams of sunlight into all the apparent colours. As an audience member, the colours one person sees may very well be totally different to the colours the people next to them see. The spirit speed in this case is infinitely variable and becomes more complex, with each mirror making the experience unique for each individual.

These mirrors are about truth and acceptance, and for me being given the gift of permission - permission to use my mirror.

In the aftermath of this revelation one can find one's voice - whether actor or singer - waiting for that moment of clarity, of truthfulness - this is the light that is reflected like the sun in the mirrors that we hold as performers.

We all have these mirrors, actors and audience, - they are our spirits!

Your work will continue to invigorate, inspire and challenge my spirit and I.
London 2010
(see Ross' pic at back of book)

Einstein, in his Relativity Theories, worked out that time was not an absolute but a measurement the same as length, breadth and depth. It was the 4th Dimension. He figured out that the only absolute was the speed of light because it never varied no matter how or where or when it was measured. It superseded Newton's 17thc theories and it was so 'different' and ethereal that it was another few decades before it could be proved. Still today, it's incomprehensible to the man in the street. It's pretty high falutin' stuff, and for most situations it isn't necessary as the old grandpa clock governs our lives, okeydoke. But it does peel open a tiny aperture to give bods like me a glimpse into explanations that can give spirit a dimension or two.
I am proposing, here, to take a quantum leap and go a tad further than Albert E. and say that spirit is faster than the speed

of light, it's **the fifth dimension**! If it is instantaneous, it means that it is always there it is a constant. In order to verify this facetious presumption, I need an experimental space and some propositions. Luckily I have a laboratory<u>! Our Frank Suzuki Performance Aesthetics is just the ticket for such quests, as it is designed for theatre as a spiritual arena where such notions are proposed and probed.</u>

Along with the vigorous workouts that we do, are long periods of reflection and homologation, and it is during these that infuse some of the propositions that I come across in lots of books on varied spiritual searchers like Neal Cassady, G.I. Gurdjieff and Willy Blake. I have written a whole chapter on WB in this book and now I want to concentrate on a small aspect of his attitude.

In a dense book about him, I tripped over the following comment......Blake believed that he, and others who chose to cultivate the power, could have visionary intercourse with spirits of the dead, because he believed in the **timeless union of all things** in the Divine Mind, and hence that the living could **command the world memory** to a greater or lesser extent.......

Two phrases sprang out like squawks from a squeaker ball!

The timeless union of all things in the divine mind...........

What could be more apposite to spirit speed than the above phrase? I don't want to go into the divine mind too much as it is tricky terrain and you can't even mention DOG these days as it freaks semi sub-Marxists out, but the first bit is vurry interesting in the light of Mr Einstein's toil, as stated above. But, if you're in a Jungian frame of reference, you can interpolate 'Collective Unconscious' for 'divine mind', and you won't be so misinterpreted.

Archetype: an original model of a person, ideal example, or a prototype, a symbol universally recognised by all.......
One of Jung's big calls was that archetypes exist all the time and through time. It's just a matter of meeting them and surfing

off the conjunctions that occur.

My take on that is that Clint Eastwood's Dirty Harry is an archetype easily 'read' whether you're in the Hindu Kush or in the south side of Chicago (Jacqui and I have seen it on street TV in lawless Western Pakistan!). Once you see that image of the mean, lean body in the black stove pipe suit, the chisel toe boots, the magnum 44, the thin black tie, you immediately know what's in store.

That occurs straightaway... (surely an instance of spirit speed) no thinking needed... you unconsciously log up all the aesthetic codes in an instinctive instant. There's a huge rush of energy, of adrenalin as you are in a moment of identifying with a universal force which is outside you, but, because you recognise it, is also inside you. It would seem our psyches take great comfort from this identification with the wider shores of human experience, as those images buttress our sense of who we are and where we belong.

Command the world memory:
When the author of Blake's biog uses the term 'world memory' I take it to mean the combined memory of all the people in the world; Past Present and Future. This is another way of stating the Collective Unconscious, which was Jung's way of describing a mytho-poetic landscape to which we are more or less connected depending on our desire for verification of the meaning of the mysteries of life and death. For most people this landscape is governed by religious structure, but for those with a secular bent, the C.U., aka World Memory, provides a prospect for connecting with time past and future.

What is interesting about these two statements is that they link the idea of 'timeless' with 'memory'. And while it is most commonly understood that timeless means eternal, it can also mean instantaneous. So the idea of spirit speed with its twin nodes of instantaneous and eternal, would seem to be a fertile inspirational hypothesis......well spotted, Ross!

I'm not advocating this to be a new scientific truth, so much as a <u>provocative proposition,</u> a mild form of astral travail, which needs to be given ballast by some form of rigorous muscular activity.

In closing, WB didn't consider that the timeless union and world memory were so extra special that only he could access them....... anybody could do it.......one only had to get the timing belt in the brain ticking over...

Of course, Blake was a natural expert at this Astral Travail. In fact mates like John Varley used to spend endless night time hours sitting next to him while WB copied down pictures from the other side. This makes him the first Grand Master of Spirit Speed. Blake was a natural... any of us slobs ordinaire who would like to walk on the far side would need to be trained up a tad....hmmmm!

Molecular Provocation #8
Thespians Quantum Leaping From Newton to Einstein

Here follows a letter sent by the Kirlian Geometer, Peter Berkahn, then edited by yours truly and hit back over the net as a thought ball.

Think of this provocation as a type of two way 'thought experiment', much the same as Einstein used to use when he was trying to figure out solutions to complex problems that can't be seen. For us it is applying the paradoxical notions of nuclear physics to the complex interdependent dialectic of acting, and, by doing that, transferring the poetic logic to higher concepts like soul, which are difficult to pin down, but are known to exist. Such provocations as this may give the soul some legibility and density for performative purposes.

I gain great enjoyment in the beautiful nomenclature that the scientific space cadets came up with in their quest to formulate the brave new conjunction of sub atomic and interstellar.

Witness these labels:

- Particle Wave theory,
- Sub-atomic,
- the Plank Constant,
- String theory,
- Continuous/Discontinuous,
- Quantum Mechanics,
- Un-observability
- and the best, Heisenberg's Uncertainty Principle.

These imaginative names represent the creative nature of the search - to explain something that is hidden and doesn't make daily sense. The highly poetic nomenclature is coding that invites the unconscious mind to become a co-participant with the logical mind in the integrative quest. This letter projects poesy as a bridge from science to art.

Newtonian Physics:

In 1687 Isaac Newton formulated the basic law of classical mechanics: Every action has an equal and opposite reaction, the law of cause and effect. This dominated the scientific view for the next 3 centuries.

In Newton's view, objects affect each other gravitationally. The mass of an interstellar lump brings about a gravitational affect on other proximate heavenly lumps - eg the Earth on the Moon, the evidence for which we see in the tides. Under Newton, it's inversely related to distance alone - no way that the space between may be elastic and/or deformable. So, the space in between planets, stars, etc. was considered to be empty.

It took Einstein to show that in fact space and time are also affected by the movement and action of these masses. Here, simple cause and effect becomes compounded by the morphing of space and time.

To move beyond straightforward cause and effect, we need **Particle Wave Theory** to explain the microcosmic, sub atomic world, those invisible electrons, etc. which when compounded together, make up the macrocosmic 'big' masses.

Newtonian Acting:

In relation to acting, under Newtonian cause and effect, one actor does or says something ....the other actor reacts, throwing words back over the net. Bouncing off each other, they think they are transcendent. Not quite so! They are hitting sweetly all right, but the result is one dimensional, action and re-action!

This tennis of the emotions leaves a performance with no transformational grunt, because the audience's souls have no chance of linking with the actor's soul, due to the fact that there's no morphing of the message as it tos and fros across the stage.

The Shape of the Soul

The soul is a wonderful frontless, backless, sideless subject, and it'd be pretty neat (albeit tricky!) to give it a shape and form - to make a portrait of it, rather than just leave it in the realm of airy fairy mysticism.

The attempt to quantify the soul gives us an operational hypothesis to give the soul more tangibility; to make it more manifest. It's not the success that is necessarily important but the potential it reveals. It opens a window through which to study the actor's processes as they are triggered and occupied by the soul.

Said another way, the soul is not able to be directly measured, but we can approximate it by giving it some form and substance - all art and religion is effectively an attempt to explain or quantify soul. And so the attempted portraits themselves are probes which serve a purpose - to somehow reveal a sculpture of the soul and the effects on its owner as he progresses through his life.

In the case of an actor, his performance is the portrait.

Lateral Physics Thinking:

The latest theme in physics is **string theory**. Yes, that's right! The physical world is made up of thin pieces of string - this theory proposes that the universe is held together by 13 dimensions of strings! No one knows what the hell that means but that does not stop them dreaming up such ethereal constructs, and falling in and out of love with them!

But why can't we start working on equations that delineate the soul? Propel spirit into the realm of mathematics! Now, there are parallels between writing an equation to have the soul made measurable for us humans (micro), and writing one for the universe (macro). For example, to ask for the shape of the universe is as mega abstract as asking for a geometrical shape of the soul. Is the micro the mini map of the macro?

Are you with me?

Quantum Physics.

Black bodies absorb the most energy (black absorbs the most light, and it holds true for other electromagnetic ranges) and they emit radiation in certain frequencies, but just how these frequencies are emitted was a mystery until about 1900.

Discrete frequencies of Black Body Radiation were first estimated by **Max Planck**, and he became the first to suggest that energy was emitted in packets of **quanta** (blobs). He worked out a constant for the frequency of energy put out and it was named after him, **'The Planck Constant'**. Planck was awarded the Nobel Prize for this work - this idea of packets of energy was later expanded by Einstein who discovered that an object will lose mass when photons are directed at it, meaning that electrons are knocked off like bullets knocking chips off a concrete block.

Mr E. deduced, or guessed, that photons also operated in quantum packets. His 'thought experiment' explained light as a **Quantum-Wave (Blob-Ripple) function** in 1905. By the by, Einstein had a golden year in 1905 - he also worked out four other new things, all now sub-branches of science in biology, physics and chemistry. One was his famous equation of the century, E=MC squared.

Niels Bohr followed, getting the Nobel Prize for his discoveries on the structure of the hydrogen atom. This helped prepare the scene for **quantum wave mechanics**.

The Soul via Quantum Physics:

The Psyche, operating as both an abstract and a physical entity, can possibly be viewed as a particle-wave paradox. It has connections to our soul, and also owns, and at the same time is submerged in the substrates of our being. So the Soul can be seen as a particle wave duality - part inhabiting the body - but as well, activating from and connecting with some eternal (non time based) position. This paradox compares with light which also consists of the apparent opposites of wave and particle.

For theatre, it's up to the actor to project (particle) and occupy (wave) this as a performance. Because paradox is the glue that unites the unconscious with the conscious, the actor needs to accept paradox, not try and rationalise or straighten it, but allow both (projection and occupation) to exist as though they were wings on a plane, and therefore occupy the space between. He has to be in paradox on stage - truly self and truly the other. Truly himself and truly the role he's playing. He exists in separate particle and wave states that are connected in the 'moment' on stage - the vibrational state of the soul.

Conventional acting attitudes can't give him that experience because they only consider one or the other. They consider either the actor as prime, or the role as prime.

We can also borrow ideas from physics to show how the actors impact on each other in ways that they be both wave and particle to each other - this Einsteinian adoption for theatre provides useful insights for the actor to first of all engage, and then to reconfigure themselves in elastic space and time. And that aesthetic is projected as quanta of **spirit speed** (Mol Provoc 7) pulses to the audience and other actors.

So Quantum Physics can articulate what is happening at the most powerful soulstate level inside a performance.

Conventional Newtonian Theatre:

The Newtonian world all hinges on one dimensional causality. Likewise, in conventional performance, the acting allows the audience to only experience the emotional affect of an actor upon another actor. It doesn't create any opportunities for soul to soul interaction between the actors and the audience. Things proceed only in terms of emotional action and reaction. There is nothing deeper going on - eg we have two actors, one reveals love or hate, which initiates an obvious, predictable emotional response from the other actor.

Einsteinian Theatre Potential (Nijinsky):

A more sophisticated possibility than this Newtonian system in theatre is illustrated by this story: the Russian composer, Igor Stravinsky, is an example of an artist locked in the Newtonian world and, through composing for Russian dancer/choreographer Vaslav Nijinsky, found himself confronting an Einsteinian world where Dance is making new language - an existing but hitherto hidden language revealed by Nijinsky.

Stravinsky's assumptions about the relationship of dancer with the music sees matching the dance with the music in one dimensional terms -the dance merely copies the music - merely a slave to the structure. Stravinsky was of the opinion that Nijinsky, who choreographed his 1913 **Rite of Spring** score, was an idiot: "the poor boy knew nothing of music!" he said.

Definitely not true! It was Stravinsky who believed that the music should govern the dancer - cause and affect - though this can appear sophisticated. But faux sophistication was the trap that kept Stravinsky locked in his Newtonian Causality. It took Nijinsky's inter-dimensional dance to shift the music to a new space/time rhythm.

Only the soul can read the meaning of this other rhythm - it is Einsteinian in nature because it allows the soul a compound view of the elastic relationship between the music and the dance. Sadly, this was not seen by Stravinsky as an expanding of the melodic and rhythmic palette. This palette, however, was revealed by Nijinsky's dance aesthetic because he had created a work which was interdependent on multiple levels.

Stravinsky's 19th century attitude that music had a one dimensional effect on dance was a mirror of contemporary physics which still held to a Newtonian view that the movement of the Earth only affected the movement of its satellite, the Moon, mass affecting another mass, as though there was a giant rigid steel rod in between. No space-time plasticity in the gap. And so Stravinsky, locked in an old fashioned linear modality, completely missed the point of Nijinsky's challenge to make the space an active participant, as it were, a co-choreographer.

It is quite straightforward to understand that dance can respond to and articulate the music, but to comprehend that dance can also respond to and articulate THE SPACE requires an Einsteinian attitude. The relativity thinking is a means to break out of old linear concepts to create a new choreographic modality that compounds movement with sound, and rhythm with space.

It parallels the discovery that the space and time in between the planets underwent incredible alterations - warping and deformation- the steel rod was stretching and twisting.

So it was with Nijinsky; manipulating, not just the obvious objects (the dancers), but also the music, as if it were a mass as well. He morphed space and time via his injection of an elastic dynamic that intervened between the apparent rhythm and the audience's sense of time in the room.

Are you still with me?

Quantum Mechanics and the Brando Effect:

The mechanism of **spirit speed** (instantaneous connection between the individual and collective unconscious) still holds, but needs to be looked at from the quantum position, a post Einstein position - ie discontinuous energy changes. If the unconscious is the thinking place of the soul, as put by Ozfrankie **Jor'el Mitchell**, and emits continuous packets of energy at spirit speed to the audience, what about its discontinuous state? Is that when the soul is asleep?

Unanswerable! Just go back to the Brando head to arm affect and interpret it with the aid of **Blob/Ripple** theories.

Marlon Brando once described his performing method thus: Something transformational occurring when messages travelled from his head to his extremities when he was acting. Not only were messages going out, but something was happening to them **AS** they were going out. This is far more complex than most acting, where the situation is really only one dimension of message. In Brando's case the message is being 'massaged' - it is morphing into something else as it leaves.

To overlay the Brando experience with Quantum Mechanics is to postulate what could be happening electro-chemically between Brando's head and body whilst acting. What sort of micro radiation is triggered in the sub-atomic mechanism of the psyche,that enables it to pulsate, or 'wave out' to the audience at spirit speed so as to communicate the actor's engagement with deep soul experience? And by doing so, both actor and audience are transformed.

Such a contemplation stimulates a working hypothesis. No definitive answer is required - but a sense of it may be apprehended if we conceive that the psyche phenomena is a type of **discontinuous** (Blob or Particle) / **continuous** (Wave or Ripple) happening, where energy is conserved to maximize the sense of the actor (self definition) and also produced to allow for emanations to the audience (expressed energy).

Unobservability:

Quantum Mechanics (where sub-atomic particles can either be known where they have come from, but not where they are going, or vice versa) punched a few holes in Einstein's wave particle aspect. Why? Because it needed other small particles to hit the observed sub-particles in order to know where the particles came from. But in doing so, they changed the track of the particles they were trying to observe. The so called impartial experiment was going to irrevocably affect the observation. The unobservable was forever going to affect the observing of the observed. Likewise the audience's observation of the actor is forever going to affect the actor. By this I mean the actor's expressed energy without an audience has a certain value. When an audience observes the actor the observation changes the value, because the audience's expectation is another energy. This is analogous to a snooker ball hitting another ball that is already in motion. Given that the actor's un-witnessed energy is a type of truth, then the witnessing creates another type of truth.

Quantum Physics and the Unconscious:

Transpose quantum physics to the unconscious life of the actor - he cannot measure what he does. He requires the audience to define the 'measure'. He must therefore rely on the format of an Einstein type training to sustain an equilibrium between:

(1) His inner world (the Brando affect of quantum psyche-soul mechanics) and

(2) the other outer mechanics of acting - which can be:

(a) inclusive of Newtonian simple cause and affect - ie two actors on stage, completely ignorant of the space between, and

(b) the more complicated interdependency of Einstein's actor in space - plasma reading between actors and operating according to the training provided to them to harness all conscious and unconscious patterns of their psyche - Einsteinian and quantum-psycho-mechanical.

Plasticity of Time:

Inexactness of time is actually a gift to the actor; he does not need to predict what he is to do next at some exact moment in some exact way to form a character for the audience - the actor only needs to rely on his training and to proceed through the role - let other parties to the experience feel the time - it will come to them from the pulse and quantum packets of the actor: being himself, and sending waves of transformative energy into the audience.

The Heisenberg Uncertainty Principle:

The HUP proposes that certain pairs of properties, like **position** and **momentum** cannot both be known precisely in the same instant. That is, the more one property is known, the less precisely the other is known. To broach an analogy with acting, we can substitute self definition (position) and role (momentum). The HUP transfers to performance where it is difficult to work out where the self definition ends and the role begins, and the audience experiences both in combination.

Now note the next passage below, it is a **thought experiment**. It's important for physicists to use thought experiments, because they are attempting to quantify situations that are almost invisible. Likewise we can transpose the idea of a thought experiment to the audience's unquantifiable apprehension of a performance.

The HUP was not accepted by everyone. Its most outspoken opponent was Einstein. He devised a challenge to Niels Bohr which he made at a conference which they both attended in 1930.

Einstein suggested a box filled with radiation with a clock fitted in one side. The clock is designed to open a shutter and allow one photon to escape. Weigh the box again some time later and the photon energy and its time of escape can both be measured with arbitrary accuracy. Of course this is not meant to be an actual experiment, only a 'thought experiment'. Niels Bohr is reported to have spent an unhappy evening and Einstein a happy one, after this challenge by Einstein to the uncertainty principle.

However Niels had the final triumph, for the next day he had the solution. The mass is measured by hanging a compensation weight under the box. This in turn imparts a **momentum** to the box and there is an error in measuring the **position**. Time, according to relativity, is not absolute and the error in the position of the box translates into an error in measuring the time....

The Actor and the Audience:

We can draw a bead from the Bohr Box Thought Experiment. Can we find parallels with the Box story to that of the actor and the audience? One is viewed (the actor), the other is the viewer (the audience). The actor is a combination of position (self definition) and momentum (role), and the audience is needed for the external 'reading' of the combination - this 'reading' is where the self definition (position) and the role (momentum) become unified - the actor's completion.

Much the same as the thought box, the actor cannot 'complete' (know) himself. His performance is the display of his 'oppositional essences' released by his 'psychic shutter' as continuous and discontinuous photons that radiate out to the audience. The audience's function is to 'read', reflect on, refract and resend these 'actor photons' back to the actor as completion.

It will be for the audience to unconsciously use their collective sub-atomic mysticism to 'feel' and 'measure' the actor whilst he is using the wave-particle Brando effect to act.

How much value can we put on all this discussion?

It is not the aim of this to and fro discussion to arrive at concrete absolute answers to the questions surrounding acting, so much as to promote a new attitude which can encompass multiple contingencies. It is not simplistic science, but a probe using poetry as an unconscious thought impulse to swing the brain to another space.

This provoc has been about transposing the scientific poesy that imagines the sub-atomic world, and casts it over the field of the similarly invisible liminal world of the actor's soul. This poeticism constellates the actor's vocation to portray the cosmology and fault-lines of society's spiritual loci. Performative Art as a parallel mystical vision to super material nuclear reality, akin to Dali's nuclear mysticism.

As Quantum Mechanics was formulated to make scientific sense of the micro and the macro by including electric with mechanic, its elastic imagination can be reconfigured to re-deploy art that is not retro action and reaction, but future perfect inclusive.

Big ta for that, Kirly!

The last provoc has wrung me out and spun me out. I feel like the Black Holes I talk about…my shoulders cramped……wrists aching and slow….eyelids dry and low….the coal black night leisurely feathers into the translucent dawn. This devil reaches for the door……he's done his job…..he starts to slide into the backlots of my mind, to reside awhile in the soft fleshy folds of my cerebellum……to lie in wait for another time when he can dance the advocate's tango. He'll be back; I know he will – the provocateur of the souler plexus.

But as he sinks behind the skin, with one last wave of his languid arm, his final words fade softly….

"Not bad, Nobbsy!"

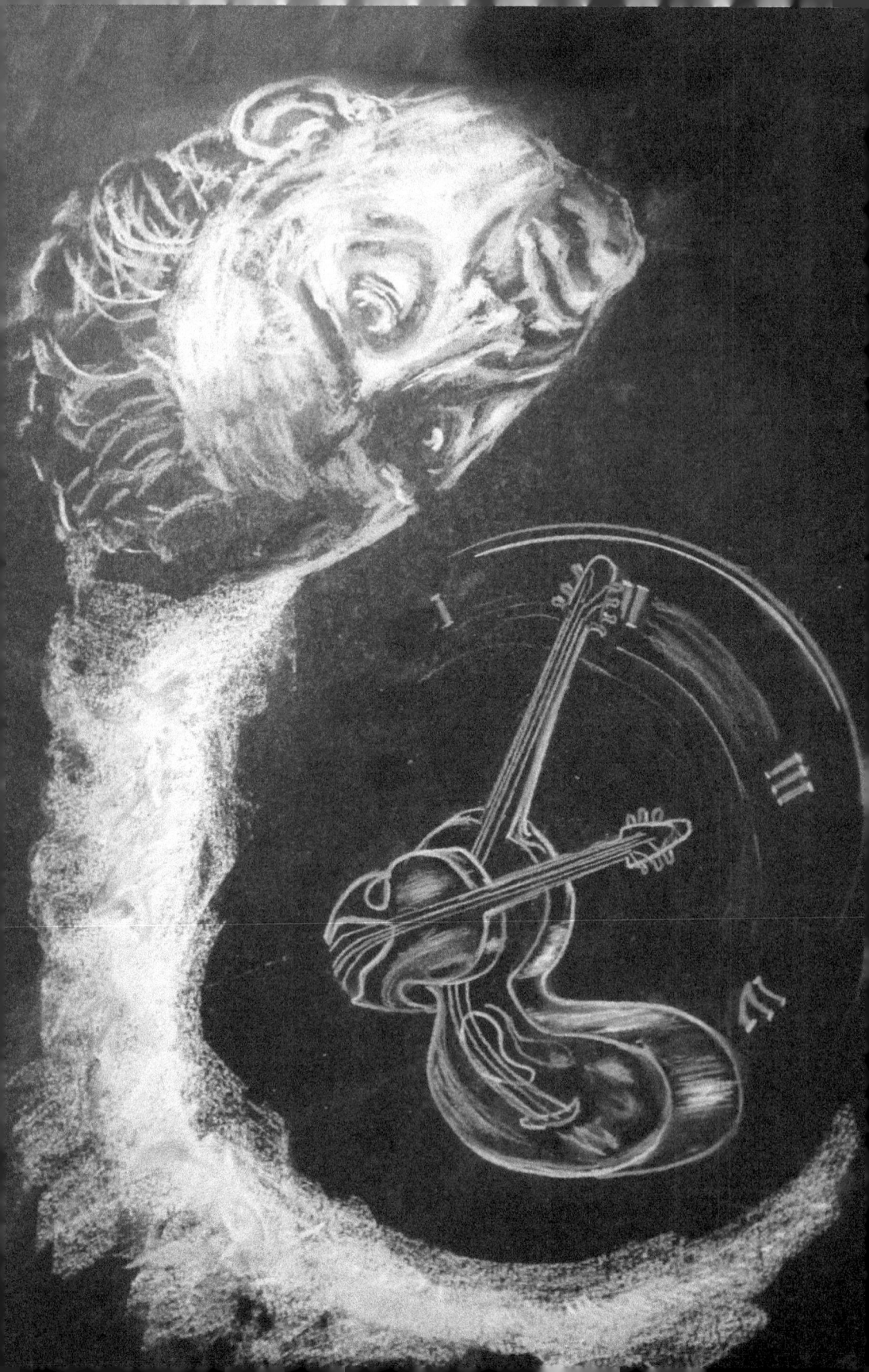

A Devil Pokes the Actor   343

Peter's illustration of Johnny Cash brings up two intertwining anecdotes to introduce the gallery of Ozfrank plays and players that close the book.

An astute Drama professor from Tasmania, by the name of Robert Lewis (who also heads a small company called Voice Lab) was doing our 2010 summer intensive and some way through it we were doing a 'Hands off the Wall' exercise. Afterwards I pondered aloud to him as to why it was so compelling to observe.

He answered: "I think its because you are taking your history with you, as you proceed" An equally compelling response!

To compound that.......a few weeks later Glenn Taylor, whilst in conversation, mentioned that he had read recently that Johnny Cash, no matter where he played, he always sounded like where he came from. And even later, after Jacqui and I had taught Robert's actors in a chilly Launceston, Robert related a company discussion about the very 'Hands off the Wall' exercise, and they had together felt that it was essential Stanislavsky that had neatly dovetailed into the FSPA.... which may be a good start for another book that an actor might be poked into.....Hmmm...

Ozfrank History Gallery

The Romance of Orpheus 1992/3

The first production directed and devised by Jacqui Carroll, when Ozfrank was Frank Productions. A very musical, very 'movement' work, with live percussion on stage creating the ambience of an operatic tribal ritual. Follows the classic tragic myth in a muscular fashion:

Pic 1 Irena Haze as Eurydice and JN as Orpheus before the tragedy starts

Then....Orpheus loses Eurydice when she dies then finds her and brings her back from the underworld...........then loses her again forever when he answers her traumatised questions.

In this production Jacqui inaugurated several templates she continues to use:

- an elastic cast structure. A few principal characters, such as Orpheus, Eurydice, and Death, with an adjustable number of chorus.
- **Pic 2 the female chorus consoling Orpheus. Clockwise from left: Fran Barbe, Sonia Davies, Christina Koch and Lisa O'Neill.**
- judicious and sparing use of text
- prominent choric elements of voice and movement
- performance duration of between 60 and 90 minutes max.
- simple sets and beautiful costumes

Macbeth: Crown of Blood 1995/2009

Various versions of Macbeth are the company's bellwether, the Frankly four wheel drive, performed in countries as disparate as Switzerland and Mongolia, on the sides of hills, in pouring rain, in castles and in Roman amphitheatres. First done in 1995 and repeated somewhere, somehow in nearly every year since. Nearly every Ozfrank actor has cut their teeth on one or more of the parts. This is Jacqui's favourite story and speeches. She pared the words down to 65 minutes, and often stages the work with as few a 4 actors (Mac, Lady Mac and a guy and a girl who play Mr and Mrs Everybody Else).

JN in foreground as the man and Tracy Shoemaker in back as Lady Macbeth

Fran Barbe playing the nurse in Switzerland, Mac lurking out back.

Japanese actor Okubo Noriaki playing Mac and Lisa O'Neill playing tyrannically terrified retainer.

In 2005 we received an email asking if we were a Japanese theatre company. After an extensive Q & A electronic interchange, we were asked to bring a part English/part Japanese production to the Adana festival in Eastern Turkey. I'm not sure they knew what they were in for, but knowing that Okubo was an actor in Suzuki's company meant that he would be au fait with the Ozfrank way, and at short notice, he fitted seamlessly into the structure of the play. Okubo was a great addition to the Ozfrank aesthetic.

Tracy Shoemaker playing Lady M. in the predominantly candlelit version in Switzerland in 2009. This production is an excellent example of Macbeth as the performance outcome of an international workshop. The participants train for up to 10 days before Jacqui rehearses and directs them as the chorus. This allows them the complete process from start to end product.

By using candles with minimal stage lights, Jacqui enhanced the quiet menacing darkness of this version.

Salome 1997/8

This was the first production that Ozfrank toured internationally, with a 1998 visit to Tadashi Suzuki's festival in Toga, a well appointed village in the Japanese Alps. The **Pic is of Sarah Kemp on the left and Caroline Dunphy on the right**, in a dance sequence in the Prologue that came to be known as the 'The Egyptians'

Rashomon 2000/2004

Premiered in 2000 and performed in the Brisbane Festival in 2004. In Rashomon, Jacqui explored the relative nature of truth. A travelling couple is attacked, the man killed, the woman raped. At the trial all the testimonies contradict each other for unexpected reasons, with a surprise ending.

Jacqui has staged the play as a series of scenes where the accused brigand, the wife and the spirit of the dead husband, all give their version of events. Jacqui was inspired by Kurosawa's film, but substituted **three sly, psychedelic cleaning ladies** (Pic 1 L to R) **Caroline Dunphy, Neridah Waters and Leah Shelton** for the 3 man peasant 'chorus'. After each testimony they make raucous comment on the elastic 'truth' of each protagonist's evidence. As one of the key musical elements, Jacqui uses the abrasive PIL inversion tune 'This is not a Love Song" as an entree into each scene.

Pic 2 is **Kathleen Doyle as the monk bearing witness.**

Oedipus Rex 2003

This is Jacqui's second and current version premiered in a Croatian castle. It is a theatrical Oratorio staged on multiple levels, with text taken from Sophocles and Cocteau. It is another 4 wheel drive Ozfrank production, able to be staged in demanding terrain with a large or small chorus. A highly emotive, but austere plaint augmented with stunning music by Zbigniew Preisner and Midori Tanaka among others. The pic features **Emma Pursey as Jocasta in the temple** supplicating to the gods, with **JN behind, as Oedipus,** and surrounded by various chorus, carrying the Queen's offerings.

Doll Seventeen 2002/3

Doll Seventeen, premiered in the Brisbane Festival 2002, is Jacqui's theatrical fantasy based on Ray Lawler's **Summer of the Seventeenth Doll**, which is THE Australian classic text. With Ray's grace and permission, Jacqui excised 85% of the dialogue, reduced the cast down to 4 main characters and 3 'chorus'/property people, and featured an actress in pointe shoes and tutu as the Kewpie Doll in question. The design might be termed out of scale suburban surreal in screaming pink, with black fur walls, a revolving mirrored door, miniature pink lounge chairs and black and white cowhide seats. Using prominent music of the era such as Yma Sumac, Perez Prado and Judy Garland, combined with surprising and poignant movement, Jacqui has created a dreamscape that amplifies the essential pathos of the story which is about the inevitable passing of times golden and its un-recaptivity. The pic features in front **Lisa O'Neill as the Doll. From L to R at the back: Conan Dunning as Barney, Leah Shelton as Pearl, Caroline Dunphy as Olive** and **JN as Roo.** It is the New Year's Eve party about half way through our 80 minute version, and the Kewpie Doll is leading an old fashioned singsong.

Voodoo Macbeth 2008

Jacqui's fusing of Shakespeare's witchery with Haitian Voodoo. Mac and wife reduced to the zombified playthings of plantation slaves, voodoo dolls to be punched, kicked and pinched.....a total inversion of the classic. Unlike our standard in that M and LM hardly speak a word, but stagger soporifically and mute. A nightmare obverse of Jacqui's other - like listening to music backwards!

Pic is **JN as Mac with cracked cardboard crown being taunted by Kate Lee** with empty Fourex bottle (Queensland beer). Tacky decor, slapdash dayglo colours, naive homemade art, Duncan's corpse repelling the dagger in a Heath Robinson incubus, a disrespectful perspective from the witches' point of view with derisive repudiation of Bardolatory. (Pic taken at a 'show and tell').

The Royal Fair 2001/2

This work was a co-production between Ozfrank and the Istrian National Theatre, Croatia. Jacqui's version is an irreverent and playful retelling of a play by Croatia's esteemed playwright Miroslav Krleza, which surprised the locals. The pic features **JN and Conan Dunning as recently dead suicides** discussing the unexpected calmness of the after life.

Midsummer Night's Romeos 2003

MNR was first created in Japan as a co-production with the Suzuki Company of Toga. It was Jacqui's first foray into nonlinear theatrical essay, a mix of William Shakespeare's two great love plays, R&J and 'The Dream'. Pic shows **Lisa O'Neill as Hippolyta on the cloud bed, being assailed by Cupid's Agent Marc Carlis**, while **Caroline Dunphy as Cupid/Puck** glares in the distance. (The first time the Teddys star in an Ozfrank show).

Manga Ulysses 2006

A cultural exchange co-prod with Southbank Institute of Technology in Brisbane undertaken as an educational project featuring Japanese actor, Okubo Noriaki as Ulysses, Ozfrank actors as principals and 24 students in a steep six week learning curve. Manga, like its name, is a modern light weight recount of the myth, updating with rock and roll and chirpy design. Ordinarily the language of the training is never used on stage, but this work was deliberately designed to take several training exercises, and use them as episodes in the saga. The pic is of the **non standard sirens, seductively weaving umbrellas to the elegaic overture of Traviata.**

Hamlet Stooged! 2006

This pic is taken in Chicago and shows **Leah Shelton as Ophelia (left), Ira Seidenstein as Yorick (middle), Michael Coughlan as Hamlet (front) and Chad Beckett as the dog Horatio (right).**

Note the punky attire from the main two, dog costume for dog, and bowler hatted clowny look for Yorick (which matches the doll that later appears).The moment is about 2/3rds through the 55 min piece, where **H** tells **O** that he doesn't love her and suggests she goes to work in a rub 'n tug (massage parlour) - a rather naughty take on "Get thee to a Nunnery!"

The Reckoning of Badengood 2009

BGD is a replay of the 14thC miracle play **Everyman,** with newer words that aren't so olde worlde. The costumes are simple T shirts and pants, with easily read labels in big letters. These plays were the moral lectures of the 14th century performed for the great unwashed and made digestible by the addition of sundry entertainments. The story is that **God** is mighty displeased

Pic is of Glenn Taylor as God voicing displeasure.

God sends Death to teach humanity a lesson by taking an ordinary guy (who is both good and bad) on a life journey to his death, wherein he discovers that all his worldly attributes (friends, family and effects) mean nothing, and all that matters at the end is the good deeds (personified by Kate) he leaves as a legacy. She appears for the first time in the last scene from inside the set, as though, unknown to Badengood, she has been there all the time. Being the only woman in the cast, her surprising emergence shows she is Badengood's feminine unconscious, his anima.

The Reckoning of Badengood 2009/10

The top pic comes from a three day video shoot done in Brisbane and shows the scene where Badengood visits his family, who are **Bro, Benjamin Williams (left) and Sis, Glenn Johnson (right).** They are sitting in front of the 'patio', which is represented by a tent/caravan type awning with trad stripes that I found out the back of the studio in a wonderful instance of design serendipity.

BGD is the fourth production that Jacqui has taken to Suzuki's festivals in Toga. She was asked by Mr. Suzuki to create a brand new production as an example of our her latest style, and she chose BGD because she thought that Japanese audiences would never have seen any samples of early western theatre.

The second Pic was taken at Sunshine beach State High School at an out of town try out prior to the visit to Japan.

The pic is of James Anderson playing the title role of Christian Badengood in the penultimate scene. He is shadowed by Kate Lee, playing Good Deeds.

This pic of James and Kate is of the moment where he passes through to the other side, accompanied by Kate as a memory. Even though it's an oft told, old tale, the new lingo shows that the sentiments still rule true as true.

To Have Done with the Judgment of God 2008

To Have Done with the Judgment of God is a radio play, written by Antonin Artaud in 1947, but never performed in his lifetime due to its scatological and sacrilegious content. Jacqui decided to create this experimental piece for 5 men, to explore movement and voice patterns that emanate from instinctive bodily responses rather than style or narrative. **The five men showing their muscular bums (not sure which) are Kieran Law, Glenn Taylor, Noel Sheridan, Donovan Holbrook and JN.**

Cave: Mark 1: 2007

This pic is taken from the second of the 3 studies that Jacqui experimented with, before embarking on the final version called **Up Jumped the Devil**. These studies were essentially probes that illustrated the songs. They had no story line as such, and it was only when Jacqui came up with the idea of the reverse pilgrim's progress, that the songs and story coalesced. This pic is of one such probe. **It shows Caroline Dunphy in a disturbing montage of complicitous torture with Ramsay Hatfield, Marc Carlis and Conan Dunning.**

Up Jumped the Devil 2009

Jacqui Carroll's reverse Pilgrim's Progress articulating 8 songs by gothic rockster Nick Cave. It stars **Ross Hobson** as **Walker**, on death row for killing the love of his life. This dark music theatre piece is a giant flashback, the exploded instant before the high voltage chair flashes its deadly spark. This work features a 5 piece electric chamber orchestra, and a cast of masked carnival characters, all phantasms of Walker's psychotic divided mind.

Ross Hobson serenading his box of broken dreams.

Caroline Dunphy as one half of the Queens of the Crimson Sting.

Cave Songs featured were Up Jumped the Devil, The Carny, I let Love in, Lucy, The Ship Song, Loverman, The Mercy Seat and The Weeping Song.

Up Jumped the Devil 2009

'Devil' took over a year to develop, with columns as sets (see cover pic), trapdoors, stairs, a coffin, quiz show wheel, electric chair, 2 sets of large wings, a special silver floor, a cargo net, candles, car batteries.

The top pic is Tracy Shoemaker, as Walker's Anima, with Walker's giant polystyrene tombstone, replete with tilting candles. Its existence as a prop is another wonderful example of design serendipity. I found it floating in the Brisbane River!

One of the most intriguing sequences that Jacqui staged was the double mask routine, where the actors, as carnival characters populating Walker's fevered brain, don white masks. After a while the white ones come off to reveal cheap but spooky clear plastic ones that enhance the surreal nature of the scene.

The bottom pic is Ross Hobson as Walker facing Nick Cilento carrying Caroline Dunphy and Kate Lee as the Queens of the Crimson Sting, mysteriously masked in neutral white.

Authors and publishers to acknowledge:

Martin Buzacott
The Death of the Actor
Shakespeare on page and stage
Routledge
1991

David Mamet
True and False
Heresy and Common Sense for the Actor
Faber & Faber
1997

Stephen Wangh
An Acrobat of the Heart
A physical approach to acting
Inspired by the work of Jerzy Grotowski
Vintage Books a division of Random House
2000

Steven Berkoff
Free Association
An autobiography
Faber & Faber
1996

Francine The Gerbil proudly presents **Frankly Acting**

Frankly Acting is the first book written by John Nobbs. In it he outlines the development of the **Frank Suzuki Performance Aesthetics** as a variant of the classic Suzuki Training system.

It has two main outlooks. One is an articulation of the kinesiological intelligence of the original system developed by Tadashi Suzuki. The second is the translation into the FSPA where its eastern mores morph into more easily understood western modalities that prove Suzuki's training pertinence as the most appropriate universal actor training system for the 21st century. It alone invokes the dialectics of materiel and spirit, and addresses the paradox of actor and role.

The book outlines a situation where, by maintaining the core functions but adding regional themes and textures, the original system can be reconfigured for any and every acting situation.

In **Frankly Acting** John instances his personal inspirations, interrogations, ingestions, and tells the reader how they manifested as training exercises - a snail trail template for others similarly inclined.....

To purchase email <info@ozfrank.com>

www.ingramcontent.com/pod-product-compliance
Lightning Source LLC
Chambersburg PA
CBHW060106170426
43198CB00010B/792